THE CATECHETICAL INSTRUCTIONS OF

ST THOMAS AQUINAS

SINAG-TALA
PUBLISHERS, INC.
Manila

First published in English in February, 1939 by Joseph F. Wagner, Inc., New York City.

Nihil Obstat: E.A.Connolly, S.S., J.C.D.
        Censor Deputatus

Imprimatur: † Most Reverend Michael J. Curley, D.D.
        Archbishop of Baltimore

9 February, 1939

(This book has been re-set in Novarese 10 points medium for greater clarity, but none of the original content has been changed.)

ISBN 971 117 022 1

COVER: St Thomas Aquinas (1225-1294). Recognized as the leading philosopher of the Roman Catholic Church, Aquinas' authority was officially established by Pope Leo XIII in the encyclical *Aeterni Patris* (1879).

PRINTED IN THE PHILIPPINES

SINAG-TALA PUBLISHERS, INC.
Greenhills, P.O. Box 536
Manila 3113, Philippines

CONTENTS

Explanation of the Sacraments

Explanation of the Lord's Prayer

Explanation of the Hail Mary

INTRODUCTION

Some are of the opinion that the teaching of religion requires no preparation and that anything is good enough for the child. Asking catechism questions and listening to the child's recitation of the memorized answers—exercises which are considered as constituting the whole process of catechization—are in their estimation, after all, very simple tasks. And if the child stumbles and hesitates, a little prompting will elicit the desired answer. Unfortunately these exercises of verbal memory, instead of inflaming the child with a love of God, leave him as cold as do the drills of the multiplication table. The unassimilated abstract forms, instead of promoting spiritual growth, become nonfunctional memory loads. Religion, presented by methods such as these, strikes the child as a mere formality and as a hard law, and he applies himself to it more out of necessity than out of love and a joyous enthusiasm.

The teacher must carefully prepare the religion lesson if he wishes to give an accurate and adequate explanation of the catechismal truths. The child's intellectual powers are not sufficiently developed to grasp correctly a religious truth without appropriate explanations. The adult has by experience acquired many ideas and can interpret the new in terms of the old. But this is not true of the child. For him the bread of divine truth and life must be broken slowly. At the same time his mind is an "unmarked virgin slate" which registers new impressions with the pliability of wax and retains them with the durability of marble. If a child, through a faulty presentation on the part of the teacher, assimilates an erroneous idea in his early years, he may retain it for the rest of his life. The child will be confirmed in his error by the teacher's authority which he accepts unquestioningly, and by his own imitative tendency which makes him readily repeat whatever the teacher says. If the instructor is to be a messenger of truth and not of error, he must have access to doctrinal commentaries in which the truths of faith are explained in a simple, accurate and authoritative manner.

The catechist must supply those concrete explanations which the Catechism and religion books are obliged in their brevity to leave out. Theological manuals in use by priests and seminarians usually state a thesis and then prove it from the infallible decrees of the Church, from the Scriptures and Fathers, and finally from reason. The thesis should logically be placed at the end of such a discussion, since it is an abstract conclusion based upon many concrete facts. The doctrinal statements in our Catechisms and religion books are also conclusions—conclusions based upon facts derived from various sources. To expect the child to grasp these abstract formulas without first becoming acquainted with the concrete facts on which they are based, is to expect greater intellectual acumen in the child than in the theologian. Catechists must, with the help of appropriate handbooks, build up the rich doctrinal background which the Catechism and religion books presuppose.

In his translation entitled "The Catechetical Instructions of St. Thomas Aquinas," the Rev. Joseph B. Collins, S.S., S.T.D., Professor of Theology and Catechetics at the Catholic University of America, has made available to teachers of religion a theologically accurate explanation of the Catechism. It is Dr. Collins' latest contribution to the catechetical movement in America. The appearance of this translation of St. Thomas' catechetical works will be greeted with genuine satisfaction by all. In these days of renewed interest in Thomism, especially on the part of laymen, it will be comforting to know that the vast knowledge of the Church's greatest theologian is now made accessible—in a condensed and simple form—not only to teachers of religion but to the laity at large.

The work presents several peculiarities. Suggestive of the medieval custom of dividing the contents of catechetical manuals, the work contains an explanation of the Creed, the Sacraments, the Commandments, the Our Father, and the Hail Mary. The principle of doctrinal correlation is frequently in evidence. Thus, a brief explanation of the Sacraments is correlated with the Tenth Article of the Creed—"The Communion of Saints, the Forgiveness of Sins"; for it is through the Sacraments that Christ, our Head, communicates graces to the members of His Mystical Body. As in the great theological syntheses of the Middle Ages, the presentation of truth is comparatively cold and abstract. The medieval theologians deemed it inadvisable to appeal to the imagination and to the emotions in the quest of truth. But they were by no means unacquainted with the ethical appeal of the truths they were discussing. In no one's career, perhaps, was the golden thread of doctrine so closely woven into the tissues of a perfect life as in that of St. Thomas. Of him it may be said that he wished to know in order that he might love; then, because he loved, he wished to scrutinize ever more closely the object of his affections. His sublime hymns on the Eucharist are best proof that lofty speculation does not suppress or warp the affective element in human nature.

Today, as in other ages, "truths are decayed, they are diminished among the children of men." The environment in which we live and the atmosphere which we breathe are tainted with irreligion and unbelief. May the perusal of this book produce in the readers that strong faith, fond hope, and burning love of God which animated the soul of the great theologian, the Angelic Doctor, St. Thomas Aquinas!

RUDOLPH G. BANDAS, S.T.D. ET M.

TRANSLATOR'S PREFACE

St. Thomas Aquinas

St. Thomas Aquinas was born about the year 1225[1]. The name Aquinas derived from the territory of his father, Count Landulf of Aquina, in the vicinity of Naples. The mother of Thomas was Theodora, Countess of Teano, and his family was related to the Emperors Henry VI and Frederick II, and to the Kings of France, Aragon, and Castile. "He could have quartered half the kingdoms of Europe in his shield," wrote Chesterton, "if he had not thrown away the shield. He was Italian and French and German and in every way European."[2] At the early age of five Thomas was sent to school at the Benedictine Monastery of Monte Cassino. He showed at once the great gifts of intellect with which he had been endowed. His biographers attest to the piety and inquiring nature of this young pupil, who would surprise his master with the oft-repeated question: "What is God?" The early Benedictine training left Thomas with a life-long devotion to the Liturgy, and prepared him for further studies at the famed University of Naples where he was enrolled in or about the year 1239. While at Naples Thomas met with the members of the Order of St. Dominic, which had been founded some twenty years earlier. He made known his desire to be a Dominican about 1240, and instantly met with strong opposition from his family, but especially from his mother. At length he received the Dominican habit in April, 1244, and was chosen to continue his studies at the Dominican school of studies at the University of Paris.

---

[1] P. Mandonnet, "Date de la naissance de S. Thomas d'Aquin," in *Revue Thomiste* (1914), 652-662.

[2] G. K. Chesterton, "St. Thomas Aquinas" (1933), 43.

Countess Theodora completely disapproved of his journey, and sent two of her sons and a detachment of soldiers to intercept Friar Thomas on his way to Paris. In this she was successful, and for nearly two years he was held a virtual prisoner in the family castle. This period was well spent by Thomas in study and meditation. Here he was constantly urged to forsake his vocation, and on one occasion he was tempted by a woman who had been thrust into his chamber by his own brothers. Thomas arose and grasping a burning brand from the fire, forced the temptress from his room. Then with characteristic vigor he burned deep in the door the potent sign of the cross. In later years he confided to his secretary and companion, Reginaldo of Piperno, that immediately after this event he was granted his urgent prayer for the gift of perpetual-chastity, and thereafter had complete freedom from the motions of concupiscence. It seems probable that this gave first basis for his title of Angelic Doctor.

In 1245 St. Thomas began to attend the lectures in theology of St. Albert the Great at the University of Paris. He made extraordinary progress in his studies, and three years later he accompanied St. Albert to Cologne there to continue his study. He was engaged in teaching in 1250. This same year marks his ordination to the priesthood. Thomas accompanied his teacher, Albert the Great, back to Paris in 1252, where he continued his lecturing and at the same time prepared for the examinations for the degree of Master in Theology. He was awarded the degree in 1257 from the University of Paris. He continued to lecture at this world-famous institution during these early years in his career, which was marked by developing intellectual power and originality and growing familiarity with the vast field of theological and philosophical learning.

St. Thomas was called to Rome in 1259, and for nine busy years was teaching, lecturing, and writing as the theologian of the Papal Court. He continued his study of Aristotle, and was deeply engrossed in the literature of the

Fathers of the Church. "He worked with the spirit of a missionary," says Maritain, "in the cause of Truth against error."[3] His chief writings of this period were a number of philosophical works, commentaries on various Books of the Old and New Testaments, theological disputations; above all, in 1267 or 1268 he completed the first Part of his masterpiece, the Summa Theologica.

St. Thomas was already widely known as a great theologian and scholar in this century which abounded in great theologians and scholars. Recalled to Paris to replace a stricken Master of Theology at the University, he began the last period of his life. He was to live less than six more years. They were crowded years of writing, teaching, and preaching. His Sermons, which fill a good-sized volume, were begun in the early years of his priestly life, and he continued to preach until his death. He was an authority on the spiritual life, and personally experienced the trials and consolations of the trained ascetic and the true contemplative. His writings on ascetic and mystical theology are original and permanent contributions to the science of the Saints. It is related of him that, after having written the sublime treatise on the Holy Eucharist, he was seen to fall into an ecstasy, and a voice from the crucifix above the altar was heard to say: "Thou hast written well of Me, Thomas. What reward wilt thou have?" To this the Saint replied: "None Lord, other than Thyself."

Thomas remained in Paris for three years, from 1269 to 1272, in the full maturity of his powers and the manifold outpourings of his genius. All of the Second Part of the Summa Theologica was written at this time, and the Third Part

[3] J. Maritain, "The Angelic Doctor." 35.
[4] For the vexed question of exact dates in the life of St. Thomas, I have relied chiefly on Cayre, "Precis de Patrologie" (Paris, 1930), II. pp. 526-536, who in turn is largely indebted to the researches of Mandonnet.

was begun. In 1272 he was recalled to Naples by order of the king to teach at the University of Naples which he had attended as a boy. He put the finishing touches on his numerous projects, completed the Third Part of the *Summa* up to Question XC, and then laid down his pen already worn out at the early age of 48. "I can do no more," he said on the morning of December 6, 1273. He had experienced an ecstasy during Mass and said to Reginald, his secretary: "Such secrets have been revealed to me that all I have written now appears of little value." During the following Lenten season, Thomas gave to the students and townsfolk of Naples the series of catechetical instructions on the Creed, Commandments, and Prayer which make up part of this volume. They are his last words. He died on March 1274, at Fossanuova in Northern Italy while on his way to attend the Council of Lyons. St. Thomas Aquinas lived in an age of great scholars and great Saints. He is the "prince and Master of all."[5]

St. Thomas was canonized in 1323. St. Pius X proclaimed him Doctor of the Universal Church in 1567. When Pope Leo XIII wrote his famous Encyclical, "A Eterni Patris," on the restoration of Christian philosophy, he urged his readers with all the force of his apostolic office" to restore the golden wisdom of St. Thomas and to spread it far and wide for the defense and beauty of the Catholic Faith, for the good of society, and for the advantage of all sciences." The same Pontiff, in a Brief dated August 4, 1880, designated St. Thomas, Patron of all Catholic universities, and his successors, including Pope Pius XI, have ordered Catholic teachers to make the explanations of Christian Doctrine by St. Thomas the basis for all their teaching.

---

[5] Pope Leo XIII in Encyclical, "Eterni Patris," August 4, 1879.

Chief Works of St. Thomas

More than sixty separate works, some of great length and some brief, came from the fertile mind of the Angelic Doctor.[6] Most important and, one would wish, most familiar of all his writings is the *Summa Theologica*. This is a complete scientific exposition of theology and at the same time a summary of Christian philosophy. St. Thomas considered this work simply as a manual of Christian Doctrine for the use of students. He thus announced its division: "Since the chief aim of this sacred science is to give a knowledge of God, not only as He is in Himself, but also as He is the Beginning of all things and the End of all, especially of all rational creatures—we shall treat first of God; secondly, of rational creatures' advance towards God; thirdly, of Christ who as Man is the Way by which we tend to God." These are the leading ideas of his *Summa*, and upon them he based the three Parts of this great work.

The *Summa contra Gentiles*, whose full title is "Treatise on the Truth of the Catholic Faith against Unbelievers" (1258-1261), is the most profound and doubtless the most powerful apologetical work ever written. It is St. Thomas' *Summa philosophica*, taking philosophy in the modern sense. The long list of Commentaries on the Sacred Scriptures are exhaustive, of great depth, and of permanent value. The "Perfection of the Spiritual Life" is one of the classics in the field of ascetical and mystical theology, and together with pertinent parts of the "Summa" forms a complete explanation of the Christian higher life.[7] St. Thomas also

---

[6] For a complete list of St. Thomas' writings: Cayre, *loc. cit.*; Maritain, "The Angelic Doctor," pp. 179-183; "Catholic Encyclopedia," XIV, 666 sqq.
[7] Cf. Hugh Pope O. P., "On Prayer and the Contemplative Life by St. Thomas" (Benziger Bros., 1914).

wrote the admirable "Office for the Feast of Corpus Christi" with its familiar prayers and hymns.[8]

The Opuscula

The Opuscula or "Little Treatises" are very numerous. In the course of time works were listed among the Opuscula which were not written by St. Thomas. In the "official" catalogue of Reginald of Piperno the Opuscula number seventy. They may be roughly classified as philosophical and theological, on moral and canonical questions, on Liturgy and the religious life, and catechetical instructions. There are some Opuscula not listed in the "official" catalogue which are now considered authentic. The five Opuscula which are translated in the present volume are undoubtedly authentic.[9] The Explanations of the Creed, the Our Father, and the Ten Commandments are numbers 66, 65, 67, 68 respectively in the catalogue which was prepared for the process of canonization of St. Thomas. The Explanation of the Hail Mary is listed in the catalogue of Bernard Guidonis and in later lists. This is noteworthy, since Bernard had before him the official list. Both Mandonnet and Grabmann consider the work authentic.[10] St. Thomas gave these Ex-

---

[8] It contains the *Pange lingua* with the "Tantum ergo" among its verses, *Sacris Solemnis* with the lines of "Panis angelicus," *Verbum supernum* with its concluding verse, "O salutaris hostia." The antiphon of the Office is the beautiful "O Sacrum Convivium." The prayer said by the celebrant at Benediction of the Blessed Sacrament. "Deus qui nobis sub Sacramento mirabili, etc.," is also part of this Office. The Eucharistic poem, *Adoro te devote*, is also probably by St. Thomas, who is rightly called the Doctor of the Eucharist.

[9] The authoritative studies on the authenticity of the *Opuscula* are: M. Mandonnet, O. P., *"Des Ecrits Authentiques de S. Thomas d'Aquin"* (Fribourg, 1910), and "Les Opuscules de S. Thomas D'Aquin," in *Revue Thomiste* (1927), 121-157; M. Grabmann, "Die echten Schriften des hl. Thomas v. Aquin" (Münster, 1920).

[10] Mandonnet, *"Des Ecrits,"* etc., 66; Grabmann, *op. cit.*, 232-337.

planations to the students and people of Naples during his last Lenten season on earth. The talks on the Ten Commandments were written down by Peter d' Andrea, and the Explanation of the other prayers were faithfully reported by his secretary and companion, Reginald of Piperno.

The "Explanation of the Seven Sacraments" is the second part of the treatise, "De fidei articulis et septem sacramentis," which St. Thomas wrote at the request of the Archbishop of Palermo in 1261-1262. It is noteworthy that the famed "Decretum pro Armenis" (Instruction for the Armenians), issued by the authority of the Council of Florence, is taken almost verbatim from the second part of this *Opusculum* (i.e., the "Explanation of the Seven Sacraments"). It is not a definition of the Council, but a practical instruction, as Denzinger points out.[11]

The latest editions of the *Opuscula* are the Vives edition (Paris) of 1871-80 and the Parma edition of 1852-73. This latter edition is reedited by Mandonnet with a new order and an introduction (Lethielleux, Paris, 1927). The "catechetical" *Opuscula* are here given in one volume in English for the first time. An English translation of two of these under the title, "On the Commandments" and "On the Lord's Prayer," was made by the Reverend H. A. Rawes in England in 1891. It is now out of print and practically inaccessible. Recently an English translation was by Rev. Lawrence Shapcote, O. P., in two small volumes with the titles, "The Three Greatest Prayers" and "The Commandments of God" (Burns and Oates, 1937). The "Explanation of the Seven Sacraments," however, is here given for the first time in English.

---

[11] "Enchiridion Symbolorum," n. 695.

St. Thomas in the History of Catechetics

The original and traditional meaning of *catechesis* (from the Greek: teaching by word of mouth) was oral teaching or instruction by word. It is used in this sense in the New Testament (e.g., in Luke i. 4; Acts, xviii. 25). "Catechetical" referred solely to this form of oral explanation of Christian Doctrine. This is the meaning that "catechetical instruction" had in the time of St. Thomas and throughout the Middle Ages.[12] "In this connection," says one authority, "it must be remembered that the term 'catechetical' was very often applied to sermons and instructions for grown people, not for children."[13] The conception of "catechetical" and "catechism" as referring to the question and answer method of teaching became general only during the Counter-Reformation. Thus, St. Augustine's classic work on teaching religion, "De rudibus catechizandis" (on Instructing the Ignorant), is straight exposition without question and answers. The famed "Roman Catechism" (Catechism of the Council of Trent) is not in question and answer form. Hence, the catechetical instructions of St. Thomas, which are oral explanations of Christian Doctrine, entitle him to a place in the history of catechetics with St. Augustine, Gerson, St. Charles Borromeo, St. Peter Canisius and others.[14]

The method of explaining Christian Doctrine by giving detailed attention to the Creed, the Commandments, the

---

[12] "By the catechism of St. Thomas is generally understood his explanation of the Apostles' Creed, the Lord's Prayer, the Hail Mary, and the Decalogue" (Gatterer-Kruz, "The Theory and Practice of the Catechism," 1914, p. 47).

[13] Spirago-Messmer, "Spirago's Method of Christian Doctrine" (1901), 508.

[14] John Gerson, the saintly chancellor of the University of Paris, wrote "On Leading the Little Ones to Christ" in the early fifteenth century. St. Charles Borromeo, Archbishop of Milan, was one of the founders of the Confraternity of Christian Doctrine and one of the authors of the Roman Catechism. St. Peter Canisius, the great Jesuit teacher of religion in the Counter-Reformation, wrote the well-known Canisian Catechisms.

Our Father and Hail Mary, goes back to the early centuries of the Church. One of the first great works which embody this fourfold division is the "Catechetical Instructions" of St. Cyril of Jerusalem (d 386). This division became general throughout the medieval period, and the "Creed, Code, Sacraments and Prayer" came to be a formula of the faith. Numerous Synods and Councils of the Church at this time decreed that sermons and instructions must be given the faithful according to this fourfold division.[15] The "Roman Catechism" follows this arrangement, as do most of the Catechisms of modern times.

The catechetical instructions of St. Thomas were used generally throughout the thirteenth and fourteenth centuries as manuals and text-books for priests and teachers of religion.[16] "The Explanations of St. Thomas", wrote Spirago, "are remarkable for their conciseness and their simplicity of language; they are especially noteworthy because the main parts of the catechetical course of instruction are brought into connection with one another so that they appear as one harmonious whole."[17] The influence of these works is especially prominent in the "Roman Catechism" which the Council of Trent ordered written for parish priests and for all teachers of religion. Many of the explanatory passages in both works are almost identical.

[15] Cf. Callan-McHugh, "Catechism of the Council of Trent," Introduction, xiv and xvi. See also Spirago-Messmer, *op. cit., 507.*

[16] Spirago-Messmer, *op. cit., 513-514.*

[17] *Ibid.*

Translator's Note

The edition used in this translation is the Parma, edited by P. Mandonnet, O. P., *Opuscula Omnia* (Lethielleux, Paris, 1927). Where the Vives edition is used, the change is noted in the footnotes. The edition of the "Roman Catechism" (Catechism of the Council of Trent) used in the commentary is "Catechismus Concilii Tridentini ad Parochos," Romae, Ex. Typog. Polyglotta, S. Cong. de Prop. Fide, 1891. To Reverend E. A. Connolly, S. S., for reading the manuscript and for many helpful suggestions the Translator is very grateful.

JOSEPH B. COLLINS, S.S., D.D., PH.D

Codex Aureus, *from the monastery of St. Emmeran, ca. 870 (Bavarian State Library, Munich). Depicted here are Christ, the four Evangelists, and four scenes from the Bible. Front board of oak, ornamented with gold leaf, precious stones, pearls and filigree work.*

EXPLANATION OF THE APOSTLES' CREED

What is Faith?

The Nature and Effects of Faith. —The first thing that is necessary for every Christian is faith, without which no one is truly called a faithful Christian.[1] Faith brings about four good effects. The first is that through faith the soul is united to God, and by it there is between the soul and God a union akin to marriage. "I will espouse thee in faith."[2] When a man is baptized the first question that is asked him is: "Do you believe in God?"[3] This is because Baptism is the first Sacrament of faith. Hence, the Lord said: "He that believeth and is baptized shall be saved."[4] Baptism without faith is of no value. Indeed, it must be known that no one is acceptable before God unless he have faith. "Without faith it is impossible to please God."[5] St Augustine explains

---

[1] "The Catechism of the Council of Trent," known as the "Roman Catechism" (and so called throughout this book), thus introduces the explanation of the twelve Articles of the Creed: "The Christian religion proposes to the faithful many truths which either singly or all together must be held with a certain and firm faith. That which must first and necessarily be believed by all is that which God Himself has taught us as the foundation of truth and its summary concerning the unity of the Divine Essence, the distinction of Three Persons, and the actions which are by particular reason attributed to each. The pastor should teach that the Apostles' Creed briefly sets forth the doctrine of these mysteries. . . The Apostles' Creed is divided into three principal parts. The first part describes the First Person of the Divine Nature and the marvelous work of the creation. The second part treats of the Second Person and the mystery of man's redemption. The third part concludes with the Third Person, the head and source of our sanctification. The varied and appropriate propositions of the Creed are called Articles, after a comparison often made by the Fathers; for just as the members of the body are divided by joints (*articuli*), so in this profession of faith whatever must be distinctly and separately believed from everything else is rightly and aptly called an Article. (Part 1 Chapter 1, 4).

[2] Osee, ii. 20

[3] In the ceremony of administering the Sacrament of Baptism, the priest asks the sponsor: "N., do you believe in God the Father Almighty, Creator of heaven and earth?

[4] Mark, xvi. 16

[5] Heb. xi. 6.

these words of St. Paul, "All that is not of faith is sin,"[6] in this way: "Where there is no knowledge of the eternal and unchanging Truth, virtue even in the midst of the best moral life is false."

The second effect of faith is that eternal life is already begun in us; for eternal life is nothing else than knowing God. This the Lord announced when He said: "This is eternal life, that they may know Thee, the only true God, and Jesus Christ whom Thou hast sent."[7] This knowledge of God begins here through faith, but it is perfected in the future life when we shall know God as He is. Therefore, St. Paul says: "Faith is the substance of things to be hoped for."[8] No one then can arrive at perfect happiness of heaven, which is the true knowledge of God, unless first he knows God through faith. "Blessed are they that have not seen and have believed."[9]

The third good that comes from faith is that right direction which it gives to our present life. Now, in order that one live a good life, it is necessary that he know what is necessary to live rightly; and if he depends for all this required knowledge, on his own efforts alone, either he will never attain such knowledge, or if so, only after a long time. But faith teaches us all that is necessary to live a good life. It teaches us that there is one God who is the rewarder of good and the punisher of evil; that there is a life other than this one, and other like truths whereby we are attracted to live rightly and to avoid what is evil. "The just man liveth by faith."[10] This is evident in that no one of the philosophers before the coming of Christ could, through his own powers, know God and the means necessary for salvation as well as any old woman since Christ's coming know Him through faith. And, therefore, it is said in Isaias that "the earth is

---

[6] Rom., xiv. 23.
[7] John, xvii. 3.
[8] Heb., xi. 1.
[9] John, xx. 29.
[10] Hab., ii. 4.

filled with the knowledge of the Lord."[11]

The fourth effect of faith is that by it we overcome temptations: "The holy ones by faith conquered kingdoms."[12] We know that every temptation is either from the world or the flesh or the devil. The devil would have us disobey God and not be subject to Him. This is removed by faith, since through it we know that He is the Lord of all things and must therefore be obeyed. "Your adversary the devil, as a roaring lion, goeth about seeking whom he may devour. Whom resist ye, strong in faith."[13] The world tempts us either by attaching us to it in prosperity, or by filling us with fear of adversity. But faith overcomes this in that we believe in a life to come better than this one, and hence we despise the riches of this world and we are not terrified in the face of adversity. "This is the victory which overcometh the world: our faith."[14] The flesh, however, tempts us by attracting us to the swiftly passing pleasures of this present life. But faith shows us that, if we cling to these things inordinately, we shall lose eternal joys. "In all things taking the shield of faith."[15] We see from this that it is very necessary to have faith.

"The Evidence of Things that Appear Not."—But someone will say that it is foolish to believe what is not seen, and that one should not believe in things that he cannot see. I answer by saying that the imperfect nature of our intellect takes away the basis of this difficulty. For if man of himself could in a perfect manner know all things visible and invisible, it would indeed be foolish to believe what he does not see. But our manner of knowing is so weak that no philosopher could perfectly investigate the nature of even one little fly. We even read that a certain philosopher spent thirty years in solitude in order to know the nature of the

[11] Isa., xi. 9.
[12] Heb., xi. 33.
[13] I Peter, v. 8.
[14] I John, v. 4.
[15] Eph., vi. 16.

bee. If, therefore, our intellect is so weak, it is foolish to be willing to believe concerning God only that which man can know by himself alone. And against this is the word of Job: "Behold, God is great, exceeding our knowledge."[16] One can also answer this question by supposing that a certain master had said something concerning his own special branch of knowledge, and some uneducated person would contradict him for no other reason than that he could not understand what the master said! Such a person would be considered very foolish. So, the intellect of the Angels as greatly exceeds the intellect of the greatest philosopher as much as that of the greatest philosopher exceeds the intellect of the uneducated man. Therefore, the philosopher is foolish if he refuses to believe what an Angel says, and far greater fool to refuse to believe what God says. Against such are these words: "For many things are shown to thee above the understanding of men."[17]

Then, again, if one were willing to believe only those things which one knows with certitude, one could not live in this world. How could one live unless one believed others? How could one know that this man is one's own father? Therefore, it is necessary that one believe others in matters which one cannot know perfectly of oneself. But no one is so worthy of belief as is God, and hence they who do not believe the words of faith are not wise, but foolish and proud. As the Apostle says: "He is proud, knowing nothing."[18] And also: "I know whom I have believed; and I am certain."[19] And it is written: "Ye who fear the Lord, believe Him and your reward shall not be made void."[20] Finally, one can say also that God proves the truth of the things which faith teaches. Thus, if a king sends letters signed with his seal, no one would dare to say that those

[16] Job. xxxvi. 26.
[17] Ecclus., iii. 25.
[18] I Tim., vi. 4.
[19] II Tim., i. 12.
[20] Ecclus, ii. 8.

letters did not represent the will of the king. In like manner, everything that the Saints believed and handed down to us concerning the faith of Christ is signed with the seal of God. This seal consists of those works which no mere creature could accomplish; they are the miracles by which Christ confirmed the saying of the Apostles and of the Saints.

If, however, you would say that no one has witnessed these miracles, I would reply in this manner. It is a fact that the entire world worshipped idols and that the faith of Christ was persecuted, as the histories of the pagans also testify. But now all are turned to Christ—wise men and noble and rich—converted by the words of the poor and simple preachers of Christ. Now, this fact was either a miracle or it was not. If it is miraculous, you have what you asked for, a visible fact; if it is not, then there could not be a greater miracle than that the whole world should have been converted without miracles. And we need go no further. We are more certain, therefore, in believing the things of faith than those things which can be seen, because God's knowledge never deceives us, but the visible sense of man is often in error [21].

THE FIRST ARTICLE:

"I Believe in One God."

Among all the truths which the faithful must believe, this is the first—that there is one God. We must see that *God* means the ruler and provider of all things. He, there-

---

[21] For the meaning of the word "faith" see the "Catholic Encyclopedia," vol. V. The neccesity of faith is explained in St. Thomas, *Summa Theologica*, II-II. Q. ii., 3, 4.

fore, believes in God who believes that everything in this world is governed and provided for by Him. He who would believe that all things come into being by chance does not believe that there is a God. No one is so foolish as to deny that all nature, which operates with a certain definite time and order, is subject to the rule and foresight and an orderly arrangement of someone. We see how the sun, the moon, and the stars, and all natural things follow a determined course, which would be impossible if they were merely products of chance. Hence, as is spoken of the Psalm, he is indeed foolish who does not believe in God: "The fool hath said in his heart: There is no God."[1]

There are those, however, who believe that God rules and sustains all things of nature, and nevertheless do not believe God is the overseer of the acts of man; hence they believe that human acts do not come under God's providence. They reason thus because they see in this world how the good are afflicted and how the evil enjoy good things, so that Divine Providence seems to disregard human affairs. Hence the words of Job are offered to apply to this view: "He doth not consider our things; and He walketh about the poles of heaven."[2] But this is indeed absurd. It is just as though a person who is ignorant of medicine should see a doctor give water to one patient and wine to another. He would believe that this is mere chance, since he does not understand the science of medicine which for good reasons prescribes for one wine and for another water. So is it with God. For God in His just and wise Providence knows what is good and necessary for men; and hence He afflicts some who are good and allows certain wicked men to prosper. But he is foolish indeed who believes this is due to chance, because he does not know the causes and method of God's dealing with men. "I wish that God might speak with thee, and would open His lips to thee, that He

[1] Ps. xiii. 1.
[2] Job, xxii. 14.

might show thee the secrets of wisdom, and that His law is manifold: and thou mightest understand that He exacteth much less of thee than iniquity deserveth."[3]

We must, therefore, firmly believe that God governs and regulates not only all nature, but also the actions of men. "And they said: The Lord shall not see; neither shall the God of Jacob understand. Understand, ye senseless among the people, and, you fools, be wise at last. He that planted the ear, shall He not hear, or He that formed the eye, doth He not consider? ... The Lord knoweth the thoughts of men."[4] God sees all things, both our thoughts and the hidden desires of our will. Thus, the necessity of doing good is especially imposed on man since all these thoughts, words and actions are known in the sight of God: "All things are naked and open to His eyes."[5]

We believe that God who rules and regulates all things is but *one* God. This is seen in that wherever the regulation of human affairs is well arranged, there the group is found to be ruled and provided for by one, not many. For a number of heads often brings dissension in their subjects. But since divine government exceeds in every way that which is merely human, it is evident that the government of the world is not by many gods, but by one only.[6]

Some Motives for Belief in Many Gods

There are four motives which have led men to believe in a number of gods. (1) The dullness of the human intel-

---

[3] Job, xi. 5-6.
[4] Ps. xciii. 7-11.
[5] Heb., iv. 13.
[6] "There is but one God, not many gods. We attribute to God the highest goodness and perfection, and it is impossible that what is highest and absolutely perfect could be found in many. If a being lack that which constitutes supreme perfection, it is, therefore, imperfect and cannot have the nature of God" ("Roman Catechism," *The Creed*, First Article, 7).

lect. Dull men, not capable of going beyond sensible things, did not believe anything existed except physical bodies. Hence, they held that the world is disposed and ruled by those bodies which to them seemed most beautiful and most valuable in this world. And, accordingly, to things such as the sun, the moon and the stars, they attributed and gave a divine worship. Such men are like to one who, going to a royal court to see the king, believes that whoever is sumptuously dressed or of official position is the king! "They have imagined either the sun and moon or the circle of the stars... to be the gods that rule the world. With whose beauty, if they being delighted, took them to be gods."[7]

(2) The second motive was human adulation. Some men, wishing to fawn upon kings and rulers, obey and subject themselves to them and show them honor which is due to God alone. After the death of these rulers, sometimes men make them gods, and sometimes this is done even whilst they are living. "That every nation may know that Nabuchodonosor is god of the earth, and besides him there is no other."[8]

(3) The human affection for sons and relatives was a third motive. Some, because of the excessive love which they had for their family, caused statues of them to be erected after their death, and gradually a divine honor was attached to these statues.[9] "For men serving either their affections or their kings, gave the incommunicable Name to stones and wood."[10]

(4) The last motive is the malice of the devil. The devil wished from the beginning to be equal to God, and thus he said: "I will ascend above the height of the clouds. I will be like the Most High."[11] The devil still entertains this desire.

[7] Wis., xiii. 2-3.
[8] Judith, v. 29.
[9] All this is fully explained in the fourteenth chapter of the Book of Wisdom, verses 15-21.
[10] Wis., xiv. 21.
[11] Isa., xiv. 14.

His entire purpose is to bring about that man adore him and offer sacrifices to him; not that he takes delight in a dog or cat that is offered to him, but he does relish the fact that thereby irreverence is shown to God. Thus, he spoke to Christ: "All these will I give Thee, if falling down Thou wilt adore me."[12] For this reason those demons who entered into idols said that they would be venerated as gods. "All the gods of the Gentiles are demons."[13] "The things which the heathens sacrifice, they sacrifice to devils, and not to God."[14]

Although all this is terrible to contemplate, yet at times there are many who fall into these above-mentioned four causes. Not by their words and hearts, but by their actions, they show that they believe in many gods. Thus, those who believe that the celestial bodies influence the will of man and regulate their affairs by astrology, really make the heavenly bodies gods, and subject themselves to them. "Be not afraid of the signs of heaven which the heathens fear. For the laws of the people are vain."[15] In the same category are all those who obey temporal rulers more than God, in that which they ought not; such actually set these up as gods. "We ought to obey God rather than men."[16] So also those who love their sons and kinsfolk more than God show by their actions that they believe in many gods; as likewise do those who love food more than God: "Whose god is their belly."[17] Moreover, all who take part in magic or in incantations believe that the demons are gods, because they seek from the devil that which God alone can give, such as revealing the future or discovering hidden things. We must, therefore, believe that there is but one God.

---

[12] Matt., iv. 9.
[13] Ps. cxv. 5.
[14] I Cor., x. 20.
[15] Jerem., x. 2-3
[16] Acts. v. 29.
[17] Phil., iii. 19.

THE FIRST ARTICLE (CONTINUED):

"The Father Almighty, Creator of Heaven and Earth."

It has been shown that we must first of all believe there is but one God. Now, the second is that this God is the Creator and Maker of heaven and earth, of all things visible and invisible. Let us leave more subtle reasons for the present and show by a simple example that all things are created and made by God. If a person, upon entering a certain house, should feel a warmth at the door of the house, and going within should feel a greater warmth, and so on the more he went into its interior, he would believe that somewhere within was a fire, even if he did not see the fire itself which caused this heat which he felt. So also is it when we consider the things of this world. For one finds all things, arranged in different degrees of beauty and worth, and the closer things approach to God, the more beautiful and better they are found to be. Thus, the heavenly bodies are more beautiful and nobler than those which are below them; and, likewise, the invisible things in relation to the visible. Therefore, it must be seen that all these things proceed from one God who gives His being and beauty to each and everything. "All men are vain, in whom there is not the knowledge of God: and who by these good things that are seen could not understand Him that is. Neither by attending to the works have acknowledged who was the workman. . . . For by the greatness of the beauty, and of the creature, the creator of them may be seen, so as to be known thereby."[1] Thus, therefore, it is certain for us that all things in the world are from God.

[1] **Wis.**, xiii. 1, 5.

Errors Relating to the First Article

There are three errors concerning this truth which we must avoid. First, the error of the Manicheans, who say that all visible created things are from the devil, and only the invisible creation is to be attributed to God. The cause of this error is that they hold that God is the highest good, which is true; but they also assert that whatsoever comes from good is itself good. Thus, not distinguishing what is evil and what is good, they believed that whatever is partly evil is essentially evil—as, for instance, fire because it burns is essentially evil, and so is water because it causes suffocation, and so with other things. Because no sensible thing is essentially good, but mixed with evil and defective, they believed that all visible things are not made by God who is good, but by the evil one. Against them St. Augustine gives this illustration. A certain man entered the shop of a carpenter and found tools which, if he should fall against them, would seriously wound him. Now, if he would consider the carpenter a bad workman because he made and used such tools, it would be stupid of him indeed. In the same way it is absurd to say that created things are evil because they may be harmful; for what is harmful to one may be useful to another. This error is contrary to the faith of the Church, and against it we say: "Of all things visible and invisible."[2] "In the beginning God created heaven and earth."[3] "All things were made by Him."[4]

The second error is of those who hold the world has existed from eternity: "Since the time that the fathers slept,

---

[2] In the Nicene Creed.
[3] Gen., i. 1.
[4] John, i. 3.

all things continue as they were from the beginning of the creation."[5] They are led to this view because they do not know how to imagine the beginning of the world. They are, says Rabbi Moses, in like case to a boy who immediately upon his birth was placed upon an island, and remained ignorant of the manner of child-bearing and of infants' birth. Thus, when he grew up, if one should explain all these things to him, he would not believe how a man could once have been in his mother's womb. So also those who consider the world as it is now, do not believe that it had a beginning. This is also contrary to the faith of the Church, and hence we say: "the Maker of heaven and earth."[6] For if they were *made*, they did not exist forever. "He spoke and they were made."[7]

The third is the error which holds that God made the world from prejacent matter (*ex prejacenti materia*). They are led to this view because they wish to measure divine power according to human power; and since man cannot make anything except from material which already lies at hand, so also it must be with God. But this is false. Man needs matter to make anything, because he is a builder of particular things and must bring form out of definite material. He merely determines the form of his work, and can be only the cause of the form that he builds. God, however, is the universal cause of all things, and He not only creates the form but also the matter. Hence, He makes out of nothing, and thus it is said in the Creed: "the Creator of heaven and earth." We must see in this the difference between making and creating. To create is to make something out of nothing; and if everything were destroyed, He could again make all things. He, thus, makes the blind to see, raises up the dead, and works other similar miracles. "Thy power is at hand when Thou wilt."[8]

---

[5] II Peter, iii. 4.
[6] In the Nicene Creed
[7] Ps. cxlviii. 5.
[8] Wis., xii. 18.

Good Effects of our Faith

From a consideration of all this, one is led to a fivefold benefit.

(1) We are led to a knowledge of the divine majesty. Now, if a maker is greater than the things he makes, then God is greater than all things which He has made. "With whose beauty, if they being delighted, took them to be gods, let them know how much the Lord of them is more beautiful than they... Or if they admired their power and their effects, let them understand by them that He that made them, is mightier than they."[9] Hence, whatsoever can even be affirmed or thought of is less than God. "Behold: God is great, exceeding our knowledge."[10]

(2) We are led to give thanks to God. Because God is the Creator of all things, it is certain that what we are and what we have is from God: "What hast thou that thou hast not received."[11] "The earth is the Lord's and the fullness thereof; the world and all they that dwell therein."[12] "We, therefore, must render thanks to God: What shall I render to the Lord for all the things that He hath rendered to me?"[13]

(3) We are led to bear our troubles in patience. Although every created thing is from God and is good according to its nature, yet, if something harms us or brings us pain, we believe that such come from God, not as a fault in Him, but because God permits no evil that is not for good. Affliction purifies from sin, brings low the guilty, and urges on the good to a love of God: "If we have received

---

[9] *Ibid.*, xiii. 3-4.
[10] Job, xxxvi. 26.
[11] I Cor., iv. 7.
[12] Ps. xxiii. 1.
[13] Ps. cxv. 12.

good things from the hand of God, why should we not receive evil?"[14]

(4) We are led to a right use of created things. Thus, we ought to use created things as having been made by God for two purposes: for His glory, "since all things are made for Himself"[15] (that is, for the glory of God), and finally for our profits: "Which the Lord thy God created for the service of all the nations."[16] Thus, we ought to use things for God's glory in order to please Him no less than for our own profit, that is, so as to avoid sin in using them: "All things are Thine, and we have given Thee what we received of Thy hand."[17] Whatever we have, be it learning or beauty, we must revere all and use all for the glory of God.

(5) We are led also to acknowledge the great dignity of man. God made all things for man: "Thou has subjected all things under his feet,"[18] and man is more like to God than all other creatures save the Angels: "Let us make man to Our image and likeness."[19] God does not say this of the heavens or of the stars, but of man; and this likeness of God in man does not refer to the body but to the human soul, which has free will and is incorruptible, and therein man resembles God more than other creatures do. We ought, therefore, to consider the nobleness of man as less than the Angels but greater than all other creatures. Let us not, therefore, diminish this dignity by sin and by an inordinate desire for earthly things which are beneath us and are made for our service. Accordingly, we must rule over things of the earth and use them, and be subject to God by obeying and serving Him. And thus we shall come to the enjoyment of God forever.

---

[14] Job, ii. 10.
[15] Prov., xvi. 4.
[16] Deut., iv. 19.
[17] I Paral., xxix. 14.
[18] Ps. viii. 8.
[19] Gen. i. 26.

THE SECOND ARTICLE:

"And in Jesus Christ, His only Son, our Lord."

It is not only necessary for Christians to believe in one God who is the Creator of heaven and earth and of all things; but also they must believe that God is the Father and that Christ is the true Son of God. This, as St. Peter says, is not mere fable, but is certain and proved by the word of God on the Mount of Transfiguration. "For we have not by following artificial fables made known to you the power and presence of our Lord Jesus Christ; but we were eye-witnesses of His greatness. For He received from God the Father honor and glory, this voice coming down to Him from the excellent glory: "This is My beloved Son, in whom I am well pleased. Hear ye Him." And this voice, we heard brought from heaven, when we were with Him in the holy mount."[1] Christ Jesus Himself in many places called God His Father, and Himself the Son of God. Both the Apostles and the Fathers placed in the articles of faith that Christ is the Son of God by saying: "And (I believe) in Jesus Christ, His (i.e., God's) only Son."[2]

Errors Relating to the Second Article

There were, however, certain heretics who erred in this belief. Photinus, for instance, believed that Christ is not the

---

[1] II Peter, i. 16.

[2] "Jesus Christ is the Son of God, and true God, like the Father who begot Him from all eternity. We also believe that He is the Second Person of the Blessed Trinity, in all things equal to the Father and to the Holy Spirit. Since we acknowledge the essence, will and power of all the Divine Persons to be one, then in them nothing unequal or unlike should exist or even be imagined to exist" ("Roman Catechism" Second Article, 8).

Son of God but a good man who, by a good life and by doing the will of God, merited to be called the son of God; and so Christ who lived a good life and did the will of God merited to be called the son of God. Moreover, this error would not have Christ living before the Blessed Virgin, but would have Him begin to exist only at His conception. Accordingly, there are here two errors: the first, that Christ is not the true Son of God according to His nature; and the second, that Christ in His entire being began to exist in time. Our faith, however, holds that He is the Son of God in His nature, and that He is from all eternity. Now, we have definite authority against these errors in the Holy Scriptures. Against the first error it is said that Christ is not only the Son, but also the only-begotten Son of the Father: "The only-begotten Son who is in the bosom of the Father, He hath declared Him."[3] And against the second error it is said: "Before Abraham was made, I AM."[4] It is evident that Abraham lived before the Blessed Virgin. And what the Fathers added to the other Creed [i.e., the Nicene Creed], namely, "the only-begotten Son of God," is against the first error; and "born of the Father before all ages" is against the second error.

Sabellius said that Christ indeed was before the Blessed Virgin, but he held that the Father Himself became incarnate and, therefore, the Father and the Son is the same Person. This is an error because it takes away the Trinity of Persons in God, and against it is this authority: "I am not alone, but I and the Father that sent Me."[5] It is clear that one cannot be sent from himself. Sabellius errs therefore, and in the "Symbol"[6] of the Fathers it is said: "God of

    [3] John, i. 18.
    [4] John, viii. 58.
    [5] John, viii. 16.
    [6] "Symbol" (from the Greek, *Symbolon*, and the late Latin *Symbolum*) is a formal authoritative statement of the religious belief of the Church, referring here to the Nicene Creed. This treatise of St. Thomas is indeed called by him an "Explanation of the Symbol of the Apostles," or the Apostles' Creed.

God; Light of Light," that is, we are to believe in God the Son from God the Father, and the Son who is Light from the Father who is Light.

Arius, although he would say that Christ was before the Blessed Virgin and that the Person of the Father is other than the Person of the Son, nevertheless made a three-fold attribution to Christ: (1) that the Son of God was a creature; (2) that He is not from eternity, but was formed the noblest of all creatures in time by God; (3) that God the Son is not of one nature with God the Father, and therefore that He was not true God. But this too is erroneous and contrary to the teaching of the Holy Scriptures. It is written: "I and the Father are one."[7] That is, in nature; and therefore, just as the Father always existed, so also the Son; and just as the Father is true God, so also is the Son. That Christ is a creature, as said by Arius, is contradicted in the "Symbol" by the Fathers: "True God of true God;" and the assertion that Christ is not from eternity but in time is also contrary to the "Symbol": "Begotten not made;" and finally, that Christ is not of the same substance as the Father is denied by the "Symbol": "Consubstantial with the Father."

It is therefore clear we must believe that Christ is the Only-begotten of God, and the true Son of God, who always was with the Father, and that there is one Person of the Son and another of the Father who have the same divine nature.[8] All this we believe now through faith, but we shall know it with a perfect vision in the life eternal. Hence, we shall now speak somewhat of this for our own edification.

---

[7] John, x. 30.

[8] " . . . We believe Him (Christ) to be one Son, because His divine and human natures meet in one Person. As to His divine generation, He has no brethren or coheirs, being the Only-begotten Son of the Father, and we men are the image and work of His hands" ("Roman Catechism," *loc. cit., 9-10*).

The Divine Generation

It must be known that different things have different modes of generation. The generation of God is different from that of other things. Hence, we cannot arrive at a notion of divine generation except through the generation of that created thing which more closely approaches to a likeness to God. We have seen that nothing approaches in likeness to God more than the human soul. The manner of generation in the soul is effected in the thinking process in the soul of man, which is called a conceiving of the intellect. This conception takes its rise in the soul as from a father, and its effect is called the *word* of the intellect or of man. In brief, the soul by its act of thinking begets the word. So also the Son of God is the Word of God, not like a word that is uttered exteriorly (for this is transitory), but as a word is interiorly conceived; and this Word of God is of the one nature as God and equal to God.[9]

The testimony of St. John concerning the Word of God destroys these three heresies, viz., that of Photinus in the words: "In the beginning was the Word;"[10] that of Sabellius in saying: "And the Word was with God;"[11] and that of Arius when it says: "And the Word was God."[12]

---

[9] "Among the different comparisons brought forth to show the mode and manner of this eternal generation, that which is taken from the production of thought in our mind seems to come nearest to its illustration, and hence St. John calls the Son 'the Word.' For our mind, understanding itself in some way, forms an image of itself which theologians have called the *word;* so God, in so far as we may compare human things to divine, understanding Himself, begets the Eternal Word. But it is more advantageous to consider what faith proposes, and with all sincerity of mind to believe and profess that Jesus Christ is true God and true Man—as God, begotten before all time; as Man, born in time of Mary, His Virgin Mother" ("Roman Catechism," *loc. cit.,* 9). St. Thomas treats more fully the eternal generation and Sonship of Christ in the *Summa Theol.,* I, Q. xxvii, art. 2; Q. xxxiv.

[10] John, i. 1.

[11] *Ibid.*

[12] *Ibid.*

But a word in us is not the same as the Word in God. In us the word is an *accident*;"[13] whereas in God the Word is the same as God, since there is nothing in God that is not of the essence of God. No one would say God has not a Word, because such would make God wholly without knowledge; and therefore, as God always existed, so also did his Word ever exist. Just as a sculptor works from a form which he has previously thought out, which is his word; so also God makes all things by His Word, as it were through His art: "All things were made by Him."[14]

Now, if the Word of God is the Son of God and all the words of God bear a certain likeness of this Word, then we ought to hear the word of God gladly; for such is a sign that we love God. We ought also to believe the word of God whereby the Word of God dwells in us, who is Christ: "That Christ may dwell by faith in your hearts."[15] "And you have not His word abiding in you."[16] But we ought not only to believe that the Word of God dwells in us, but also we should meditate often upon this; for otherwise we will not be benefited to the extent that such meditation is a great help against sin: "Thy words have I hidden in my heart, that I may not sin against Thee."[17] Again it is said of the just man: On His law he shall meditate day and night."[18] And it is said of the Blessed Virgin that she "kept all these words, pondering them in her heart."[19] Then also, one should communicate the word of God to others by advising, preaching and inflaming their hearts: "Let no evil speech proceed from your mouth; but that which is good, to the edification of faith."[20] Likewise, "let the word of Christ

---

[13] An accident is an attribute which is not part of the essence.
[14] John, i. 3.
[15] Eph., iii. 17.
[16] John, v. 38.
[17] Ps. cxviii. 11.
[18] Ps. i. 2.
[19] Luke, ii. 19.
[20] Eph., iv. 29.

dwell in you abundantly in all wisdom, teaching and admonishing one another."[21] So also "Preach the word; be instant in season, out of season; reprove, entreat, rebuke in all patience and doctrine."[22] Finally, we ought to put the word of God into practice: "Be ye doers of the word and not hearers only, deceiving your own selves."[23]

The Blessed Virgin observed these five points when she gave birth to the Word of God. first, she heard what was said to her: "The Holy Spirit shall come upon thee."[24] Then she gave her consent through faith: "Behold the handmaid of the Lord."[25] And she also received and carried the Word in her womb. Then she brought forth the Word of God and, finally, she nourished and cared for Him. And so the Church sings: "Only a Virgin didst nourish Him who is King of the Angels."[26]

THE THIRD ARTICLE:

"Who was conceived by the Holy Spirit, born of the Virgin Mary."

The Christian must not only believe in the Son of God, as we have seen, but also in His Incarnation. St. John, after having written of things subtle and difficult to understand,[1] points out the Incarnation to us when he says: "And the Word was made flesh."[2] Now, in order that we may under-

---

[21] Colos, iii. 16.
[22] II Tim., iv. 2.
[23] James, i. 22.
[24] Luke, i. 35.
[25] Luke, i. 38.
[26] Fourth Responsory, Office of the Circumcision, Dominican Breviary.

[1] John, i. 1-13.
[2] *Ibid.*, i. 14.

stand something of this, I give two illustrations at the outset.

It is clear that there is nothing more like the Word of God than the word which is conceived in our mind but not spoken. Now, no one knows this interior word in our mind except the one who conceives it, and then it is known to others only when it is pronounced.[3] So also as long as the Word of God was in the heart of the Father, it was not known except by the Father Himself; but when the Word assumed flesh—as a word becomes audible—then was It first made manifest and known. "Afterwards He was seen upon earth and conversed with men."[4] Another example is that, although the spoken word is known through hearing, yet it is neither seen nor touched, unless it is written on paper. So also the Word of God was made both visible and tangible when He became flesh. And as the paper upon which the word of a king is written is called the word of the king, so also Man to whom the Word of God is conjoined in one *hypostasis*[5] is called the Son of God. "Take thee a great book and write in it with a man's pen."[6] Therefore, the holy Apostles affirmed: "Who was conceived by the Holy Spirit, born of the Virgin Mary."

Errors Relating to the Third Article

On this point there arose many errors; and the holy Fathers at the Council of Nicaea added in that other Creed a number of things which suppress all these errors.

Origen said that Christ was born and came into the world to save even the devils, and, therefore, at the end of

---

[3] See above, p. 18.

[4] Baruch, iii. 38.

[5] Hypostasis is person distinct from *nature*, as in the one hypostasis of Christ as distinct from His two *natures*, human and divine; also distinct from *substance*, as in the three hypostases of the Godhead, which are the same in substance.

[6] Isa., viii. 1.

the world all the demons will be saved. But this is contrary to the Holy Scripture: "Depart from Me, you cursed, into everlasting fire which was prepared for the devil and his angels."[7] Consequently, to remove this error they added in the Creed: "Who for us men (not for the devils) and for our salvation, came down from heaven." In this the love of God for us is made more apparent.

Photinus would have Christ born of the Blessed Virgin, but added that he was a mere man who by a good life in doing the will of God merited to become the son of God even as other holy men. This, too, is denied by this saying of John: "I came down from heaven, not to do My own will but the will of Him that sent Me."[8] Now if Christ were not in heaven, He would not have descended from heaven, and were He a mere man, He would not have been in heaven. Hence, it is said in the Nicene Creed: "He came down from heaven."

Manichaeus, however, said that Christ was always the Son of God and He descended from heaven, but He was not actually but only in appearance clothed in true flesh. But this is false, because it is not worthy of the Teacher of Truth to have anything to do with what is false, and just as He showed His physical Body, so it was really His: "Handle, and see; for a spirit hath not flesh and bones, as you see Me to have."[9] To remove this error, therefore, they added: "And He was incarnate."

Ebion, who was a Jew, said that Christ was born of the Blessed Virgin in the ordinary human way.[10] But this is false, for the Angel said of Mary: "That which is conceived

---

[7] Matt., xxv. 41.

[8] John, vi. 38.

[9] Luke, xxiv. 39.

[10] "We believe and confess that the same Jesus Christ, our only Lord, the Son of God, when He assumed human flesh for us in the womb of the Virgin, was not conceived like other men, from the seed of man, but in a manner above the order of nature. i.e., by the power of the Holy Spirit; so that the same Person, remaining God as He was from all eternity, became man, what He was not before" ("Roman Catechism," Third Article, 1).

in her is of the Holy Spirit."[11] And the holy Fathers to destroy this error, added: "By the Holy Spirit."

Valentinus believed that Christ was conceived by the Holy Spirit, but would have the Holy Spirit deposit a heavenly body in the Blessed Virgin, so that she contributed nothing to Christ's birth except to furnish a place for Him. Thus, he said, this Body appeared by means of the Blessed Virgin, as though she were a channel. This is a great error, for the Angel said: "And therefore also the Holy which shall be born of thee shall be called the Son of God."[12] And the Apostle adds; "But when the fullness of time was come, God sent His Son, made of woman."[13] Hence the Creed says; "Born of the Virgin Mary."

Arius and Apollinarius held that, although Christ was the Word of God and was born of the Virgin Mary, nevertheless He did not have a soul, but in place of the soul was His divinity. This is contrary to the Scripture, for Christ says: "Now is My soul troubled."[14] And again: "My soul is sorrowful even unto death."[15] For this reason the Fathers added: "And was made man." Now, man is made up of body and soul. Christ had all that a true man has save sin. All the above mentioned errors and all others that can be offered are destroyed by this, that He was made man. The error of Eutyches particularly is destroyed by it. He held that, by a commixture of the divine nature of Christ with the human, He was neither purely divine nor purely human. This is not true, because by it Christ would not be a man. And so it is said: "He was made man." This destroys also the error of Nestorius, who said that the Son of God only by an indwelling was united to man. This, too, is false, because by this Christ would not be man but only in a man,

---

[11] Matt., i. 20.
[12] Luke, i. 35.
[13] Gal., iv. 4.
[14] John, xii, 27.
[15] Matt., xxvi. 38.

and that He became man is clear from these words: "He was in habit found as man."[16] "But now you seek to kill Me, a man who has spoken the truth to you, which I have heard of God."[17]

Good Effects of these Considerations

We can learn something from all this. (1) Our faith is strengthened. If, for instance, someone should tell us a- bout a certain foreign land which he himself had never seen, we would not believe him to the extent we would if he had been there. Now, before Christ came into the world, the Patriarchs and Prophets and John the Baptist told some- thing of God; but men did not believe them as they be- lieved Christ, who was with God, nay more, was one with God. Hence, far more firm is our faith in what is given us by Christ Himself: "No one hath seen God at any time; the only-begotten Son who is in the bosom of the Father, He hath declared Him."[18] Thus, many mysteries of our faith which before the coming of Christ were hidden from us, are now made clear.

(2) Our hope is raised up. It is certain that the Son of Man did not come to us, assuming our flesh, for any trivial cause, but for our exceeding great advantage. For He made as it were a trade with us, assuming a living body and deigning to be born of the Virgin, in order that to us might be vouchsafed part of His divinity,[19] And thus He became man that He might make man divine.[20]

---

[16] Phil., ii. 7.
[17] John, viii. 40.
[18] Ibid., i. 18.
[19] Thus, in the Mass, when the Priest puts wine and water in the chalice, he says: " . . . Grant that by the mystery of this water and wine we may be made partakers of His Divinity who vouchsafed to become partakers of our humanity, Jesus Christ, Thy Son, Our Lord."
[20] "Et sic factus est homo, ut hominem faceret Deum."

(3) Our charity is enkindled. There is no proof of divine charity so clear as that God, the Creator of all things, is made a creature; that Our Lord is become our brother, and that the Son of God is made the Son of man: "For God so loved the world as to give His only begotten Son."[21] Therefore, upon consideration of this our love for God ought to be re-ignited and burst into flame.

(4) This induces us to keep our souls pure. Our nature was exalted and ennobled by its union with God to the extent of being assumed into union with a Divine Person.[22]

Indeed, after the Incarnation the Angel would not permit St. John to adore him, although he allowed this to be done before by even the greatest partriarchs.[23] Therefore, one who reflects on this exaltation of his nature and is ever conscious of it, should scorn to cheapen and lower himself and his nature by sin. Thus, says St. Peter: "By whom He hath given us most great and precious promises; that by these you may be made partakers of the divine nature; flying the corruption of that concupiscence which is in the world.[24]

Finally, by consideration of all this, our desire to come to Christ is intensified. If a king had a brother who was away from him a long distance, that brother would desire to come to the king to see him, to be with him and to abide with him. So also Christ is our brother, and we should desire to be with Him and to be united to Him. "Where-

---

[21] John, iii. 16.

[22] "The Word, who is a Person of the divine nature, assumed human nature in such a manner that there should be one and the same Person in both the divine and human natures" ("Roman Catechism," *loc. cit.*, 2).

[23] "And after I had heard and seen, I fell down to adore before the feet of the Angel who showed me these things. And he said to me: 'See thou do it not,'" (Apoc., xxii. 8).

[24] II Peter, i, 4. "God deigned to assume the lowliness and frailty of our flesh in order to lift man up to the highest degree of dignity. . . We may now glory that the Son of God is bone of our bone, and flesh of the flesh, a privilege which is not granted to the Angels" ("Roman Catechism," *loc. cit.*, 11).

soever the body shall be, there shall the eagles also be gathered together."[25] The Apostle desired "to be dissolved and to be with Christ."[26] And it is this desire which grows in us as we meditate upon the Incarnation of Christ."

THE FOURTH ARTICLE:

"Suffered under Pontius Pilate, was crucified, died and was buried."

It is just as necessary for the Christian to believe in the passion and death of the Son of God as it is to believe in His Incarnation. For, as St. Gregory says, "there would have been no advantage in His having been born for us unless we had profited by His Redemption." That Christ died for us is so tremendous a fact that our intellect can scarcely grasp it; for in no way does it fall in the natural way of our understanding. This is what the Apostle says: "I work in your days, a work which you will not believe, if any man shall tell it to you."[1] The grace of God is so great and His love for us is such that we cannot understand what He has done for us. Now, we must believe that, although Christ suffered death, yet His Godhead did not die; it was the human nature in Christ that died. For He did not die as God, but as man .[2]

---

[25] Matt., xxiv. 28.
[26] Phil., i. 23.

[1] Acts, xiii., 41. (quoting Hab., i. 5).
[2] "As Christ was true and perfect man, He was capable of truly dying. Now, man dies when the soul is separated from the body. When, therefore, we say that Jesus died, we mean this, that His soul was disunited from His body. We do not admit, however, that the Divinity was separated from His Body. On the contrary, we firmly believe and profess that when His soul was dissociated from His body, His Divinity continued always united both to His body in the sepulchre and to His soul in limbo" ("Roman Catechism," Fourth Article, 6).

This will be clear from two examples, one of which is taken from man himself. Now, when a man dies, in the separation of the soul from the body the soul does not die but the body or flesh does die. So also in the death of Christ, His Divinity did not die, but His human nature suffered death. But if the Jews did not slay the Divinity of Christ, it would seem that their sin was not any greater than if they killed any ordinary man. In answering this we say that it is as if a king were clothed only in one garment, and if someone befouled this garment, such a one has committed as grave a crime as if he had defiled the king himself. Likewise, although the Jews could not slay God, yet in putting to death the human nature which Christ assumed, they were as severely punished as if they had put the Godhead itself to death. Another example is had from what we said before, viz., that the Son of God is the Word of God, and the Word of God made flesh is like the word of a king written on paper.[3] So if one should tear this royal paper in pieces, it would be considered that he had rent apart the word of the king. Thus, the sin of the Jews was as grievous as if they had slain the Word of God.

But what need was there that the Son of God should suffer for us? There was a great need; and indeed it can be assigned to two reasons. The first is that it was a remedy against sin, and the second is for an example of what we ought to do. It was a remedy to such an extent that in the passion of Christ we find a remedy against all the evils which we incur by our sins. And by our sins we incur five different evils.

Evil Effects of Sin

The first evil that man incurs by sin is the defilement of his soul. Just as virtue gives the soul its beauty, so sin

[3] See above, p. 4.

makes it ugly. "How happened it, O Israel, that thou art in thy enemies' land?. . . Thou art defiled with the dead."[4] But all this is taken away by the passion of Christ, whereby Christ poured out His blood as a laver wherein sinners are cleansed: "Who hath loved us and washed us from our sins in His own blood."[5] So, too, the soul is washed by the blood of Christ in baptism because then a new birth is had in virtue of His blood, and hence when one defiles one's soul by sin, one offers insult to Christ and sins more gravely than before one's baptism. "A man making void the law of Moses dieth without any mercy under two or three witnesses. How much more, do you think, he deserveth worse punishments, who hath trodden under foot the Son of God and hath esteemed the blood of the testament unclean!"[6]

Secondly, we commit an offense against God. A sensual man loves the beauty of the flesh, but God loves spiritual beauty, which is the beauty of the soul. When, however, the soul is defiled by sin, God is offended and the sinner incurs His hatred: "To God the wicked and his wickedness are hateful alike."[7] This also is removed by the passion of Christ, which made satisfaction to God the Father for sin—a thing which man of himself could never do. The charity and obedience of Christ in His suffering were greater than the sin and disobedience of the first man: "When we were enemies, we were reconciled to God by the death of His Son."[8]

Thirdly, we have been weakened by sin. When a person sins the first time, he believes that he will thereafter keep away from sin, but what happens is the very opposite. This is because by that first sin he is weakened and made more prone to commit sins, and sin more and more has power over him. Such a one, as far as he alone is concerned, has

---

[4] Bar., iii. 10-11.
[5] Apoc., i. 5.
[6] Heb., x. 28-29.
[7] Wis., xiv. 9.
[8] Rom., v. 10.

lowered himself to such a condition that he cannot rise up, and is like to a man who jumps into a well from which, without God's help, he would never be rescued. After the fall of man, our nature was weakened and corrupted, and we were made more prone to sin. Christ, however, lessened this sickness and weakness, although He did not entirely take it away. So now man is strengthened by the passion of Christ, and sin is not given such power over him. Moreover, he can rise clean from his sins when aided by God's grace conferred by the Sacraments, which receive their efficacy from the passion of Christ: "Our old man is crucified with Him, that the body of sin may be destroyed."[9] Indeed, before the passion of Christ few there were who lived without falling into mortal sin; but afterwards many have lived and are living without mortal sin.

Fourthly, we incur the punishment due to sin. For the justice of God demands that whosoever sins must be punished. This punishment, however, is in proportion to the guilt. But the guilt of mortal sin is infinite, because it is an offense against the infinite good, namely, God, whose commandments the sinner holds in contempt. Therefore, the punishment due to mortal sin is infinite. Christ, however, through His passion has taken away this punishment from us and borne it Himself: "Who His own self bore our sins in His body upon the tree."[10] "Our sins [that is, the punishment due to sin] His own self bore in His body." The passion of Christ was of such value that it sufficed to expiate for all the sins of the whole world, even of a hundred thousand worlds. And so it is that when a man is baptized, he is released from all his sins; and so also is it that the priest forgives sins; and, again, the more one conforms himself to the passion of Christ, the greater is the pardon and the grace which he gains.

Fifthly, we incur banishment from the kingdom of heaven. Those who offend kings are compelled to go into

[9] Rom., vi. 6.
[10] I Pet., ii. 24.

exile. Thus, man is expelled from heaven on account of sin Adam was driven out of paradise immediately after his sin and the gate of paradise was shut. But Christ by His sufferings and death opened this gate and recalled all the exiles to the kingdom. With the opening of the side of Christ, the gate of paradise is opened; and with the pouring out of His blood, guilt is washed away, satisfaction is made to God, infirmity is removed, punishment is expiated, and the exiles are called back to the kingdom. Hence, the thief received the immediate response: "This day thou shalt be with Me in paradise."[11] Never before was this spoken to anyone, not to Adam, not to Abraham, not to David; but *this day* (i.e., as soon as the gate is opened) the thief, having asked for pardon, received it: "Having a confidence in the entering into the holies by the blood of Christ.[12]

Christ, Exemplar of Virtues

From all this then is seen the effect of the passion of Christ as a remedy for sin. But no less does it profit us as an example. St. Augustine says that the passion of Christ can bring about a complete reformation of our lives. Whoever wishes to live perfectly need do nothing other than despise what Christ despised on the Cross, and desire what Christ desired. There is no virtue that did not have its example on the Cross.

So if you seek an example of charity, then, "greater love than this no man hath, that a man lay down his life for his friends."[13] And this Christ did upon the Cross. If, there-

---

[11] Luke, xxiii. 43.
[12] Heb., x. 19.
[13] John, xv. 13.

fore, He gave His life for us, we ought to endure any and all evils for Him: "What shall I render to the Lord for all the things that He hath rendered to me?"[14]

If you seek an example of patience, you will find it in its highest degree upon the Cross. Great patience is exemplified in two ways: either when one suffers intensely in all patience, or when one suffers that which he could avoid if he so wished. Christ suffered greatly upon the Cross: "O all ye that pass by the way, attend, and see if there be any sorrow like to My sorrow."[15] And with all patience, because, "when He suffered, He threatened not."[16] And again: "He shall be led as a sheep to the slaughter and shall be dumb before his shearer, and shall not open His mouth."[17] He could have avoided this suffering, but He did not: "Thinkest thou that I cannot ask My Father, and He will give Me presently more than twelve legions of Angels?"[18] the patience of Christ upon the Cross, therefore, was of the highest degree: "Let us run by patience to the fight proposed to us; looking on Jesus, the author and finisher of faith, who, having joy set before Him endured the cross, despising the shame."[19]

If you seek an example of humility, look upon Him who is crucified: although He was God, He chose to be judged by Pontius Pilate and to be put to death: "Thy cause has been judged as that of the wicked."[20] Truly "that of the wicked," because: "Let us condemn Him to a most shameful death."[21] The Lord chose to die for His servant: the Life of the Angels suffered death for man: "He humbled Him-

---

[14] Ps. cxv. 12.
[15] Lament., i. 12.
[16] I Pet., ii. 23.
[17] Isa., liii. 7.
[18] Matt., xxvi. 53.
[19] Heb., xii. 1-2.
[20] Job. xxxvi. 17
[21] Wis., ii. 20.

self, becoming obedient unto death, even to the death of the cross."[22]

If you seek an example of obedience, imitate Him who was obedient to the Father unto death: "For by the disobedience of one man, many were made sinners; so also by the obedience of one, many shall be made just."[23]

If you seek an example of contempt for earthly things, imitate Him who is the King of kings, the Lord of rulers, in whom are all the treasures of wisdom; but on the Cross He was stripped naked, ridiculed, spat upon, bruised, crowned with thorns, given to drink of vinegar and gall, and finally put to death. How falsely, therefore, is one attached to riches and raiment, for: "They parted My garments amongst them; and upon My vesture they cast lots."[24] How falsely to honors, since "I was covered with lashes and insults;" how falsely to positions of power, because "taking a crown of thorns, they placed it upon My brow;" how falsely to delicacies of the table , for "in My thirst they gave Me to drink of vinegar." Thus, St. Augustine, in commenting on these words, "Who, having joy set before Him, endured the Cross despising the shame,"[25] says: "The man Christ despised all earthly things in order to teach us to despise them."

THE FIFTH ARTICLE:

"He Descended into Hell."

The death of Christ was the separation of His soul from His body as it is with other men. But the Divinity was

---

[22] Phil., ii. 8.
[23] Rom., v. 19.
[24] Ps. xxi. 19.
[25] Heb., xii. 2.

so indissolubly conjoined to the Man Christ that although His soul and body were disunited, His Divinity was always most perfectly united to both the soul and body. This we have seen above. Therefore in the sepulchre His body was together with the Son of God who together with His soul descended into hell.[1]

Reasons for Christ's Descent

There are four reasons why Christ together with His soul descended into hell. First, He wished to take upon Himself the entire punishment for our sins, and thus atone for its entire guilt. The punishment for the sin of man was not alone death of the body, but there was also a punishment of soul, since the soul had its share in sin; and it was

---

[1] "Hell here means those far-removed places in which are detained those souls that have not been awarded the happiness of heaven. . . These places are not of the same nature. There is that most abominable and most dark prison where the souls of the damned, together with the unclean spirits, are punished in eternal and unquenchable fire. This is *gehenna* or the 'abyss,' and is Hell, strictly so-called. There also is the fire of Purgatory, in which the suffering souls of the just are purified for a definite time in order that they be permitted to enter into the everlasting Fatherland, where nothing unclean is admitted. . . The third and last place is that in which the souls of the just before the coming of the Lord were received; there without any pain, sustained by the blessed hope of the redemption, they enjoyed a quiet repose. *It was to these just souls who waited in the bosom of Abraham that Christ the Lord descended, and whom He delivered*" ("Roman Catechism," Fifth Article, Chapter VI, 2-3). Therefore, "He descended into hell" means that the soul of Jesus Christ, after His death, descended into Limbo, i.e., to the place where the souls of the just who died before Christ were detained, and were waiting for the time of their redemption. St. Peter writes: "He was put to death indeed in the flesh, but enlivened in the spirit, in which also coming, He preached to those spirits that were in prison" (I Peter, iii. 18-19).

"We profess that immediately after the death of Christ, His soul descended into hell, and remained there as long as His body was in the sepulchre; and we believe also that the one Person of Christ was at the same time in hell and in the tomb" ("Roman Catechism," *loc. cit.*, 1).

punished by being deprived of the beatific vision; and as yet no atonement had been offered whereby this punishment would be taken away. Therefore, before the coming of Christ all men, even the holy fathers after their death, descended into hell. Accordingly in order to take upon Himself most perfectly the punishment due to sinners, Christ not only suffered death, but also His soul descended into hell.[2] He, however, descended for a different cause than did the fathers; for they did so out of necessity and were of necessity taken there and detained, but Christ descended there of His own power and free will: "I am counted among them that go down to the pit; I am become as a man without help, free among the dead."[3] The others were there as captives, but Christ was freely there.

The second reason is that He might perfectly deliver all His friends. Christ had His friends both in the world and in hell. The former were His friends in that they possessed charity; and the latter were they who departed this life with charity and faith in the future Redeemer, such as Abraham, Isaac, Jacob, Moses, David, and other just and good men. Therefore, since Christ had dwelt among His friends in this world and had delivered them by His death, so He wished to visit His friends who were detained in hell and deliver them also: "I will penetrate to all the lower parts of the earth, and will behold all that hope in the Lord."[4]

The third reason is that He would completely triumph over the devil. Now, a person is perfectly vanquished when he is not only overcome in conflict, but also when the assault is carried into his very home, and the seat of his kingdom is taken away from him. Thus Christ triumphed over the devil,[5] and on the Cross He completely van-

---

[2] See last footnote. This place is also called Limbo.

[3] Ps. lxxxvii. 5. "They descended as captives; He as free and victorious amongst the dead, to overcome those devils by whom, in consequence of their guilt, they were held in captivity" ("Roman Catechism," loc. cit., 5).

[4] Ecclus. xxiv. 45.

[5] This refers to the temptation of Our Lord in the desert.

quished him: "Now is the judgment of this world; now shall the prince of this world (that is, the devil) be cast out."[6] To make this triumph complete, Christ wished to deprive the devil of the seat of his kingdom and to imprison him in his own house—which is hell. Christ, therefore, descended there, and despoiled the devil of everything and bound him, taking away his prey :[7] "And despoiling the principalities and powers, He hath exposed them confidently in open show, triumphing over them in Himself."[8] Likewise, Christ who had received the power and possession of heaven and earth, desired too the possession of hell, as says the Apostle: "That in the name of Jesus every knee should bow, of those that are in heaven, on earth, and under the earth."[9] "In My name they shall cast out devils."[10]

The fourth and final reason is that Christ might free the just who were in hell [or Limbo]. For as Christ wished to suffer death to deliver the living from death, so also He would descend into hell to deliver those who were there: "Thou also by the blood of Thy testament, hast sent forth Thy prisoners out of the pit wherein is no water."[11] And again: "O death, I will be thy death; O hell, I will be thy bite."[12] Although Christ wholly overcame death, yet not so completely did He destroy hell, but, as it were, He *bit* it. He did not free all from hell, but those only who were without mortal sin. He likewise liberated those without original sin, from which they, *as individuals*, were freed *by circumcision*; or before [the institution of] circumcision, they who had been saved *through their parents' faith* (which refers to those who died before having the use of reason); or *by the sacrifices*, and

---

[6] John, xii. 31.
[7] St. Thomas says that the soul of Christ descended to the hell of the jus' or to Limbo *per suam essentiam*, but to the hell of the damned only *per suan effectum* (*Summa Theol.*, III, Qu. lii, Art. 2).
[8] Col., ii. 15.
[9] Phil., ii. 10.
[10] Mark, xvi. 17.
[11] Zach., ix. 11.
[12] Osee, xiii. 14.

by their *faith in the future coming of Christ* (which refers to adults)."[13] The reason they were there in hell [i.e., Limbo] is original sin which they had contracted from Adam, and from which as members of the human race they could not be delivered except by Christ. Therefore, Christ left there those who had descended there with mortal sin, and the non-circumcised children. Thus, it is seen that Christ descended into hell, and for what reasons. Now we may gather four considerations from this for our own instruction.

What We May Learn from This

(1) A firm hope in God. No matter how much one is afflicted, one ought always to hope in the assistance of God and have trust in Him. There is nothing so serious as to be in hell. If, therefore Christ delivered those who were in hell, what great confidence ought every friend of God have that he will be delivered from all his troubles! "She [that is, wisdom] forsook not the just when he was sold, but delivered him from sinners. She went down with him into the pit. And in bonds she left him not."[14] God helps in a special manner those who serve Him, and hence the servant of God should feel secure in Him: "He that feareth the Lord shall tremble at nothing and shall not be afraid; for He is his hope."[15]

(2) We ought to conceive a fear of God and avoid all presumption. We have already seen that Christ suffered for sinners and descended into hell for them. However, He did not deliver all sinners, but only those who were free from

[13] Italics added.
[14] Wis., x. 13-14.
[15] Ecclus., xxxiv. 16.

mortal sin. He left there those who departed this life in mortal sin. Hence, anyone who descends into hell in mortal sin has no hope of deliverance; and he will remain in hell as long as the holy fathers remain in paradise, that is, for all eternity: "And these shall go into everlasting punishment; but the just, into life everlasting."[16]

(3) We ought to arouse in ourselves a mental anxiety. Since Christ descended into hell for our salvation, we ought in all care go down there in spirit by considering, for instance, its punishments as did that holy man, Ezechias: "I said: In the midst of my days I shall go to the gates of hell."[17] Indeed, he who during this life frequently descends into hell by thinking of it, will not easily fall into hell at death; for such meditation keeps one from sin, and draws one out of it. We see how men of this world guard themselves against wrongdoing because of the temporal punishment; but with how much more care ought they avoid the punishment of hell which far exceeds all else in its duration, its severity, and its varied nature! "In all thy works remember thy last end, and thou shalt never sin."[18]

(4) There comes to us in this an example of love. Christ descended into hell in order to deliver His own; and so we should go down there to rescue our own. They cannot help themselves. Therefore, let us deliver those who are in purgatory. He would be very hard-hearted who does not come to the aid of a relative who is detained in an earthly prison; but much more cruel is he who will not assist a friend who is in purgatory, for there is no comparison between the pains of this world and of that: "Have pity on me, have pity on me, at least you my friends, because the hand of the Lord hath touched me."[19] "It is therefore a holy and wholesome thought to pray for the dead, that they may be loosed from their sins."[20] We may assist these souls in

---

[16] Matt., xxv. 46.
[17] Isa., xxxviii. 10.
[18] Ecclus., vii. 40.
[19] Job. xix. 21.
[20] Mach., xii. 46.

three ways as St. Augustine tells us, viz., through Masses, prayers, and almsgiving. St. Gregory adds a fourth, that is, fasting. All this is not so amazing, for even in this world a friend can pay a debt for his friend; but this applies only to those who are in purgatory.

THE FIFTH ARTICLE (CONTINUED):

"The third day He rose again from the dead."

We must necessarily know two things: the glory of God and the punishment of hell. For being attracted by His glory and made fearful by punishments, we take warning and withdraw ourselves from sin. But for us to appreciate these facts is very difficult. Thus, it is said of God's glory: "But the things that are in heaven, who shall search out?" [1] For those who are worldly minded this is indeed difficult, because "he that is of the earth, of the earth he is, and of the earth he speaketh;"[2] but it is easier for the spiritual-minded, because, "he that cometh from above is above all," as is said in the same place. Accordingly God descended from heaven and became incarnate to teach us heavenly things. Once it was difficult to know about the punishments of hell: "no man hath been known to have returned from hell,"[3] as it is said in the person of the wicked. But this cannot be said now, for just as Christ descended from heaven to teach us heavenly things, so also He came back from the region of hell to teach us about it. It is, therefore, necessary that we believe not only that

---

[1] Wis., ix. 16.
[2] John, iii. 31.
[3] Wisd., ii. 1.

Christ was made man, and died, but also that He arose again from the dead. Therefore, it is said in the Creed: "The third day He arose again from the dead."

We find that many arose from the dead, such as Lazarus,[4] the son of the widow,[5] and the daughter of the Ruler of the synagogue.[6] But the resurrection of Christ differed from the resurrection of these and of all others in four points.

Special Character of Christ's Resurrection

(1) Christ's resurrection differed from that of all others in its cause. Those others who arose did so not of their own power, but either by the power of Christ or through the prayers of some Saint. Christ, on the contrary, arose by His own power, because He was not only Man but also God, and the Divinity of the Word was at no time separated either from His soul or from His body. Therefore, His body could, whenever He desired, take again the soul, and His soul the body: "I lay down My life, that I may take it again.

. . And I have power to lay it down; and I have power to take it up again."[7] Christ truly died, but not because of weakness or of necessity but rather of His own will entirely and by His own power. This is seen in that moment when He yielded up the ghost; He cried out with a loud voice,[8] which could not be true of others at the moment of dying, because they die out of weakness... For this the centurion said: "Indeed, this was the Son of God."[9] By that same power

---

[4] John, xi. 1-44.
[5] Luke, vii. 11-16.
[6] Mark, v. 35-43.
[7] John, x. 18.
[8] Matt., xxvii. 50.
[9] Matt., xxvii. 54.

whereby He gave up His soul, He received it again; and hence the Creed says, "He arose again," because He was not raised up as if by anyone else. "I have slept and have taken My rest; and I have risen up."[10] Nor can this be contrary to these words, "This Jesus hath God raised again,"[11] because both the Father and the Son raised Him up, since one and the same power is of the Father and the Son.

(2) Christ's resurrection was different as regards the life to which He arose. Christ arose again to a glorious and incorruptible life: "Christ is risen from the dead by the glory of the Father."[12] The others, however, were raised to that life which they had before, as is seen of Lazarus and the others.

(3) Christ's resurrection was different also in effect and efficacy. In virtue of the resurrection of Christ all shall rise again: "And many bodies of the saints that had slept arose."[13] The Apostle declares that "Christ is risen from the dead, the first fruits of them that sleep."[14] But also note that Christ by His Passion arrived at glory: "Ought not Christ to have suffered these things and so to enter into His glory?"[15] And this is to teach us how we also may arrive at glory: "Through many tribulations we must enter into the kingdom of God."[16]

(4) Christ's resurrection was different in point of time. Christ arose on the third day; but the resurrection of the others is put off until the end of the world. The reason for this is that the resurrection and death and nativity of Christ were "for our salvation,"[17] and thus He wished to rise again at a time when it would be of profit to us. Now, if He had

[10] Ps. iii. 6.
[11] Acts, ii. 32.
[12] Rom., vi. 4.
[13] Matt., xxviii. 52.
[14] I Cor., xv. 20.
[15] Luke, xxiv. 26.
[16] Acts, xiv. 21.
[17] From the Nicene Creed.

risen immediately, it would not have been believed that He died; and similarly, if He had put it off until much later, the disciples would not have remained in their belief, and there would have been no benefit from His Passion. He arose again, therefore, on the third day, so that it would be believed that He died, and His disciples would not lose faith in him.[18]

What We May Learn from the Resurrection

From all this we can take four things for our instruction. Firstly, let us endeavor to arise spiritually, from the death of the soul which we incur by our sins, to that life of justice which is had through penance: "Rise, thou that sleepest, and arise from the dead; and Christ shall enlighten thee."[19] This is the first resurrection: "Blessed and holy is he that hath part in the first resurrection."[20]

Secondly, let us not delay to rise until our death, but do it at once, since Christ arose on the third day: "Delay not to be converted to the Lord; and defer it not from day to day."[21] You will not be able to consider what pertains to salvation when weighed down by illness, and, moreover, by persevering in sin, you will lose part of all the good which is done in the Church, and you will incur many evils. Indeed, the longer you possess the devil, the harder it is to put him away, as St. Bede tells us.

---

[18] "Christ did not remain in the grave during all these three days, but as He lay in the sepulchre during an entire natural day, during part of the preceding day, and part of the following day, he is said, in very truth, to have lain in the grave for three days, and on the third day to have risen again from the dead" ("Roman Catechism," *loc. cit.*, 10).

[19] Eph., v. 14.

[20] John, xx. 6.

[21] Ecclus., v. 8.

Thirdly, let us rise up again to an incorruptible life in that we may not die again, but resolve to sin no more: "Knowing that Christ, rising again from the dead, dieth now no more. Death shall no more have dominion over Him. . . So do you also reckon that you are dead to sin, but alive unto God, in Christ Jesus our Lord. Neither yield ye your members as instruments of iniquity unto sin; but present yourselves to God, as those that are alive from the dead."[22]

Fourthly, let us rise again to a new and glorious life by avoiding all that which formerly were the occasions and the causes of our death and sin: "As Christ is risen from the dead by the glory of the Father, so we also may walk in newness of life."[23] This new life is the life of justice which renews the soul and leads it to the life of glory.

THE SIXTH ARTICLE:

"He ascended into heaven, and sitteth at the right hand of God, the Father Almighty."

Besides the resurrection of Christ, we must also believe in His ascension; for He ascended into heaven on the fortieth day. Hence, the Creed says: "He ascended into heaven." Concerning this we ought to observe three things, viz., that it was sublime, reasonable, and beneficial.

The Sublimity of the Ascension

It was certainly sublime that Christ ascended into heaven. This is expounded in three ways. Firstly, He

[22] Rom., vi. 9, 11-14.
[23] *Ibid.*, 4.

ascended above the physical heaven: "He... ascended above all the heavens."[1] Secondly, He ascended above all the spiritual heavens, i.e., spiritual natures: "Raising [Jesus] up from the dead and setting Him on His right hand in the heavenly places. Above all principality and power and virtue and dominion and every name that is named, not only in this world but also in that which is to come. And He hath subjected all things under His feet."[2] Thirdly, He ascended up to the very throne of the Father: "Lo, one like the Son of man came with the clouds of heaven. And He came even to the Ancient of days."[3] "And the Lord Jesus, after He had spoken to them, was taken up into heaven and sitteth on the right hand of God."[4] Now, it is not to be taken in the literal sense, but figuratively, that Christ is at the right hand of God. Inasmuch as Christ is God, He is said to sit at the right hand of the Father, that is, in equality with the Father; and as Christ is man, He sits at the right hand of the Father, that is, in a more preferable place.[5] The devil once feigned to do this: "I will ascend above the height of the clouds. I will be like the Most High."[6] But Christ alone succeeded in this, and so it is said: "He ascended into heaven, and sitteth at the right hand of the Father." "The Lord said to my Lord: Sit Thou at My right hand."[7]

[1] Eph., iv. 10.
[2] *Ibid.*, i. 20-22.
[3] Dan., vii. 13.
[4] Mark, xvi. 19.
[5] "In these words we observe a figure of speech, that is, the changing of a word from its literal to a figurative meaning, something which is not infrequent in the Scriptures; for when accommodating its language to human ideas, it attributes human affections and human members to God, who is pure spirit and can admit of nothing corporeal. For, just as among men, he who sits at the right hand is considered to occupy the most honored place; so, transferring the idea to heavenly things to express the glory which Christ as Man enjoys above all others, we say that He sits at the right hand of His Eternal Father. Now, this does not mean actual position and figure of body, but declares the fixed and permanent possession of royal and supreme power and glory which Christ received from the Father" ("Roman Catechism," Sixth Article, 3).
[6] Isa., xiv. 13-14.
[7] Ps. cix. 1.

The Reasonableness of the Ascension

The Ascension of Christ into heaven is in accord with reason: (1) because heaven was due to Christ by His very nature. It is natural for one to return to that place from whence he takes his origin. The beginning of Christ is from God, who is above all things: "I came forth from the Father and am come into the world; again I leave the world and I go to the Father."[8] "No man hath ascended into heaven, but He that descended from heaven, the Son of man who is in heaven."[9] The just ascend into heaven, but not in the manner that Christ ascended, i.e., by His own power; for they are taken up by Christ:[10] "Draw me, we will run after Thee."[11] Or, indeed, we can say that no man but Christ has ascended into heaven, because the just do not ascend except in so far as they are the members of Christ who is the head of the Church. "Wheresoever the body shall be, there shall the eagles also be gathered together."[12]

(2) Heaven is due to Christ because of His victory. For He was sent into the world to combat the devil, and He did overcome him. Therefore, Christ deserved to be exalted above all things: "I also have overcome and am set down with My Father in His throne."[13]

---

[8] John, xvi. 28.

[9] *Ibid.*, iii. 13.

[10] "He ascended by His own power, not by the power of another as did Elias, who was taken up into heaven in a fiery chariot (IV Kings, ii. 1); or as the prophet Habacuc (Dan., xiv. 35); or Philip, the deacon, who was borne through the air by the divine power and traversed the distant regions of the earth (Acts, viii. 39). Neither did He ascend into heaven solely by the exercise of His supreme power as God, but also, by virtue of the power which He possessed as Man; although human power alone was insufficient to raise Him from the dead, yet the virtue with which the blessed soul of Christ was endowed, was capable of moving the body as it pleased, and His body, now glorified, readily obeyed the soul that moved it" ("Roman Catechism," *loc. cit.*, 2).

[11] Cant., i. 3.

[12] Matt., xxiv. 28.

[13] Apoc., iii. 21.

(3) The Ascension is reasonable because of the humility of Christ. There never was humility so great as that of Christ, who, although He was God, yet wished to become man; and although He was the Lord, yet wished to take the form of a servant, and, as St. Paul says: "He was made obedient unto death,"[14] and descended even into hell. For this He deserved to be exalted even to heaven and to the throne of God, for humility leads to exaltation: "He that humbleth himself shall be exalted."[15] "He that descended is the same also that ascended above all the heavens."[16]

The Benefits of the Ascension

The Ascension of Christ was very beneficial for us. This is seen in three ways. Firstly, as our Leader, because He ascended in order to lead us; for we had lost the way, but He has shown it to us. "For He shall go up that shall open the way before them,"[17] and thus we may be made certain of possessing the heavenly kingdom: "I go to prepare a place for you."[18] Secondly, that He might draw our hearts to Himself: "For where thy treasure is, there is thy heart also."[19] Thirdly, to let us withdraw from worldly things: "Therefore; if you be risen with Christ, seek the things that are above, where Christ is sitting at the right hand of God. Mind the things that are above, not the things that are upon the earth."[20]

[14] Phil., ii. 8.
[15] Luke, xiv. 11.
[16] Eph., iv. 10.
[17] Mich., ii. 13.
[18] John, xiv. 2.
[19] Matt., vi. 21.
[20] Col., iii. 1.

THE SEVENTH ARTICLE:

"From thence He shall come to judge the living and the dead."

It is of the office of the King and Lord to pronounce judgment: "The king that sitteth on the throne of judgment scattereth away all evil with His look."[1] Since Christ, therefore, ascended into heaven and sits at the right hand of God as Lord of all, it is clear that His is the office of Judge. For this reason we say in the rule of Catholic faith that "He shall come to judge the living and the dead." Indeed the Angels have said that: "This Jesus who is taken up from you into heaven shall so come as you have seen Him going into heaven."[2]

We shall consider three facts about the judgment: (1) the form of the judgment; (2) the fear of the judgment; (3) our preparation for the judgment.

The Form of the Judgment

Now, concerning the form of the judgment there is a threefold question. Who is the judge, who are to be judged, and upon what will they be judged? Christ is the judge: "It is He who is appointed by God to be judge of the living and of the dead."[3] We may here interpret "the dead" to mean sinners and "the living" to mean the just; or "the living" to refer to those who at that time were living and "the dead" to mean those who had died. Christ of a certain is Judge, not only in that He is God, but also in that He is man. The

---

[1] Prov., xx. 8.
[2] Acts, i. 11.
[3] Acts, x. 42.

first reason for this is because it is necessary that they who are to be judged may see the Judge. But the Godhead is so wholly delightful that no one could behold it without great enjoyment; and hence the damned are not permitted to see the Judge, nor in consequence to enjoy anything. Christ, therefore, of necessity will appear in the form of man so that He may be seen by all: "And He hath given Him power to do judgment, because He is the Son of man."[4] Again Christ deserved this office as Man, for as Man He was unjustly judged, and therefore God constitutes Him Judge of the entire world: "Thy cause hath been judged as that of the wicked. Cause and judgment Thou shalt recover."[5] And, lastly, if God alone should judge men, they, being terrified, would despair; but this despair disappears from men if they are to be judged by a Man: "And then they shall see the Son of man coming in a cloud."[6]

Who are to be Judged?

All are to be judged—those who are, who were, and who will be: "We must all be manifested before the judgment seat of Christ that every one may receive the proper things of the body, according as he hath done, whether it be good or evil."[7] There are, says St. Gregory, four different classes of people to be judged. The chief difference is between the good and the wicked.

Of the wicked, some will be condemned but not judged. They are the infidels whose works are not to be discussed because, as St. John says: "He that doth not believe is already judged."[8] Others will be both condemned

[4] John, v. 27.
[5] Job, xxxvi. 17.
[6] Luke, xxi. 27.
[7] II Cor., v. 10.
[8] John, iii. 18.

and judged. They are those possessing the faith who departed this life in mortal sin: "For the wages of sin is death."[9] They shall not be excluded from the judgment because of the faith which they possessed.

Of the good also, some will be saved and shall not be judged. They are the poor in spirit for God's sake who rather shall judge others: "Amen, I say to you that you, who have followed Me, in the regeneration when the Son of man shall sit on the seat of His majesty, you also shall sit on twelve seats judging the twelve tribes of Israel."[10] Now, this is not to be understood only of the disciples, but of all those who are poor in spirit; for otherwise Paul, who labored more than others, would not be among this number. These words, therefore, must refer also to all the followers of the Apostles and to all apostolic men: "Know you not that we shall judge Angels?"[11] "The Lord will enter into judgment with the ancients of His people and its princes."[12]

Others shall both be saved and judged, that is, they who die in a state of righteousness. For although they departed this life in justice, nevertheless they fell somewhat amiss in the business of temporal matters, and hence shall be judged but saved. The judgment will be upon all their deeds good and bad: "Walk in the ways of thy heart, . . . and know that for all these God will bring thee into judgment."[13] "And all things that are done, God will bring into judgment for every error, whether it be good or evil."[14] Even idle words shall be judged: "But I say to you that every idle word that men shall speak, they shall render an account for it in the day of judgment."[15] And thoughts

[9] Rom., vi. 23.
[10] Matt., xix. 28.
[11] I Cor., vi. 3.
[12] Isa., iii. 14.
[13] Eccles., xi. 9.
[14] *Ibid.*, xii. 14.
[15] Matt., xii. 36.

also: "For inquisition shall be made into the thought of the ungodly."[16] Thus, the form of the judgment is clear.

The Fear of the Judgment

The judgment ought indeed to be feared. (a) Because of the wisdom of the Judge. God knows all things, our thoughts, words and deeds, and "all things are naked and open to his eyes."[17] "All the ways of men are open to His eyes."[18] He knows our words: "The ear of jealousy heareth all things."[19] Also our thoughts: "The heart is perverse above all things and unsearchable. Who can know it? I am the Lord, who search the heart and prove the reins; who give to every one according to his way and according to the fruit of his devices."[20] There will be infallible witnesses—men's own consciences: "Who show the work of the law written in their hearts, their conscience bearing witness to them; and their thoughts between themselves accusing or also defending one another, in the day when God shall judge the secrets of men."[21]

(b) Because of the power of the Judge, who is almighty in Himself: "Behold, the Lord God will come with strength."[22] And also almighty in others: "The whole world shall fight with Him against the unwise."[23] Hence, Job says: Whereas there is no man that can deliver out of Thy hand."[24] "If I ascend into heaven, Thou art there; if I descend into hell, Thou art present," says the Psalmist.[25]

[16] Wis., i. 9.
[17] Heb., iv. 13.
[18] Prov., xvi. 2.
[19] Wis., i. 10.
[20] Jerem., xvii. 9-10.
[21] Rom., ii. 15-16.
[22] Isa., xl. 10.
[23] Wis., v. 21.
[24] Job, x. 7.
[25] Ps. cxxxviii. 8.

(c) Because of the inflexible justice of the Judge. The present is the time for mercy; but the future is the time solely for justice; and so the present is our time, but the future is God's time: "When I shall take a time, I shall judge justices."[26] "The jealousy and rage of the husband will not spare in the day of revenge. Nor will he yield to any man's prayers; nor will he accept for satisfaction ever so many gifts."[27]

(d) Because of the anger of the Judge. He shall appear in different ways to the just and to the wicked. To the just, He will be pleasant and gracious: "They will behold the King of beauty."[28] To the wicked He will be angry and pitiless, so that they may say to the mountains: "Fall upon us and hide us from the wrath of the Lamb."[29] But this anger of God does not bespeak in Him any perturbation of soul, but rather the effect of His anger which is the eternal punishment inflicted upon sinners.

Our Preparation for the Judgment

Now, against this fear of the judgment we ought to have four remedies. The first is good works: "Wilt thou then not be afraid of the power? Do that which is good, and thou shalt have praise from the same."[30] The second is confession and repentance for sins committed; and this ought to include sorrow in thinking of them, feeling of shame in confessing them, and all severity in making satisfaction for them. And these will take away the eternal punishment. The third is giving of alms, which makes all things clean: "Make unto you friends of the mammon of iniquity; that

---

[26] Ps. lxxiv. 3.
[27] Prov., vi. 34-35.
[28] Isa., xxxiii. 17.
[29] Apoc., vi. 16.
[30] Rom., xiii. 3.

when you shall fail, they may receive you into everlasting dwellings."[31] The fourth is charity, viz., the love of God and our neighbor, for "charity covereth a multitude of sins."[32]

THE EIGHTH ARTICLE:

"I Believe in the Holy Spirit."

As we have said, the Word of God is the Son of God just as in a way the word of man is the concept of his intellect.[1] But sometimes man has a word which is dead. This is when, for instance, he conceives what he ought to do, but he has not the will to do it; or when one believes but does not practise; then his *faith* is said to be *dead*, as St. James points out.[2] The word of God, however, is alive: "For the word of God is living."[3] It is necessary, therefore, that in God there be will and love. Thus, St. Augustine says: "The word of God which we plan to speak is knowledge with love."[4] Now as the Word of God is the Son of God, God's love is the Holy Spirit. Hence, it is that one possesses the Holy Spirit when he loves God: "The charity of God is poured forth in our hearts, by the Holy Spirit who is given to us."[5]

[31] Luke, xvi. 9.
[32] I Peter, iv. 8.

[1] See above, p. 18.
[2] "So faith also, if it have not works, is dead in itself" (James, ii. 17).
[3] Heb., iv. 12.
[4] *De Trinitate,* ix. 10.
[5] Rom., v. 5.

Teaching of the Nicene Creed

There are some who held false opinions concerning the Holy Spirit. They said, for instance, that He was only the servant and minister of God. Hence, to remove these errors the holy Fathers added five phrases concerning the Holy Spirit.[6]

"The Holy Spirit, the Lord."—The first is, that although there are other spirits, such as the Angels who are ministers of God (Art they not all ministering spirits?)[7] nevertheless the Holy Spirit is the Lord. "God is a Spirit,"[8] and, "Now the Lord is a Spirit,"[9] and also, "Where the Spirit of the Lord is, there is liberty."[10] The reason is that He makes us love God and cease to love the world. Thus, the Creed says: "In the Holy Spirit, the Lord."

And Life-Giver." —The second phrase is there because the soul's life is to be united to God, inasmuch as God is the life of the soul, and as truly as the soul is the life of the body.[11] Now, the Holy Spirit unites the soul to God through love, because He is the love of God, and therefore He gives life. "It is the spirit that quickeneth."[12] Therefore, it is said: "and Life-giver."

"Who Proceeds from the Father and the Son." —"The third is that the Holy Spirit is one in substance with the Father and the Son; because as the Son is the Word of the Father, so the Holy Spirit is the love both of the Father and the Son, and, therefore, He proceeds from them both. Moreover, just as the Word of God is of the same substance as the Father,

---

[6] "And I believe in the Holy Spirit, (1) the Lord and (2) Life-giver, (3) who proceeds from the Father and the Son: (4) who together with the Father and the Son is adored and glorified: (5) who spoke by the Prophets" (The Nicene Creed).

[7] Heb., i. 14.

[8] John, iv. 24.

[9] II Cor., iii. 17.

[10] *Ibid.*

[11] *"Cum ipse Deus sit vita animae, sicut anima vita corporis."*

[12] John, vi. 64.

so also is Love |Holy Spirit| of the same substance as the Father and the Son." Hence, it is said: "who proceedeth from the Father and the Son." From this it is seen that the Holy Spirit is not a Creature.

"Who. . . is Adored and Glorified." —The fourth phrase is that the Holy Spirit as regards adoration is equal to the Father and the Son: "The true adorers shall adore the Father in spirit and truth."[13] "Teach ye all nations; baptizing them in the name of the Father and of the Son and of the Holy Spirit."[14] Hence, it is said: "Who together with the Father and the Son is adored."[15]

"Who Spoke by the Prophets." —The fifth phrase, wherein the Holy Spirit is declared equal to God, is that the Holy prophets spoke on behalf of God. It is clear that, if the Holy Spirit were not God, then it would not be said that the prophets had spoken of God on His behalf. Thus, says St. Peter: "The holy men of God spoke, inspired by the Holy Spirit."[16] Also: "The Lord God hath sent me, and His Spirit."[17] And so it is said: "Who spoke by the prophets."

In all this two errors are condemned. The Manicheans said that the Old Testament was not from God. But this is false because the Holy Spirit spoke through the prophets. Likewise, the error of Priscillian and Montanus was that they believed that the prophets did not speak by the Holy Spirit but were somewhat beside themselves.

[13] John, iv. 23.

[14] Matt., xxviii. 19.

[15] "The Holy Spirit is equally God with the Father and the Son, equally omnipotent, eternal, perfect, the supreme good, infinitely wise, and of the same nature with the Father and the Son. . . If the Father is God, and the Son, God, we must confess that the Holy Spirit, who is united with them in the same degree of honor, is also God. . . The Holy Spirit is God, the third Person in the divine nature, distinct from the Father and the Son, and produced by their will" ("Roman Catechism," Eighth Article, 4-5).

[16] II Peter, i. 21.

[17] Isa., xlviii. 16.

Benefits from the Holy Spirit

Many benefits come to us from the Holy Spirit. (1) He cleanses us from our sins. The reason is that one must repair that which one has made. Now, the soul is created by the Holy Spirit, because God has made all things through Him; for God, by loving His goodness, created everything: "Thou lovest all things that are, and hatest none of the things which Thou hast made."[18] Thus, Dionysius says: "Divine love did not permit Him to be without offspring."[19] It is necessary, therefore, that the hearts of men, destroyed by sin be made new by the Holy Spirit: "Thou shalt send forth Thy Spirit, and they shall be created; and Thou shalt renew the face of the earth."[20] Nor is it any wonder that the Spirit cleanses, since all sins are taken away by love: "Many sins are forgiven her, because she hath loved much."[21] "Charity covereth all sins."[22] And likewise: "Charity covereth a multitude of sins."[23]

(2) The Holy Spirit enlightens the intellect, since all that we know, we know through the Holy Spirit: "But the Paraclete, the Holy Spirit, whom the Father will send in My name, He will teach you all things and bring all things to your mind, whatsoever I shall have said to you."[24] Also: "His unction teacheth you all things."[25]

(3) He assists us and, to a certain extent, compels us to keep the commandments. No one can keep the commandments unless he loves God: "If any one love Me, he will keep My word."[26] Thus, the Holy Spirit makes us love

---

[18] Wis., xi. 25.
[19] *Div. Nom.*, IV.
[20] Ps. ciii. 30.
[21] Luke, vii. 47.
[22] Prov., x. 12.
[23] I Peter, iv. 8.
[24] John, xiv. 26.
[25] I John, ii. 27.
[26] John, xiv. 23.

God: "And I give you a new heart and put a new spirit within you; and I will take away the stony heart out of your flesh and will give you a heart of flesh. And I will put My Spirit in the midst of you; and I will cause you to walk in My commandments and to keep My judgments and do them."[27]

(4) He strengthens in us the hope of eternal life, because He is the pledge to us of this our destiny: "You were signed with the Holy Spirit of promise who is the pledge of our inheritance."[28] He is, as it were, the surety of our eternal life. The reason is that eternal life is due to man inasmuch as he is become the son of God; and this is brought about in that he is made like unto Christ; and this, in turn follows from his having the Spirit of Christ, and this is the Holy Spirit: "For you have not received the spirit of bondage again in fear; but you have received the spirit of adoption of sons, whereby we cry: Abba (Father). For the Spirit Himself giveth testimony to our spirit that we are the sons of God."[29] And also: "Because you are sons, God hath sent the Spirit of His Son into your hearts, crying: Abba, Father."[30]

(5) He counsels us when we are in doubt, and teaches us what is the will of God: "He that hath an ear let him hear what the Spirit saith to the churches."[31] Likewise: "I may hear him as a master."[32]

[27] Ezech., xxxvi. 26-27.
[28] Eph., i. 13.
[29] Rom., viii. 15-16.
[30] Gal., iv. 6.
[31] Apoc., ii. 7.
[32] Isa., l. 4.

THE NINTH ARTICLE:

"I Believe in the Holy Catholic Church."

We see that in a man there are one soul and one body; and of his body there are many members. So also the Catholic Church is one body and has different members. The soul which animates this body is the Holy Spirit.[1] Hence, after confessing our faith in the Holy Spirit, we are bid to believe in the Holy Catholic Church. Thus, in the Symbol it is said, "the Holy Catholic Church."

It must be known that "church" is the same as assembly.[2] So, the Holy Church is the same as the assembly of the faithful, and every Christian is a member of this Church, of which it is written: "Draw near to Me, ye unlearned; and gather yourselves together into the house of discipline."[3]

The Church has four essential conditions, in that she is one, holy, catholic, and strong and firm.[4]

---

[1] "For as the body is one and hath many members; and all the members of the body, whereas they are many, yet are one body, so also is Christ. For in one Spirit were we all baptized into one body. . . For the body also is not one member, but many" (I Cor., xii. 12-14). For St. Paul's admirable description of the Church, Christ's mystical body, see all of this chapter.

[2] "The word *ecclesia* (church) which is borrowed by the Latins from the Greek, has been applied since the preaching of the Gospel to sacred things. The word *ecclesia* (church) means a calling forth, but writers afterwards used it to mean a council or assembly. . . However, in the ordinary sense used in the Scriptures, the word was afterwards used to designate the Christian society only, and the Assemblies of the faithful; that is, of those who were called by faith to the light of truth, and the knowledge of God" ("Roman Catechism," Ninth Article, 2).

[3] Ecclus., li. 31.

[4] "The disctinctive *marks* of the Church are also to be made known to the faithful, that they thus may be able to appreciate the extent of the blessing conferred by God on those who have the happiness to be born and educated in her fold" ("Roman Catechism," *loc. cit.,* 2).

The Unity of the Church

Of the first, it must be known that the Church is one. Although various heretics have founded various sects, they do not belong to the Church, since they are but so many divisions. Of her it is said: "One is My dove; My perfect one is but one."[5] The unity of the Church arises from three sources:

(1) *the unity of faith.* All Christians who are of the body of the Church believe the same doctrine. "I beseech you. . . that you all speak the same thing that there be no schisms among you."[6] And: "One Lord, one faith, one baptism;"[7]

(2) *the unity of hope.* All are strengthened in one hope of arriving at eternal life. Hence, the Apostle says: "One body and one Spirit, as you are called in one hope of your calling;"[8]

(3) *the unity of charity.* All are joined together in the love of God, and to each other in mutual love: "And the glory which Thou hast given Me, I have given them; that they may be one, as We also are one."[9] It is clear that this is a true love when the members are solicitous for one another and sympathetic towards each other: "We may in all things grow up in Him who is the head, Christ. From whom the whole body, being compacted, and fitly joined together, by what every joint supplieth, according to the operation in the measure of every part, maketh increase of the body unto the edifying of itself in charity."[10] This is because each one ought to make use of the grace God grants him, and be of service to his neighbor. No one ought to be indifferent to the Church, or allow himself to be cut off and expelled from

---

[5] Cant., vi. 8.
[6] I Cor., i. 10.
[7] Eph., iv. 5.
[8] *Ibid.* 4.
[9] John, xvii. 22.
[10] Eph., iv. 15-16.

it; for there is but one Church in which men are saved, just as outside of the ark of Noah no one could be saved.

The Holiness of the Church

Concerning the second mark, holiness, it must be known that there is indeed another assembly, but it consists of the wicked: "I hate the assembly of the malignant."[11] But such a one is evil; the Church of Christ, however, is holy: "For the temple of God is holy, which you are."[12] Hence, it is said: "the Holy Church."

The faithful of this Church are made holy because of four things: (1) Just as a church is cleansed materially when it is consecrated, so also the faithful are washed in the blood of Christ: "Jesus Christ... who hath loved us and washed us from our sins in His own blood."[13] And: "That He might sanctify the people by his blood, suffered outside the gate."[14] (2) Just as there is the anointing of the church, so also the faithful are anointed with a spiritual unction in order to be sanctified. Otherwise they would not be Christians, for Christ is the same as Anointed. This anointing is the grace of the Holy Spirit: "He that confirmeth us with you in Christ and that hath anointed us, is God."[15] And: "You are sanctified... in the name of our Lord Jesus Christ."[16] (3) The faithful are made holy because of the Trinity who dwells in the Church; for wheresoever God dwells, that place is holy. "The place whereon thou standest is holy."[17] And: "Holiness becometh Thy house, O Lord."[18] (4) Lastly, the faithful are sanctified because God

[11] Ps. xxv. 5.
[12] I Cor., iii. 17.
[13] Apoc., i. 5.
[14] Heb., xiii. 12.
[15] II Cor., i. 21.
[16] I Cor., vi. 11.
[17] Josue, v. 16; cfr. also Gen., xxviii. 16.
[18] Ps. xcii. 5.

is invoked in the Church: "But Thou, O Lord, art among us, and Thy name is called upon by us; forsake us not."[19] Let us, therefore, beware, seeing that we are thus sanctified, 'est by sin we defile our soul which is the temple of God: "Know you not that you are the temple of God and that the Spirit of God dwelleth in you? But if any man violate the temple of God, him shall God destroy."[20]

The Catholicity or Universality of the Church

The Church is Catholic, that is, universal. Firstly, it is universal in place, because it is worldwide. This is contrary to the error of the Donatists.[21] For the Church is a congregation of the faithful; and since the faithful are in every part of the world, so also is the Church: "Your faith is spoken of in the whole world."[22] And also: "Go ye into the whole world and preach the gospel to every creature."[23] Long ago, indeed, God was known only in Judea; now, however, He is known throughout the entire world. The Church has three parts: one is on earth, one is in heaven, and one is in purgatory. Secondly, the Church is universal in regard to all the conditions of mankind; for no exceptions are made, neither master nor servant, neither man nor woman: "Neither bond nor free; there is neither male nor female."[24] Thirdly, it is universal in time. Some have

---

[19] Jerem., xiv. 9.

[20] I Cor., iii 16-17. "It should not be considered surprising that the Church, although among her children are many sinners, is called holy. For as those who profess any art, even though they may violate its rules, are still artists, so the faithful, although offending in many things and violating the promises which they have made, are still called holy, because they are made the people of God, and are consecrated to Christ by baptism and faith' ("Roman Catechism," loc. cit., 15).

[21] A sect which existed chiefly in Africa for about a century (311-411).

[22] Rom., i. 8.

[23] Mark, xvi. 15.

[24] Gal., iii. 28.

said that the Church will exist only up to a certain time. But this is false, for the Church began to exist in the time of Abel and will endure up to the end of the world: "Behold, I am with you all days, even to the consummation of the world."[25] Nay more, even after the end of the world, it will continue to exist in heaven.

The Apostolicity of the Church

The Church is firm. A house is said to be firm if it has a solid foundation. The principal foundation of the Church is Christ: "For other foundation no men can lay but that which is laid, which is Christ Jesus."[26] The secondary foundation, however, is the Apostles and their teaching. Therefore, the Church is firm. It is said in the Apocalypse that the city has "twelve foundations," and therein were "written the names of the twelve Apostles."[27] From this the Church is called Apostolic. Likewise, to indicate this firmness of the Church St. Peter is called the crowning head.[28]

The firmness of a house is evident if, when it is violently struck, it does not fall. The Church similarly can never be destroyed, neither by persecution nor by error. Indeed, the Church grew during the persecutions, and both those who persecuted her and those against whom she threatened[29] completely failed: "And whosoever shall fall upon this stone, shall be broken; but on whomsoever it shall fall, it shall grind him to powder."[30] As regards errors, indeed, the

---

[25] Matt., xxviii. 20.

[26] I Cor., iii. 11.

[27] Apoc., xxi. 14.

[28] As it is spoken of by Our Lord: "And I say to thee that thou art Peter; and upon this rock I will build My Church, and the gates of hell shall not prevail against it" (Matt., xvi. 18).

[29] That is, enemies of the Church who in one or other ways resisted the authority or teachings of the Church.

[30] Matt., xxi. 44.

more errors arise, the more surely truth is made to appear: "Men corrupt in mind, reprobate in faith; but they shall proceed no further."[31]

Nor shall the Church be destroyed by the temptations of the demons. For she is like a tower towards which all flee who war against the devil: "The name of the Lord is a strong tower."[32] The devil, therefore, is chiefly intent on destroying the Church, but he will not succeed, for the Lord has said: "The gates of hell shall not prevail against it."[33] This is as if He said: "They shall make war against thee, but they shall not overcome thee." And thus it is that only the Church of Peter (to whom it was given to evangelize Italy when the disciples were sent to preach) was always firm in faith. On the contrary, in other parts of the world there is either no faith at all or faith mixed with many errors. The Church of Peter flourishes in faith and is free from error. This, however, is not to be wondered at, for the Lord has said to Peter: "But I have prayed for thee, that thy faith fail not; and thou, being once converted, confirm thy brethren."[34]

THE TENTH ARTICLE:

"The Communion of Saints, the Forgiveness of Sins."

As in our natural body the operation of one member works for the good of the entire body, so also is it with a

[31] II Tim., iii. 8.
[32] Prov.. xviii. 10.
[33] Matt., xvi. 18.
[34] Luke, xxii. 32.

spiritual body, such as is the Church. Because all the faithful are one body, the good of one member is communicated to another: "And every one members, one of another."[1] So, among the points of faith which the Apostles have handed down is that there is a common sharing of good in the Church. This is expressed in the words, "the Communion of Saints."[2] Among the various members of the Church, the principal member is Christ, because He is the Head: "He hath made Him head over all the Church, which is His body."[3] Christ communicates His good, just as the power of the head is communicated to all the members.

The Seven Sacraments: A Review

This communication takes place through the Sacraments of the Church in which operate the merits of the passion of Christ, which in turn operates for the conferring of grace unto the remission of sins. These Sacraments of the Church are seven in number.

Baptism.—The first is Baptism which is a certain spiritual regeneration. Just as there can be no physical life

---

[1] Rom. xii. 5.

[2] "The evangelist St. John, writing to the faithful on the divine mysteries, tells them that he undertook to instruct them on the subject; 'that you,' he says, 'may have fellowship with us, and our fellowship be with the Father and with His son, Jesus Christ' (I John, i. 3). Now, this fellowship consists in the Communion of Saints. . . This Article is, as it were, a sort of explanation of the preceding one, which takes up the unity, sanctity, and catholicity of the Church. For the unity of the Spirit, by which she is governed, establishes among all her members a community of spiritual blessings, whereas the fruit of all the Sacraments, particularly Baptism, the door, as it were, by which we are admitted into the Church, are so many connecting links which bind and unite them to Jesus Christ." The "Roman Catechism" makes the Communion of Saints the last part of the Ninth Article of the Creed; and the Tenth Article is the Forgiveness of Sins ("Roman Catechism," *loc. cit.*, 24-25).

[3] Eph., i. 22.

unless man is first born in the flesh, so spiritual life or grace cannot be had unless man is spiritually reborn. This rebirth is effected through Baptism: "Unless a man be born again of water and the Holy Spirit, he cannot enter into the kingdom of God."[4] It must be known that, just as a man can be born but once, so only once is he baptized. Hence, the holy Fathers put into the Nicene Creed: "I confess one baptism." The power of Baptism consists in this, that it cleanses from all sins as regards both their guilt and their punishment. For this reason no penance is imposed on those who are baptized, no matter to what extent they had been sinners. Moreover, if they should die immediately after Baptism, they would without delay go to heaven. Another result is that, although only priests *ex officio* may baptize, yet any one may baptize in case of necessity, provided that the proper form of Baptism is used. This is: "I baptize thee in the name of the Father, and of the Son, and of the Holy Spirit." This Sacrament receives its power from the passion of Christ. "All we who are baptized in Christ Jesus are baptized in His death."[5] Accordingly there is a threefold immersion in water after the three days in which Christ was in the sepulchre.[6]

Confirmation.—The second Sacrament is Confirmation. Just as they who are physically born need certain powers to act, so those who are reborn spiritually must have the strength of the Holy Spirit which is imparted to them in this Sacrament. In order that they might become strong, the Apostles received the Holy Spirit after the Ascension of Christ: "Stay you in the city till you be endowed with power

---

[4] John, iii. 5.

[5] Rom., vi. 3.

[6] Immersion is the act of dipping or plunging the subject into the water used in the administration of Baptism. It was a method generally employed in the early Church, and was still in vogue at the time of St. Thomas. The Greek Church still retains it; but though valid, for obvious reasons immersion is practically no longer employed in the Latin Church. It is practised by some sects today in America.

from on high."[7] This power is given in the Sacrament of Confirmation. They, therefore, who have the care of children should be very careful to see that they be confirmed, because great grace is conferred in Confirmation. He who is confirmed will, when he dies, enjoy greater glory than one not confirmed, because greater grace will be his.

Holy Eucharist.—The Eucharist is the third Sacrament. In the physical life, after man is born and acquires powers, he needs food to sustain and strengthen him. Likewise in the spiritual life, after being fortified, he has need of spiritual food; this is the Body of Christ: "Except you eat the flesh of the Son of man and drink His blood, you shall not have life in you."[8] According to the prescribed law of the Church, therefore, every Christian must at least once a year receive the Body of Christ, and in a worthy manner and with a clean conscience: "For he that eateth and drinketh unworthily [that is, by being conscious of unconfessed mortal sin on his soul, or with no intent to abstain from it] eateth and drinketh judgment to himself."[9]

Penance.—The fourth Sacrament is Penance. In the physical life, one who is sick and does not have recourse to medicine, dies; so in the spiritual order, one becomes ill because of sin. Thus, medicine is necessary for recovery of health; and this is the grace which is conferred in the Sacrament of Penance: "Who forgiveth all thy iniquities; who healeth all thy diseases."[10] Three things must be present in the Sacrament of Penance: contrition, which is sorrow for sin together with a resolution not to sin again; confession of sins, as far as possible entire; and satisfaction which is accomplished by good works.

Extreme Unction.—Extreme Unction is the fifth Sacrament. In this life there are many things which prevent one

---

[7] Luke, xxiv. 49.
[8] John, vi. 54.
[9] I Cor, xi. 29.
[10] Ps. cii. 3.

from a perfect purification from one's sins. But since no one can enter into eternal life until he is well cleansed, there is need of another Sacrament which will purify man of his sins, and both free him from sickness and prepare him for entry into the heavenly kingdom. This is the Sacrament of Extreme Unction. That this Sacrament does not always restore health to the body is due to this, that perhaps to live is not to the advantage of the soul's salvation. "Is any man sick amongst you? Let him bring in the priests of the Church and let them pray over him, anointing him with oil in the name of the Lord. And the prayer of faith shall save the sick man. And the Lord shall raise him up; and if he be in sins, they shall be forgiven him."[11] It is now clear that the fullness of life is had from these five Sacraments.

Holy Orders.—It is necessary that these Sacraments be administered by chosen ministers. Therefore, the Sacrament of Orders is necessary, by whose powers these Sacraments are dispensed. Nor need one note the life of such ministers, if here and there one fail in his office, but remember the virtue of Christ through whose merits the Sacraments have their efficacy, and in whose Name the ministers are but dispensers: "Let a man so account of us as of the ministers of Christ and the dispensers of the mysteries of God."[12] This then is the sixth Sacrament, namely, Orders.

Matrimony.—The seventh Sacrament is Matrimony, and in it men, if they live uprightly, are saved; and thereby they are enabled to live without mortal sin. Sometimes the partners in marriage fall into venial sin, when their concupiscence does not extend beyond the rights of matrimony; but if they do go beyond such rights, they sin mortally.[13]

---

[11] James, v. 14-15.

[12] I Cor., iv. 1.

[13] See the "Explanation of the Sacraments," p. 152; and "The Commandments," p. 116.

The Forgiveness of Sins

By these seven Sacraments we receive the remission of sins,[14] and so in the Creed there follows immediately: "the forgiveness of sins." The power was given to the Apostles to forgive sins. We must believe that the ministers of the Church receive this power from the Apostles; and the Apostles received it from Christ; and thus the priests have the power of binding and loosing. Moreover, we believe that there is the full power of forgiving sins in the Church although it operates from the highest to the lowest, i.e., from the Pope down through the prelates.[15]

The Communion of Saints

We must also know that not only the efficacy of the Passion of Christ is communicated to us, but also the merits of His life; and, moreover, all the good that all the Saints have done is communicated to all who are in the state of grace, because all are one: "I am a partaker of all them that fear Thee."[16] Therefore, he who lives in charity

[14] Baptism and Penance are called Sacraments of the dead, because *they take away sin* and give the first grace of justification. The other five Sacraments are called Sacraments of the living, because one who receives them worthily is already living the life of grace. But the Sacraments of the living produce the first grace when the subject, guilty of a grievous fault, approaches the Sacraments in good faith, that is to say, with the invincible ignorance of his fault, and with attrition (cfr. Pourrat, "Theology of the Sacraments," St. Louis, 1914, p. 201).

[15] "For Our Lord did not give the power of so sacred a ministry to all, but to bishops and priests only . The same must be said regarding the manner in which the power is to be exercised; for sin can be forgiven only through the Sacraments, when duly administered. The Church has received no power otherwise to remit sins. Hence it follows that in the forgiveness of sins both priests and Sacraments are, as it were, the instruments which Christ, Our Lord, the Author and giver of salvation, makes use of to accomplish in us pardon of sin and the grace of justification" ("Roman Catechism," *loc. cit,* 6).

[16] Ps. cxviii. 63.

participates in all the good that is done in the entire world; but more specially does he benefit for whom some good work is done; since one man certainly can satisfy for another.[17] Thus, through this communion we receive two benefits. One is that the merits of Christ are communicated to all; the other is that the good of one is communicated to another. Those who are excommunicated, however, because they are cut off from the Church, forfeit their part of all the good that is done, and this is a far greater loss than being bereft of all material things. There is a danger lest the devil impede this spiritual help in order to tempt one; and when one is thus cut off, the devil can easily overcome him. Thus it was in the primitive Church that, when one was excommunicated, the devil even physically attacked him.[18]

THE ELEVENTH ARTICLE:

"The Resurrection of the Body."

Not only does the Holy Spirit sanctify the Church as regards the souls of its members, but also our bodies shall rise again by His power: "We believe in Him that raised up Jesus Christ, Our Lord, from the dead."[1] And: "By a man

---

[17] "But there is also another Communion in the Church which demands attention: every pious and holy action done by one belongs to and becomes profitable to all, through charity which "seeks not her own' " ("Roman Catechism," *loc. cit.*, 25).

[18] "The advantage of so many and such exalted blessings bestowed by Almighty God are especially enjoyed by those who lead a Christian life in charity and are just and beloved of God" ("Roman Catechism," *loc. cit.*, 26).

[1] Rom., iv. 24.

came death: and by a Man the resurrection of the dead."[2]
In this there occur four considerations: (1) the benefits
which proceed from our faith in the resurrection; (2) the
qualities of those who shall rise, taken all in general; (3)
the condition of the blessed; (4) the condition of the
damned.

The Benefits of the Resurrection

Concerning the first, our faith and hope in the resurrection is beneficial in four ways. Firstly, it takes away the
sorrow which we feel for the departed. It is impossible for
one not to grieve over the death of a relative or friend; but
the hope that such a one will rise again greatly tempers the
pain of parting: "And we will not have you ignorant,
brethren, concerning them that are asleep, that you be not
sorrowful, even as others who have no hope."[3]

Secondly, it takes away the fear of death. If one does
not hope in another and better life after death, then without doubt one is greatly in fear of death and would willingly
commit any crime rather than suffer death. But because we
believe in another life which will be ours after death, we do
not fear death, nor would we do anything wrong through
fear of it: "That, through death He might destroy him who
had the empire of death, that is to say, the devil. And might
deliver them who through fear of death were all their
lifetime subject of servitude."[4]

Thirdly, it makes us watchful and careful to live uprightly. If, however, this life in which we live were all, we

---

[2] I Cor., xv. 21. "In this Article the resurrection of mankind is called
'the resurrection of the body.' The Apostles had for object thus to convey an
important truth, the immortality of the soul. Lest, therefore, contrary to the
Sacred Scriptures, which in many places clearly teach the soul to be immortal,
any one may imagine that it dies with the body, and denies that both are to be
raised up, the Creed speaks only of 'the resurrection of the body' " ("Roman
Catechism," Eleventh Article, 2).

[3] I Thess., iv. 12.

[4] Heb., ii. 14.

would not have this great incentive to live well, for whatever we do would be of little importance, since it would be regulated not by eternity, but by brief, determined time. But we believe that we shall receive eternal rewards in the resurrection for whatsoever we do here. Hence, we are anxious to do good: "If in this life only we have hope in Christ, we are of all men most miserable."[5]

Finally, it withdraws us from evil. Just as the hope of reward urges us to do good, so also the fear of punishment, which we believe is reserved for wicked deeds, keeps us from evil; "But they that have done good things shall come forth unto the resurrection of life; but they that have done evil, unto the resurrection of judgment."[6]

Qualities of the Risen Bodies

There is a fourfold condition of all those who shall take part in the resurrection.

(a) *The Identity of the Bodies of the Risen.*—It will be the same body as it is now, both as regards its flesh and its bones. Some, indeed, have said that it will not be this same body which is corrupted that shall be raised up; but such view is contrary to the Apostle: "For this corruptible must put on incorruption."[7] And likewise the Sacred Scripture says that by the power of God this same body shall rise to life: "And I shall be clothed again with my skin; and in my flesh I shall see my God."[8]

[5] I Cor., xv. 19.
[6] John, v. 29.
[7] I Cor., xv. 53.
[8] Job, xix. 26. "The identical body which belongs to each one of us during life shall, though corrupt, and dissolved into its original dust, be raised up again to life. . . Man is, therefore, to rise again in the same body with which he served God, or was a slave to the devil; that in the same body he may experience rewards and a crown of victory, or endure the severest punishments and everlasting torments" ("Roman Catechism," *loc. cit.*, 7).

(b) *The Incorruptibility of the Risen Bodies.*—The bodies of the risen shall be of a different quality from that of the mortal body, because they shall be incorruptible, both of the blessed, who shall be ever in glory, and of the damned, who shall be ever in punishments: "For this corruptible must put on incorruption; and this mortal must put on immortality."[9] And since the body will be incorruptible and immortal, there will no longer be the use of food or of the marriage relations: "For in the resurrection they shall neither marry nor be married, but shall be as the Angels of God in heaven."[10] This is directly against the Jews and Mohammedans: "Nor shall he return any more into his house."[11]

(c) *The Integrity of the Risen Bodies.*—Both the good and the wicked shall rise with all soundness of body which is natural to man. He will not be blind or deaf or bear any kind of physical defect: "The dead shall rise again incorruptible,"[12] this is to mean, wholly free from the defects of the present life.[13]

(d) *The Age of the Risen Bodies.*—All will rise in the condition of perfect age, which is of thirty-two or thirty-three years. This is because all who were not yet arrived at this

[9] I Cor., xv. 53.

[10] Matt., xxii. 30.

[11] Job. vii. 10. "To omit many other points, the chief difference between the state of all bodies when risen from the dead, and what they had previously been, is that before the resurrection they were subject to dissolution; but when reanimated they shall all, without distinction of good and bad, be invested with immortality. This marvellous restoration of nature is the result of the glorious victory of Christ over death" ("Roman Catechism," *loc. cit.,* 12).

[12] I Cor., xv. 52.

[13] "Not only will the body rise, but it will rise endowed with whatever constitutes the reality of its nature and adorns and ornaments man. . . The members, because essential to the integrity of human nature, shall all be restored. . . For the resurrection, like the creation, is clearly to be accounted among the chief works of God. And as at the creation all things came perfect from the hand of God, so at the resurrection all things shall be perfectly restored by the same omnipotent hand" ("Roman Catechism," *loc. cit.,* 9).

age, did not possess this perfect age, and the old had already lost it. Hence, youths and children will be given what they lack, and what the aged once had will be restored to them: "Until we all attain the unity of faith and of the knowledge of the Son of God, unto a perfect man, unto the measure of the age of the fullness of Christ."[14]

Condition of the Blessed

It must be known that good will enjoy a special glory because the blessed will have glorified bodies which will be endowed with four gifts.

(a) *Brilliance.*—"Then shall the just shine as the sun in the kingdom of their Father."[15]

(b) *Impassibility* (i.e., Incapability of Receiving Action).—"It is sown in dishonor; it shall rise in glory."[16] "And God shall wipe away all tears from their eyes; and death shall be no more. Nor mourning, nor crying, nor sorrow shall be anymore, for the former things are passed away."[17]

(c) *Agility.*—"The just shall shine and shall run to and fro like sparks among the reeds."[18]

---

[14] Eph., iv. 13.

[15] Matt., xiii. 43. "This brightness is a sort of refulgence reflected from the supreme happiness of the soul; it is an emanation of the beatitude which it enjoys and which shines through the body. Its communication is like to the manner in which the soul itself is made happy, by a participation of the happiness of God" ("Roman Catechism," *loc. cit.*, 13).

[16] I Cor., xv. 43.

[17] Apoc., xxi. 4. "The first is *impassibility*, which shall place them beyond the reach of pain or inconvenience of any sort. . . This quality the Scholastics called 'impassibility,' not incorruption, in order to distinguish it as a property peculiar to a glorified body. The bodies of the damned shall not be impassible, though incorruptible; they shall be capable of experiencing heat and cold and of feeling pain." ("Roman Catechism," *ibid.*).

[18] Wis., iii. 7. *Agility,* as it is called, is a quality by which the body shall be freed from the heaviness that now presses it down; and shall acquire a capability of moving with the utmost ease and quickness wheresoever the soul pleases" ("Roman Catechism," *ibid.*).

(d) *Subtility.*—"It is sown a natural body; it shall rise a spiritual body."[19] This is in the sense of not being altogether a spirit, but that the body will be wholly subject to the spirit.

Condition of the Damned

It must also be known that the condition of the damned will be the exact contrary to that of the blessed. Theirs is the state of eternal punishment, which has a fourfold evil condition. The bodies of the damned will not be brilliant: "Their countenances shall be as faces burnt."[20] Likewise they shall be *passible*, because they shall never deteriorate and, although burning eternally in fire, they shall never be consumed: "Their worm shall not die and their fire shall not be quenched."[21] They will be weighed down, and the soul of the damned will be as it were chained therein: "To bind their kings with fetters, and their nobles with manacles of iron."[22] Finally, they will be in a certain manner fleshly both in soul and body: "The beasts have rotted in their dung."[23]

[19] I Cor., xv. 44. "Another quality is that of *subtility;* a quality which subjects the body to the absolute dominion of the soul, and to an entire obedience to her control" ("Roman Catechism," *ibid.*).

[20] Isa., xiii. 8.

[21] *Ibid.*, 'lxvi. 24.

[22] Ps. cxlix. 8.

[23] Joel, i. 17.

THE TWELFTH ARTICLE:

"Life everlasting. Amen."

The end of all our desires, eternal life, is fittingly placed last among those things to be believed; and the Creed says: "life everlasting. Amen." They wrote this to stand against those who believe that the soul perishes with the body. If this were indeed true, then the condition of man would be just the same as that of the beasts. This agrees with what the Psalmist says: "Man when he was in honor did not understand; he hath been compared to senseless beasts, and made like to them."[1] The human soul, however, is in its immortality made like unto God, and in its sensuality alone is it like the brutes. He, then, who believes that the soul dies with the body withdraws it from this similarity to God and likens it to the brutes. Against such it is said: "They knew not the secrets of God, nor hoped for the wages of justice, nor esteemed the honor of holy souls. For God created man incorruptible, and to the image of His own likeness He made him."[2]

What is Everlasting Life?

We must first consider in this Article what is everlasting life. And in this we must know that in everlasting life man is united to God. God Himself is the reward and the end of all our labors: "I am thy protector, and thy reward exceeding great."[3] This union with God consists, firstly, in a perfect vision: "We see now through a glass in a dark

---

[1] Ps. xlviii. 21.
[2] Wis., ii. 22-23. Note also: "And though in the sight of men they suffer torments their hope is full of immortality" (*ibid.*, iii. 4).
[3] Gen., xv. 1.

manner, but then face to face."[4] Secondly, in a most fervent love; for the better one is known, the more perfectly is one loved: "The Lord hath said it, whose fire is in Sion, and His furnace in Jerusalem."[5] Thirdly, in the highest praise. "We shall see, we shall love, and we shall praise," as says St. Augustine.[6] "Joy and gladness shall be found therein, thanksgiving and the voice of praise. "[7]

Then, too, in everlasting life is the full and perfect satisfying of every desire; for there every blessed soul will have to overflowing what he hoped for and desired. The reason is that in this life no one can fulfill all his desires, nor can any created thing fully satisfy the craving of man. God only satisfies and infinitely exceeds man's desires; and, therefore, perfect satiety is found in God alone. As St. Augustine says: "Thou hast made us for Thee, O Lord, and our heart is restless until it rests in Thee."[8] Because the blessed in the Fatherland will possess God perfectly, it is evident that their desires will be abundantly filled, and their glory will exceed their hopes. The Lord has said: "Enter thou into the joy of the Lord."[9] And as St. Augustine says: "Complete joy will not enter into those who rejoice, but all those who rejoice will enter into joy." "I shall be satisfied when Thy glory shall appear."[10] And again: "Who satisfieth thy desire with good things."[11]

---

[4] I Cor., xiii. 12. "The blessed always see God present, and by this greatest and most exalted of gifts, 'being made partakers of the divine nature' (II Peter, i. 4), they enjoy true and solid happiness" ("Roman Catechism," Twelfth Article, 9).

[5] Isa., xxxi. 9. Note: This second consideration is found in the Vives edition, Chapter XV.

[6] *"Ibi vacabimus, et videbimus: videbimus, et amabimus; amabimus, et laudabimus"* ("There we shall rest and we shall see; we shall see and we shall love; we shall love and we shall praise," in "The City of God," Book XXII, Chapter xxx).

[7] Isa., li. 3.

[8] "Confessions," Book I, 1.

[9] Matt., xxv. 21.

[10] Ps. xvi. 15.

[11] Ps. cii. 5.

The Fullness of Desires

Whatever is delightful will be there in abundant fullness. Thus, if pleasures are desired, there will be the highest and most perfect pleasure, for it derives from the highest good, namely, God: "Then shalt thou abound in delights in the Almighty."[12] "At the right hand are delights even to the end."[13] Likewise, if honors are desired, there too will be all honor. Men wish particularly to be kings, if they be laymen; and to be bishops, if they be clerics. Both these honors will be there: "And hath made us a kingdom and priests."[14] Behold how they are numbered among the children of God."[15] If knowledge is desired, it will be there most perfectly, because we shall possess in the life everlasting knowledge of all the natures of things and all truth, and whatever we desire we shall know. And whatever we desire to possess, that we shall have, even life eternal: "Now, all good things come to me together with her."[16] "To the just their desire shall be given."[17]

Again, most perfect security is there. In this world there is no perfect security; for in so far as one has many things, and the higher one's position, the more one has to

---

[12] Job, xxii. 26.

[13] Ps. xv. 11. "To enumerate all the delights with which the souls of the blessed will be filled, would be an endless task. We cannot even conceive them in thought. The happiness of the Saints is filled to overflowing of all those pleasures which can be enjoyed or even desired in this life, whether they pertain to the powers of the mind or the perfection of the body" ("Roman Catechism," *loc. cit.,* 12).

[14] Apoc., v. 10.

[15] Wis., v. 5. "How distinguished that honor must be which is conferred by God Himself, who no longer calls them servants, but friends, brethren, and sons of God. Hence, the Redeemer will address His elect in these infinitely loving and highly honorable words: 'Come, ye blessed of My Father, possess you the kingdom prepared for you' " ("Roman Catechism," *loc. cit.,* 11).

[16] Wis., vii. 11.

[17] Prov., x. 24.

fear and the more one wants. But in the life everlasting there is no anxiety, no labor, no fear. "And My people shall sit in the beauty of peace,"[18] and "shall enjoy abundance, without fear of evils."[19]

Finally, in heaven there will be the happy society of all the blessed, and this society will be especially delightful. Since each one will possess all good together with the blessed, and they will love one another as themselves, and they will rejoice in the others' good as their own. It will also happen that, as the pleasure and enjoyment of one increases, so will it be for all: "The dwelling in thee is as it were of all rejoicing."[20]

What is Everlasting Death?

The perfect will enjoy all this in the life everlasting, and much more that surpasses description. But the wicked, on the other hand will be in eternal death suffering pain and punishment as great as will be the happiness and glory of the good. The punishment of the damned will be increased, firstly, by their separation from God and from all good. This is the pain of loss which corresponds to aversion, and is a greater punishment than that of sense: "And the unprofitable servant, cast ye out into the exterior darkness."[21] The wicked in this life have interior darkness, namely sin; but then they shall also have exterior darkness.

Secondly, the damned shall suffer from remorse of conscience: "I will reprove thee, and set before thy face."[22] "Groaning for anguish of spirit."[23] Nevertheless, their re-

---

[18] Isa., xxxii. 10. This is in the Vives edition, Chapter xv.
[19] Prov., i. 33.
[20] Ps. lxxxvi. 7.
[21] Matt., xxv. 30.
[22] Ps. xlix. 21.
[23] Wis., v. 3.

pentance and groaning will be of no avail, because it rises not from hatred of evil, but from fear and the enormity of their punishments. Thirdly, there is the great pain of sense. It is the fire of hell which tortures the soul and the body; and this, as the Saints tell us, is the sharpest of all punishments. They shall be ever dying, and yet never die; hence it is called eternal death, for as dying is the bitterest of pains, such will be the lot of those in hell: "They are laid in hell like sheep; death shall feed upon them."[24] Fourthly, there is the despair of their salvation. If some hope of delivery from their punishments would be given them, their punishment would be somewhat lessened; but since all hope is withdrawn from them, their sufferings are made most intense: "Their worm shall not die, and their fire shall not be quenched."[25]

We thus see the difference between doing good and doing evil. Good works lead to life, evil drags us to death. For this reason, men ought frequently to recall these things to mind, since they will incite one to do good and withdraw one from evil. Therefore, very significantly, at the end of the Creed is placed "life everlasting," so that it would be more and more deeply impressed on the memory. To this life everlasting may the Lord Jesus Christ, blessed God for ever, bring us! Amen.

---

[24] Ps. xlviii. 15.
[25] Isa., lxvi. 24.

THE TEN COMMANDMENTS

I. I am the Lord thy God, who brought thee out of the land of Egypt, out of the house of bondage. Thou shalt not have strange gods before Me. Thou shalt not make to thyself a graven thing, nor the likeness of any thing that is in heaven above, or in the earth beneath, nor of those things that are in the waters under the earth. Thou shalt not adore them, nor serve them. I am the Lord thy God, mighty jealous, visiting the iniquity of the fathers upon the children, unto the third and fourth generation of them that hate Me; and showing mercy unto thousands of them that love Me, and keep My commandaments.

II. Thou shalt not take the name of the Lord thy God in vain.

III. Remember that thou keep holy the Sabbath day.

IV. Honor thy father and thy mother.

V. Thou shalt not kill.

VI. Thou shalt not commit adultery.

VII. Thou shalt not steal.

VIII. Thou shalt not bear false witness against thy neighbor.

IX. Thou shalt not covet thy neighbor's wife.

X. Thou shalt not covet thy neighbor's house, nor his field, nor his servant, nor his handmaid, nor his ox, nor his ass, nor anything that is his.[1]

---

[1] Exod., xx. 2-17, and Deut., v. 6-21.

Moses receiving the Ten Commandments.

EXPLANATION OF
THE TEN COMMANDMENTS

THE FIRST COMMANDMENT:

"Thou Shalt Not Have Strange Gods Before Me."

The entire law of Christ depends upon charity. And charity depends on two precepts, one which concerns loving God and the other concerns loving our neighbor.

Now God, in delivering the law to Moses, gave him Ten Commandments written upon two tablets of stone. Three of these Commandments that were written on the first tablet referred to the love of God; and the seven commandments written on the other tablet related to the love of our neighbor. The whole law, therefore, is founded on these two precepts.[1]

The First Commandment which relates to the love of God is: "Thou shalt not have strange gods." For an understanding of this Commandment, one must know how of old it was violated. Some worshipped demons. "All the gods of the Gentiles are devils."[2] This is the greatest and most detestable of all sins. Even now there are many who transgress this Commandment: all such as practise divinations and fortune-telling. Such things, according to St. Augustine, cannot be done without some kind of pact with the devil. "I would not that you should be made partakers with devils."[3]

---

[1] "The Decalogue is the summary and epitome of the entire law of God," is the opinion of St. Augustine (*Quest. cxl. super Exod.*, lib. ii). "Although the Lord had spoken many things, yet He gave only two tablets of stone to Moses. . . If carefully examined and well understood, it will be found that on them depend whatever else is commanded by God. Again, these ten commandments are reducible to two, the love of God and our neighbor, on which 'depend the whole law and the prophets' " ("Roman Catechism," *The Decalogue,* Chapter I, 1).

[2] Ps. xcv. 5.

[3] I Cor., x. 20.

Some worshipped the heavenly bodies, believing the stars to be gods: "They have imagined the sun and the moon to be the gods that rule the world."[4] For this reason Moses forbade the Jews to raise their eyes, or adore the sun and moon and stars: "Keep therefore your souls carefully... lest perhaps lifting up thy eyes to heaven, thou see the sun and the moon, and all the stars of heaven, and being deceived by error thou adore and serve them, which the Lord thy God created for the service of all the nations."[5] The astrologers sin against this Commandment in that they say that these bodies are the rulers of souls, when in truth they were made for the use of man whose sole ruler is God.

Others worshipped the lower elements: "They imagined the fire or the wind to be gods."[6] Into this error also fall those who wrongly use the things of this earth and love them too much: "Or covetous person (who is a server of idols)."[7]

Some men have erred in worshipping their ancestors. This arose from the three causes.

(1) *From Their Carnal Nature.*—"For a father being afflicted with a bitter grief, made to himself the image of his son who was quickly taken away; and him who then had died as a man, he began now to worship as a god, and appointed him rites and sacrifices among his servants."[8]

(2) *Because of Flattery.*—Thus being unable to worship certain men in their presence, they, bowing down, honored them in their absence by making statues of them and worshipping one for the other: "Whom they had a mind to honor... they made an image... that they might honor as present him that was absent."[9] Of such also are those men

---

[4] Wis., xiii. 2.
[5] Deut., iv. 15, 19.
[6] Wis., xiii. 2.
[7] Eph ., v. 5.
[8] Wis., xiv. 15.
[9] *Ibid.,* 17.

who love and honor other men more than God: "He that loveth his father and mother more than Me, is not worthy of Me."[10] "Put your trust not in princes; in the children of man, in whom there is no salvation."[11]

(3) *From Presumption.*—Some because of their presumption made themselves be called gods; such, for example, was Nabuchodonosor (Judith, iii. 13). "Thy heart is lifted up and thou hast said: I am God."[12] Such are also those who believe more in their own pleasures than in the precepts of God. They worship themselves as gods, for by seeking the pleasures of the flesh, they worship their own bodies instead of God: "Their god is their belly."[13] We must therefore, avoid all these things.

Why We Should Adore One God

"Thou shalt not have strange gods before Me." As we have already said, the first Commandment forbids us to worship other than the one God. We shall now consider five reasons for this.

God's Dignity.—The first reason is the dignity of God which, were it belittled in any way, would be an injury to God. We see something similar to this in the customs of men. Reverence is due to every degree of dignity. Thus, a traitor to the king is he who robs him of what he ought to maintain. Such, too, is the conduct of some towards God:" They changed the glory of the incorruptible God into the likeness of the image of a corruptible man."[14] This is highly displeasing to God: "I will not give My glory to another, nor My praise to graven things."[15] For it must be known that

---

[10] Matt., x. 37.
[11] Ps. cxlv. 3.
[12] Ezech., xxviii. 2.
[13] Phil., iii. 19.
[14] Rom., i. 23.
[15] Isa., xlii. 8.

the dignity of God consists in His omniscience, since the name of God, *Deus*, is from "seeing," and this is one of the signs of divinity: "Show the things that are to come hereafter, and we shall know that ye are gods."[16] "All things are naked and open to His eyes."[17] But this dignity of God is denied Him by practitioners of divination, and of them it is said: "Should not the people seek of their God, for the living and the dead?"[18]

God's Bounty.—We receive every good from God; and this also is of the dignity of God, that He is the maker and giver of all good things: "When thou openest Thy hand, they shall all be filled with good."[19] And this is implied in the name of God, namely, *Deus*, which is said to be distributor, that is, *dator* of all things, because He fills all things with His goodness. You are, indeed ungrateful if you do not appreciate what you have received from Him, and, furthermore, you make for yourself another god; just as the sons of Israel made an idol after they had been brought out of Egypt: "I will go after my lovers."[20] One does this also when one puts too much trust in someone other than God, and this occurs when one seeks help from another: "Blessed is the man whose hope is in the name of the Lord."[21] Thus, the Apostle says: "Now that you have known God... how turn you again to the weak and needy elements?... You observe days and months and times and years."[22]

The Strength of Our Promise.—The third reason is taken from our solemn promise. For we have renounced the devil, and we have promised fidelity to God alone. This is a promise which we cannot break: "A man making void the law of Moses dieth without mercy under two or three

[16] *Ibid.*, xli. 23.
[17] Heb., iv. 13.
[18] Isa., viii. 19.
[19] Ps. ciii. 28.
[20] Osee, ii. 5.
[21] Ps. xxxix. 5.
[22] Gal., iv. 9, 10.

witnesses. How much more think ye he deserveth punishment who hath trodden under foot the Son of God and hath esteemed the blood of the testament unclean, by which he was sanctified, and hath offered an affront to the Spirit of grace!"[23] "Whilst her husband liveth, she shall be called an adulteress, if she be with another man."[24] Woe, then, to the sinner who enters the land by two ways, and who "halts between two sides."[25]

Against Service of the Devil.—The fourth reason is because of the great burden imposed by service to the devil: "You shall serve strange gods day and night, who will give you no rest."[26] The devil is not satisfied with leading to one sin, but tries to lead on to others: "Whosoever sins shall be a slave of sin."[27] It is, therefore, not easy for one to escape from the habit of sin. Thus, St. Gregory says: "The sin which is not remitted by penance soon draws man into another sin."[28] The very opposite of all this is true of service to God; for His Commandments are not a heavy burden: "My yoke is sweet and My burden light."[29] A person is considered to have done enough if he does for God as much as what he has done for the sake of sin: "For as you have yielded your members to serve uncleanness and iniquity, unto iniquity; so now yield your members to serve justice unto sanctification."[30] But on the contrary, it is written of those who serve the devil: "We wearied ourselves in the way of iniquity and destruction, and have walked through hard ways."[31] And again: "They have labored to commit iniquity."[32]

[23] Heb., x. 28-29.
[24] Rom., vii. 3.
[25] III Kings, xviii. 21.
[26] Jerem., xvi. 13.
[27] John, viii. 34.
[28] *Super Ezech.*, xi.
[29] Matt., xi. 30.
[30] Rom., vi. 19.
[31] Wis., v. 7.
[32] Jerem., ix. 5.

Greatness of the Reward.—The fifth reason is taken from the greatness of the reward or prize. In no law are such rewards promised as in the law of Christ. Rivers flowing with milk and honey are promised to the Mohammedans, to the Jews the land of promise, but to Christians the glory of the Angels: "They shall be as the Angels of God in heaven."[33] It was with this in mind that St. Peter asked: "Lord, to whom shall we go? Thou hast the words of eternal life."[34]

---

[33] Matt., xxii, 30.

[34] John, vi. 69. "The faithful should continually remember these words, 'I am the Lord thy God.' They will learn from these words that their Lawgiver is none other than their Creator, by whom they were made and are preserved. . . 'Who brought thee out of the land of Egypt, out of the house of bondage' appear at first to relate solely to the Jews liberated from the bondage of Egypt. But if we ponder on the meaning of the salvation of the entire human race, these words will be seen to apply still more specifically to all Christians who are liberated by God, not from the bondage of Egypt, but from the bondage of sin and 'the powers of darkness, and are translated into the kingdom of His beloved Son' (Col., i. 13). . . And when it is said, 'Thou shalt not have strange gods before Me,' it is the same as to say: 'Thou shalt worship Me who am the true God; thou shalt not worship strange gods' . . . It should be accurately taught that the veneration and invocation of the Angels, of the Saints, and of the blessed souls who enjoy the glory of heaven—and, moreover, the honor which the Catholic Church has always paid even to the bodies and ashes of the Saints—are not forbidden by this Commandment" ("Roman Catechism," *First Commandment*, 1, 2, 5, 8).

THE SECOND COMMANDMENT:

"Thou Shalt Not Take the Name of the Lord Thy God in Vain."

This is the Second Commandment of the law. Just as there is but one God whom we must worship, so there is only one God whom we should reverence in a special manner. This, first of all, has reference to the name of God. "Thou shalt not take the name of the Lord thy God in vain."[1]

The Meaning of "In Vain"

"In vain" has a threefold meaning. Sometimes it is said of that which is false: "They have spoken vain things every one to his neighbor."[2] One, therefore, takes the name of God in vain when one uses it to confirm that which is not true: "Love not a false oath."[3] "Thou shalt not live because thou hast spoken a lie in the name of the Lord."[4] Any one so doing does injury to God, to himself, and to all men.

It is an insult to God because, when you swear by God, it is nothing other than to call Him to witness; and when

---

[1] "He who requires that honor be paid Him, also demands that we speak of Him with reverence, and He forbids the contrary. . . There are those who are so blinded by darkness of error as not to fear to blaspheme His name, whom the Angels glorify. Men are not deterred by this Commandment from shamelessly and daringly outraging His divine majesty every day, or rather every hour and moment of the day. Who does not know that every assertion is accompanied with an oath and teems with curses and imprecations? To such lengths has this impiety been carried that one scarcely buys or sells, or transacts ordinary business of any sort, without having recourse to swearing, and who, even in matters the most unimportant and trivial, does not profane the most holy name of God thousands of times" ("Roman Catechism," *Second Commandment*, 2). See also teaching of St. Thomas in *Summa Theol.*, II-II, Q. lxxxix, art. 3, 5, 6.

[2] Ps. xi. 3.

[3] Zach., viii. 17.

[4] *Ibid.*, xiii. 3.

you swear falsely, you either believe God to be ignorant of the truth and thus place ignorance in God, whereas "all things are naked and open to His eyes,"[5] or you think that God loves a lie, whereas He hates it: "Thou wilt destroy all that speak a lie."[6] Or, again, you detract from His power, as if He were not able to punish a lie.

Likewise, such a one does an injury to himself, for he binds himself to the judgment of God. It is the same thing to say. "By God this is so," as to say, "May God punish me if it is not so!"

He, finally, does an injury to other men. For there can be no lasting society unless men believe one another. Matters that are doubtful may be confirmed by oaths: "An oath in confirmation puts an end to all controversy."[7] Therefore, he who violates this precept does injury to God, is cruel to himself, and harmful to other men.

Sometimes "vain" signifies useless: "The Lord knoweth the thoughts of men, that they are vain."[8] God's name, therefore, is taken in vain when it is used to confirm vain things.

In the Old Law it was forbidden to swear falsely: "Thou shalt not take the name of the Lord thy God in vain."[9] And Christ forbade the taking of oaths except in case of necessity: "You have heard that it was said to them of old: Thou shalt not forswear thyself... But I say to you not to swear at all."[10] And the reason for this is that in no part our body are we so weak as in the tongue, for "the tongue no man can tame."[11] And thus even in light matter one can perjure

[5] Heb., iv. 13.
[6] Ps. v. 7.
[7] Heb., vi. 16.
[8] Ps. xciii. 11.
[9] Deut., v. 11.
[10] Matt., v. 33-34.
[11] James, iii. 8.

himself. "Let your speech be: Yea, yea; No, no. But I say to you not to swear at all."[12]

Note well that an oath is like medicine, which is never taken continually but only in times of necessity. Hence, the Lord adds: "And that which is over and above these is evil."[13] Let not the mouth be accustomed to swearing, for in it there are many falls. And let not the name of God be usual in thy mouth, and meddle not with the names of saints. For thou shalt not escape free from them."[14]

Sometimes "in vain" means sin or injustice: "O ye sons of men, how long will you be dull of heart? Why do you love *vanity*?"[15] Therefore, he who swears to commit a sin, takes the name of his God in vain. Justice consists in doing good and avoiding evil. Therefore, if you take an oath to steal or commit some crime of this sort, you sin against justice. And although you must not keep this oath, you are still guilty of perjury. Herod did this against John.[16] It is likewise against justice when one swears not to do some good act, as not to enter a church or a religious community. And although this oath, too, is not binding, yet, despite this, the person himself is a perjuror.

---

[12] Matt., v. 34, 37.

"It cannot be stated that these words condemn oaths universally and under all circumstances, since the Apostles and Our Lord Himself made frequent use of oaths (Deut., vi. 13; Ps. lxii. 12; II Cor., i. 23; Philem., 8; Apoc., x. 6). The object of the Lord was rather to reprove the perverse opinion of the Jews, which was to the effect that the only thing to be avoided in an oath was a lie. . . For oaths have been instituted on account of human frailty. They bespeak the inconstancy of him who takes it or the stubbornness of him who refuses to believe without it. However, an oath can be justified by necessity. When Our Lord says, 'Let your speech be: Yea, yea; No, no,' He evidently forbids the habit of swearing in familiar conversation and on trivial matters" ("Roman Catechism," *loc. cit.*, 19).

[13] Matt., v. 37.

[14] Ecclus., xxiii. 9, 10.

[15] Ps. iv. 3.

[16] Mark, vi.

Conditions of a Lawful Oath

One cannot, therefore, swear to a falsehood, or without good reason, or in any way against justice: "And thou shalt swear: As the Lord liveth, in truth, and in judgment and in justice."[17]

Sometimes "vain" also means foolish: "All men are *vain*, in whom there is not the knowledge of God."[18] Accordingly, he who takes the name of God foolishly, by blasphemy, takes the name of God in vain: "And he that blasphemeth the name of the Lord, dying let him die."[19]

Taking God's Name Justly

"Thou shalt not take the name of the Lord thy God in vain." However, the name of God may be taken for six purposes. First, to confirm something that is said, as in an oath. In this we show God alone is the first Truth, and also we show due reverence to God. For this reason it was commanded in the Old Law that one must not swear except by God.[20] They who swore otherwise violated this order: "By the name of strange gods you shall not swear."[21] Although at times one swears by creatures, nevertheless, it must be known that such is the same as swearing by God. When you swear by your soul or your head, it is as if you bind yourself to be punished by God. Thus: "But I call God to witness upon my soul."[22] And when you swear by the

---

[17] Jerem., iv. 2. "Although to constitute an oath it is sufficient to call God to witness, yet to make a holy and just oath many other conditions are required. . . The words [of Jeremias, cited above) briefly sum up all the conditions that constitute the perfection of an oath, namely, truth, judgment, justice" ("Roman Catechism," *loc. cit.*, 11).

[18] Wis., xiii. 1.

[19] Levit., xxiv. 16.

[20] Deut., vi. 13.

[21] Exod., xxiii. 13.

[22] II Cor., vi. 23.

Gospel, you swear by God who gave the Gospel. But they sin who swear either by God or by the Gospel for any trivial reason.

The second purpose is that of sanctification. Thus, Baptism sanctifies, for as St. Paul says: "But you are washed, but you are sanctified, but you are justified in the name of our Lord Jesus Christ, and the Spirit of God."[23] Baptism, however, does not have power except through the invocation of the Trinity: "But Thou, O Lord, art among us, and Thy name is called upon by us."[24]

The third purpose is the expulsion of our adversary: hence, before Baptism we renounce the devil: "Only let Thy name be called upon us: take away our reproach."[25] Wherefore, if one return to his sins, the name of God has been taken in vain.

Fourthly, God's name is taken in order to confess it: "How then shall they call on Him, in whom they have not believed?"[26] And again: "Whosoever shall call upon the name of the Lord, shall be saved."[27] First of all, we confess by word of mouth that we may show forth the glory of God: "And every one that calleth upon My name, I have created him for My glory."[28] Accordingly, if one says anything against the glory of God, he takes the name of God in vain. Secondly, we confess God's name by our works, when our very actions show forth God's glory: "That they may see your good works, and may glorify your Father who is in heaven."[29] "Through you the name of God is blasphemed among the Gentiles."[30]

---

[23] I Cor., vi. 11.
[24] Jerem., xiv. 9.
[25] Isa., iv. 1.
[26] Rom., x. 14.
[27] *Ibid.*, 13.
[28] Isa., xliii. 7.
[29] Matt., v. 16.
[30] Rom., ii. 24.

Fifthly it is taken for our defense: "The name of the Lord is a strong tower; the just runneth to it and shall be exalted."[31] "In My name they shall cast out devils."[32] "There is no other name under heaven given to men, whereby we must be saved".[33]

Lastly, it is taken in order to make our works complete. Thus says the Apostle: "All whatsoever you do in word or work, do all in the name of the Lord Jesus Christ."[34] The reason is because "our help is in the name of the Lord."[35] Sometimes it happens that one begins a work imprudently by starting with a vow, for instance, and then not completing either the work or the vow. And this again is taking God's name in vain. "If thou hast vowed anything to God, defer not to pay it."[36] "Vow and pay to the Lord your God; all ye that are round about Him bring presents."[37] "For an unfaithful and foolish promise displeaseth Him."[38]

THE THIRD COMMANDMENT:

"Remember that You Keep Holy the Sabbath Day."

This is the Third Commandment of the law, and very suitably is it so. For we are first commanded to adore God in our hearts, and the Commandment is to worship one God: "Thou shalt not have strange gods before Me." In the

---

[31] Prov., xviii. 10.
[32] Mark, xvi. 17.
[33] Acts, iv. 12.
[34] Col., iii. 17.
[35] Ps. cxxiii. 8.
[36] Eccles., v. 3.
[37] Ps. lxxv. 12.
[38] Eccles., v. 3.

Second Commandment we are told to reverence God by word: "Thou shalt not take the name of the Lord thy God in vain." The Third commands us to reverence God by act. It is: "Remember that thou keep holy the Sabbath day."[1] God wished that a certain day be set aside on which men direct their minds to the service of the Lord.

Reasons for this Commandment

There are five reasons for this Commandment. The first reason was to put aside error, for the Holy Spirit saw that in the future some men would say that the world had always existed. "In the last days there shall come deceitful scoffers, walking after their own lusts, saying: Where is His promise or His coming? For since the time that the fathers slept, all things continue as they were from the beginning of creation. For this they are willfully ignorant of, that the heavens were before, and the earth out of water, and through water, created by the word of God."[2] God, therefore, wished that one day should be set aside in memory of the fact that He created all things in six days, and that on the seventh day He rested from the creation of new creatures. This is why the Lord placed this Commandment in the law, saying: "Remember that thou keep holy the Sabbath day."

The Jews kept holy the Sabbath in memory of the first creation; but Christ at His coming brought about a new creation. For by the first creation an earthly man was created, and by the second a heavenly man was formed: "For in Christ Jesus neither circumcision availeth any thing, nor uncircumcision, but a new creature."[3] This new creation is

---

[1] St. Thomas also treats of this Commandment in the *Summa Theologica,* I-II, Q. cii, art. 4, 10; *ibid.,* I-II, Q. cxxii, art 4.

[2] II Peter, iii. 3-5.

[3] Gal., vi. 15.

through grace, which came by the Resurrection: "That as Christ is risen from the dead, by the glory of the Father, so we also may walk in newness of life. For if we have been planted together in the likeness of His death, so shall we also be in the likeness of His resurrection."[4] And thus, because the Resurrection took place on Sunday, we celebrate that day, even as the Jews observed the Sabbath on account of the first creation.[5]

The second reason for this Commandment is to instruct us in our faith in the Redeemer. For the flesh of Christ was not corrupted in the sepulchre, and thus it is said: "Moreover My flesh also shall rest in hope."[6] "Nor wilt Thou give Thy holy one to see corruption."[7] Wherefore, God wished that the Sabbath should be observed, and that just as the sacrifices of the Old Law signified the death of Christ, so should the quiet of the Sabbath signify the rest of His body in the sepulchre. But we do not now observe these sacrifices, because with the advent of the reality and the truth, figures of it must cease, just as the darkness is dispelled with the rising of the sun. Nevertheless, we keep the Saturdays in veneration of the Blessed Virgin, in whom remained a firm faith on that Saturday while Christ was dead.

---

[4] Rom., vi. 4-5.

[5] "The Apostles, therefore, resolved to consecrate the first of the seven days of the week to the divine worship, and they called it 'the Lord's Day.' St. John makes mention of 'the Lord's Day' in the Apocalypse (i. 10), and St. Paul commands collections to be made 'on the first day of the week' (I Cor., xvi. 2). . . . From all this we learn that even then the Lord's day was kept holy in the Church. . . The Church of God has thought it well to transfer the celebration and observance of the Sabbath to Sunday. On that day light first shone on the world when the Lord arose on that day, and the gate of eternal life was thrown open to us and we were called out of darkness into light. . . We also learn from the Holy Scriptures that the first day of the week was held sacred for other reasons, viz., on that day the creation began, and on that day the Holy Spirit descended upon the Apostles" ("Roman Catechism," *Third Commandment*, 7, 18).

[6] Ps. xv. 9.

[7] *Ibid.*, 10.

The third reason is that this Commandment was given to strengthen and foreshadow the fulfillment of the promise of rest. For rest indeed was promised to us: "And it shall come to pass on that day, that when God shall give thee rest from thy labor, and from thy vexation, and from the hard bondage, wherewith thou didst serve before."[8] "My people shall sit in the beauty of peace, and in the tabernacle of confidence, and in wealthy rest."[9]

We hope for rest from three things: from the labors of the present life, from the struggles of temptations, and from the servitude of the devil. Christ promised this rest to all those who will come to Him: "Come to Me, all ye that labor and are burdened, and I will refresh you. Take up My yoke upon you, and learn of Me, because I am meek and humble of heart; and you shall find rest to your souls. For My yoke is sweet and My burden light."[10]

However, the Lord, as we know, worked for six days and on the seventh He rested, because it is necessary to do a perfect work: "Behold with your eyes how I have labored a little, and have found much rest to Myself."[11] For the period of eternity exceeds the present time incomparably more than a thousand years exceeds one day.

Fourthly, this Commandment was given for the increase of our love: "For the corruptible body is a load upon the soul."[12] And man always tends downwards towards earthly things unless he takes means to raise himself above them. It is indeed necessary to have a certain time for this; in fact, some do this continually: "I will bless the Lord at all times, His praise shall ever be in my mouth."[13] And again: "Pray without ceasing."[14] These shall enjoy the everlasting

---

[8] Isa., xiv. 3.
[9] *Ibid.*, xxxii. 18.
[10] Matt., xi. 28-30.
[11] Ecclus., li. 35.
[12] Wis., ix. 15.
[13] Ps. xxxiii. 2.
[14] I Thess., v. 17.

Sabbath. There are others who do this (i.e., excite love for God) during a certain portion of the day: "Seven times a day I have given praise to Thee."[15] And some, in order to avoid being entirely apart from God, find it necessary to have a fixed day, lest they become too lukewarm in their love of God: "If you call the Sabbath delightful. . . then shalt thou be delighted in the Lord."[16] Again: "Then shalt thou abound in delights of the Almighty, and shalt lift up thy face to God."[17] And accordingly this day is not set aside for the sole exercise of games, but to praise and pray to the Lord God. Wherefore, St. Augustine says that it is a lesser evil to plough than to play on this day.[18]

Lastly, we are given this Commandment in order to exercise works of kindliness to those who are subject to us. For some are so cruel to themselves and to others that they labor ceaselessly all on account of money. This is true especially of the Jews, who are most avaricious. "Observe the day of the Sabbath to sanctify it. . . that thy man-servant and thy maid-servant may rest, even as thyself."[19] This Commandment, therefore, was given for all these reasons.

From What We Should Abstain on the Sabbath

"Remember that you keep holy (sanctify) the Sabbath day." We have already said that, as the Jews celebrated the Sabbath, so do we Christians observe the Sunday and all principal feasts. Let us now see in what way we should keep these days. We ought to know that God did not say to "keep" the Sabbath, but to remember to keep it holy. The word "holy" may be taken in two ways. Sometimes "holy"

---

[15] Ps. cxviii, 164.
[16] Isa., lviii. 13-14.
[17] Job. xxii. 26.
[18] This is a reference to the great public spectacles and games.
[19] Deut., v. 12-14.

(sanctified) is the same as pure: "But you are washed, but you are sanctified"[20] (that is, made holy). Then again at times "holy" is said of a thing consecrated to the worship of God, as, for instance, a place, a season, vestments, and the holy vessels. Therefore, in these two ways we ought to celebrate the feasts, that is, both purely and by giving ourselves over to divine service.

We shall consider two things regarding this Commandment. First, what should be avoided on a feast day, and secondly, what we should do. We ought to avoid three things. The first is servile work.

Avoidance of Servile Work.—"Neither do ye any work; sanctify the Sabbath day."[21] And so also it is said in the Law: "You shall do no servile work therein."[22] Now, servile work is bodily work; whereas "free work" (i.e., non-servile work) is done by the mind, for instance, the exercise of the intellect and such like. And one cannot be servilely bound to do this kind of work.

When Servile Work Is Lawful.—We ought to know, however, that servile work can be done on the Sabbath for four reasons. The first reason is necessity. Wherefore, the Lord excused the disciples plucking the ears of corn on the Sabbath, as we read in St. Matthew (xii. 3-5). The second reason is when the work is done for the service of the Church; as we see in the same Gospel how the priests did all things necessary in the Temple on the Sabbath day. The third reason is for the good of our neighbor; for on the Sabbath the Saviour cured one having a withered hand, and He refuted the Jews who reprimanded Him, by citing the example of the sheep in a pit (*ibid.*). And the fourth reason is the authority of our superiors. Thus, God commanded the Jews to circumcise on the Sabbath [23]

[20] I Cor., vi. 11.
[21] Jerem., xvii. 22.
[22] Levit., xxiii. 25.
[23] John, vii. 22-23.

Avoidance of Sin and Negligence on the Sabbath.—Another thing to be avoided on the Sabbath is sin: "Take heed to your souls, and carry no burdens on the Sabbath day."[24] This weight and burden on the soul is sin: "My iniquities as a heavy burden are become heavy upon me."[25] Now, sin is a servile work because "whosoever committeth sin is the servant of sin."[26] Therefore, when it is said. "You shall do no servile work therein,"[27] it can be understood of sin. Thus, one violates this Commandment as often as one commits sin on the Sabbath; and so both by working and by sin God is offended.[28] "The Sabbaths and other festivals I will not abide." And why? "Because your assemblies are wicked. My soul hateth your new moons[29] and your solemnities; they are become troublesome to me."[30]

Another thing to avoid on the Sabbath is idleness: "For idleness hath taught much evil."[31] St. Jerome says: "Always do some good work, and the devil will always find you occupied."[32] Hence, it is not good for one to keep only the principal feasts, if on the others one would remain idle. "The King's honor loveth judgment,"[33] that is to say, discretion. Wherefore, we read that certain of the Jews were in hiding, and their enemies fell upon them; but they, believing that they were not able to defend themselves on the Sabbath, were overcome and killed.[34] The same thing hap-

[24] Jerem., xviii. 21.

[25] Ps. xxxvii. 5.

[26] John, viii. 34.

[27] Levit., iii. 25.

[28] St. Thomas' comparison of sin and servile work follows from the words: "Whosoever committeth sin is the servant of sin," quoted above. This does not mean that commission of sin on the Sabbath changes the species of the sin or gravely increases its malice.

[29] This refers to the celebration and special sacrifices offered on the first day of the month. The Lord here is displeased not with the external ritual itself, but with the lack of proper internal dispositions on the part of the Jews.

[30] Isa., i. 13.

[31] Ecclus., xxxiii. 29.

[32] *Ep. ad Rusticum.*

[33] Ps. xcviii. 4.

[34] I Mach., ii 31-38.

pens to many who are idle on the feast days: "The enemies have seen her, and have mocked at her Sabbaths."[35] But all such should do as those Jews did, of whom it is said: "Whosoever shall come up against us to fight on the Sabbath day, we will fight against him."[36]

With What the Sabbath and Feasts Should Be Occupied

"Remember that thou keep holy the Sabbath day." We have already said that man must keep the feast days holy; and that "holy" is considered in two ways, namely, "pure" and "consecrated to God." Moreover, we have indicated what things we should abstain from on these days. Now it must be shown with what we should occupy ourselves, and they are three in number.

The Offering of Sacrifice.—The first is the offering of sacrifices.[37] In the Book of Numbers (XXVIII) it is written how God ordered that on each day there be offered one lamb in the morning and another in the evening, but on the Sabbath day the number should be doubled. And this showed that on the Sabbath we should offer sacrifice to God from all that we possess: "All things are Thine; and we have given Thee what we received from Thy hand."[38] We should offer, first of all, our soul to God, being sorry for our

---

[35] Lam., i. 7.

[36] I Mach., ii. 41.

[37] For the Catholic, of course, the great Sacrifice is that of the Mass. And we are bound to assist at Mass on Sundays and Holydays of obligation unless we are excused for serious reason. "The pastor should not omit to teach the faithful what works and actions they should perform on the festival days. These are: to go to church and there with true piety and devotion assist at the celebration of the Holy Sacrifice of the Mass; and to approach frequently the Sacraments of the Church which were instituted for our salvation" ("Roman Catechism," *Third Commandment*, 25).

[38] I Paral., xxix. 14.

sins: "A sacrifice to God is an afflicted spirit;"[39] and also pray for His blessings: "Let my prayer be directed as incense in Thy sight."[40] Feast days were instituted for that spiritual joy which is the effect of prayer. Therefore, on such days our prayers should be multiplied.

Secondly, we should offer our body, by mortifying it with fasting:[41] "I beseech you therefore, brethren, by the mercy of God, that you present your bodies a living sacrifice,"[42] and also by praising God: "The sacrifice of praise shall honor Me."[43] And thus on these days our hymns should be more numerous. Thirdly, we should sacrifice our possessions by giving alms: "And do not forget to do good, and to impart; for by such sacrifice God's favor is obtained."[44] And this alms ought to be more than on other days because the Sabbath is a day of common joys: "Send portions to them that have not prepared for themselves, because it is the holy day of the Lord."[45]

Hearing of God's Word.—Our second duty on the Sabbath is to be eager to hear the word of God. This the Jews did daily: "The voices of the prophets which are read every Sabbath."[46] Therefore Christians, whose justice should be more perfect, ought to come together on the Sabbath to hear sermons and participate in the services of the Church! "He that is of God, heareth the words of God."[47] We likewise ought to speak with profit to others: "Let no evil speech proceed from your mouth; but that which is good

[39] Ps. l. 19.
[40] Ps. cxl. 2.
[41] St. Thomas here refers not to the "fast of affliction" (*jejunium afflictionis*) but to the "fast of joy" (*jejunium exultationis*), which is a joyful lifting of the mind to higher things and proceeds from the Holy Spirit who is the spirit of liberty (cfr. *Summa Theol.*, III, Q. cxlvii, art. 5).
[42] Rom., xii. 1.
[43] Ps. xlix. 23.
[44] Heb., xiii. 16.
[45] II Esdras, viii. 10.
[46] Acts, xiii. 27.
[47] John, viii. 47.

unto sanctification."[48] These two practices are good for the soul of the sinner, because they change his heart for the better:" Are not My words as a fire, saith the Lord, and as a hammer that breaketh the rock in pieces?"[49] The opposite effect is had on those, even the perfect, who neither speak nor hear profitable things: "Evil communications corrupt good manners. Awake, ye just, and sin not."[50] "Thy words have I hidden in my heart."[51] God's word enlightens the ignorant: "Thy word is a lamp to my feet."[52] It inflames the lukewarm: "The word of the Lord inflamed him."[53]

The Spiritual Sabbath

The contemplation of divine things may be exercised on the Sabbath. However, this is for the more perfect.[54] "O taste, and see that the Lord is sweet,"[55] and this is because of the quiet of the soul. For just as the tired body desires rest, so also does the soul. But the soul's proper rest is in God: "Be Thou unto me a God, a protector, and a house of refuge."[56] "There remaineth therefore a day of rest for the people of God. For he that is entered into his rest, the same also hath rested from his works, as God did from His."[57]

[48] Eph., iv. 29.
[49] Jerem., xxiii. 29.
[50] I Cor., xv. 33.
[51] Ps. cxviii. 11.
[52] *Ibid.,* 105.
[53] Ps. civ. 19.
[54] "The spiritual Sabbath consists in a holy and mystical rest wherein, the carnal man (*vetus homo,* Rom., vi. 4) being buried with Christ, the new man is renewed to life and carefully applies himself to exercise the spirit of Christian piety" ("Roman Catechism," *Third Commandment,* 15).
[55] Ps. xxxiii. 9.
[56] Ps. xxx. 3.
[57] Heb., iv. 9-10.

When I go into my house, I shall repose myself with her" (i.e., Wisdom).[58]

However, before the soul arrives at this rest, three other rests must precede. The first is the rest from the turmoil of sin: "But the wicked are like the raging sea which cannot rest."[59] The second rest is from the passions of the flesh, because "the flesh lusteth against the spirit, and the spirit against the flesh."[60] The third is rest from the occupations of the world: "Martha, Martha, thou art careful and art troubled about many things."[61]

The Heavenly Sabbath[62]

And then after all these things the soul rests peacefully in God: "If thou call the Sabbath delightful. . . then shalt thou be delighted in the Lord,"[63] The Saints gave up everything to possess this rest, "for it is a pearl of great price which a man having found, hid it, and for joy thereof goeth and selleth all that he hath, and buyeth that field."[64] This rest in truth is eternal life and heavenly joy: "This is my rest for ever and ever; here will I dwell, for I have chosen it."[65] And to this rest may the Lord bring us all!

---

[58] Wis., viii. 16.
[59] Isa., lvii. 20.
[60] Gal., v. 17.
[61] Luke, x. 41.
[62] "The heavenly Sabbath, as St. Cyril observes on the words of St. Paul, 'There remaineth therefore a day of rest for the people of God' (Eph., v. 8.), is that life in which, living with Christ, we shall experience all joy, and all sin will be wiped away (*In Joan,* lib. 4). And in this vision of God the souls of the saints shall obtain every good" ("Roman Catechism," *loc. cit.,* 16).
[63] Isa., lviii. 13-14.
[64] Matt., xiii. 44-46.
[65] Ps. cxxxi. 14.

THE FOURTH COMMANDMENT:

"Honor thy father and thy mother, that thou mayest be long-lived upon the land which the Lord thy God will give thee."[1]

Perfection for man consists in the love of God and of neighbor. Now, the three Commandments which were written on the first tablet pertain to the love of God; for the love of neighbor there were the seven Commandments on the second tablet. But we must "love, not in word nor in tongue, but in deed and in truth."[2] For a man to love thus, he must do two things, namely, avoid evil and do good. Certain of the Commandments prescribe good acts, while others forbid evil deeds. And we must also know that to avoid evil is in our power; but we are incapable of doing good to everyone. Thus, St. Augustine says that we should love all, but we are not bound to do good to all. But among those to whom we are bound to do good are those in some way united to us. Thus, "if any man have not care of his own and especially of those of his house, he hath denied the faith."[3] Now, amongst all our relatives there are none closer than our father and mother. "We ought to love God first," says St. Ambrose, "then our father and mother." Hence, God has given us the Commandment: "Honor thy father and thy mother."[4]

The Philosopher also gives another reason for this honor to parents, in that we cannot make an equal return to our parents for the great benefits they have granted to us; and, therefore, an offended parent has the right to send his son away, but the son has no such right.[5] Parents,

---

[1] Exod., xx. 12; Deut., v. 16.

[2] I John, iii. 18.

[3] I Tim., v. 8.

[4] St. Thomas also treats of the Fourth Commandment in *Summa Theol.*, II-II, QQ. cxxii, ci.

[5] Aristotle, "Ethics."

indeed, give their children three things. The first is that they brought them into being: "Honor thy father, and forget not the groanings of thy mother; remember that thou hadst not been born but through them."[6] Secondly, they furnished nourishment and the support necessary for life. For a child comes naked into the world, as Job relates (i. 24), but he is provided for by his parents. The third is instruction: "We have had fathers of our flesh for instructors."[7] "Hast thou children? Instruct them."[8]

Parents, therefore, should give instruction without delay to their children, because "a young man according to his way, even when he is old will not depart from it."[9] And again: "It is good for a man when he hath borne the yoke from his youth."[10] Now, the instruction which Tobias gave his son (Tob., iv) was this: to fear the Lord and to abstain from sin. This is indeed contrary to those parents who approve of the misdeeds of their children. Children, therefore, receive from their parents birth, nourishment, and instruction.

What Children Owe Parents

Now, because we owe our birth to our parents, we ought to honor them more than any other superiors, because from such we receive only temporal things: "He that feareth the Lord honoreth his parents, and will serve them as his masters that brought him into the world. Honor thy father in work and word and all patience, that a blessing may come upon thee from him."[11] And in doing this you

---

[6] Ecclus., vii.29-30.
[7] Heb., xii. 9.
[8] Ecclus., vii. 25.
[9] Prov., xxii. 6.
[10] Lam., iii. 27.
[11] Ecclus., iii. 10.

shall also honor thyself, because "the glory of a man is from honor of his father, and a father without honor is the disgrace of his son."[12]

Again, since we receive nourishment from our parents in our childhood , we must support them in their old age: "Son, support the old age of thy father, and grieve him not in his life. And if his understanding fail, have patience with him; and despise him not when thou art in thy strength. . . Of what an evil fame is he that forsaketh his father! And he is cursed of God that angereth his mother."[13] For the humiliation of those who act contrary to this, Cassiodorus relates how young storks, when the parents have lost their feathers by approaching old age and are unable to find suitable food, make the parent storks comfortable with their own feathers, and bring back food for their worn-out bodies. Thus, by this affectionate exchange the young ones repay the parents for what they received when they were young."[14]

We must obey our parents, for they have instructed us "Children, obey your parents in all things."[15] This except of course, those things which are contrary to God. St. Jerome says that the only loyalty in such cases is to be cruel:[16] "If any man hate not his father and mother. . . he cannot be My disciple."[17] This is to say that God is in the truest sense our Father: "Is not He thy Father who hath possessed thee, and hath made thee, and created thee?"[18]

[12] *Ibid.*, 13.
[13] *Ibid.*, 14, 15, 18.
[14] *Epist.*, lib. II.
[15] Col., iii. 20.
[16] *Ad Heliod.*
[17] Luke, xiv. 26.
[18] Deut., xxxii. 6.

Rewards for Keeping This Commandment

"Honor thy father and thy mother." Among all the Commandments, this one only has the additional words: "that thou mayest be long lived upon the land:" The reason for this is lest it be thought that there is no reward for those who honor their parents, seeing that it is a natural obligation. Hence it must be known that five most desirable rewards are promised those who honor their parents.

Grace and Glory.—The first reward is grace for the present life, and glory in the life to come, which surely are greatly to be desired: "Honor thy father... that a blessing may come upon thee from God, and His blessing may remain in the latter end".[19] The very opposite comes upon those who dishonor their parents; indeed, they are cursed in the law by God.[20] It is also written: "He that is unjust in that which is little, is unjust also in that which is greater."[21] But this our natural life is as nothing compared with the life of grace. And so, therefore, if you do not acknowledge the blessing of the natural life which you owe to your parents, then you are unworthy of the life of grace, which is greater, and all the more so for the life of glory, which is the greatest of all blessings.

A Long Life.—The second reward is a long life: "That thou mayest be long lived upon the land." For "he that honoreth his father shall enjoy a long life."[22] Now, that is a long life which is a full life, and it is not observed in time but in activity, as the Philosopher observes. Life, however, is full inasmuch as it is a life of virtue; so a man who is virtuous and holy enjoys a long life even if in body he dies young. "Being perfect in a short space, he fulfilled a long

---

[19] Ecclus., iii. 9-10.
[20] Deut., xxvii. 16.
[21] Luke, xvi. 10.
[22] Ecclus., iii. 7.

time; for his soul pleased God."[23] Thus, for example, he is a good merchant who does as much business in one day as another would do in a year. And note well that it sometimes happens that a long life may lead up to a spiritual as well as a bodily death, as was the case with Judas. Therefore, the reward for keeping this Commandment is a long life for the body. But the very opposite, namely, death is the fate of those who dishonor their parents. We receive our life from them; and just as the soldiers owe fealty to the king, and lose their rights in case of any treachery, so also they who dishonor their parents deserve to forfeit their lives: "The eye that mocketh at his father and that despiseth the labor of his mother in bearing him, let the ravens pick it out, and the young eagles eat it.[24] Here "the ravens" signify officials of kings and princes, who in turn are the "young eagles." But if it happens that such are not bodily punished, they nevertheless cannot escape death of the soul. It is not well, therefore, for a father to give too much power to his children: "Give not to son or wife, brother or friend, power over thee while thou livest; and give not thy estate to another, lest thou repent"[25]

The third reward is to have in turn grateful and pleasing children. For a father naturally treasures his children, but the contrary is not always the case: "He that honoreth his father shall have joy in his own children."[26] Again: "With what measure you mete, it shall be measured to you again."[27] The fourth reward is a praiseworthy reputation: "For the glory of a man is from the honor of his father."[28] And again: "Of what an evil fame is he that forsaketh his father?"[29] A fifth reward is riches: "The father's blessing

---

[23] Wis., iv. 13.
[24] Prov., xxx. 17.
[25] Ecclus., xxxiii. 20.
[26] *Ibid.*, iii. 6.
[27] Matt., vii. 2.
[28] Ecclus., iii. 13.
[29] *Ibid.*, 18.

establisheth the houses of his children, but the mother's curse rooteth up the foundation."[30]

The Different Applications of "Father"

"Honor thy father and thy mother." A man is called father not only by reason of generation, but also for other reasons, and to each of these there is due a certain reverence. Thus, the Apostle and the Saints are called fathers because of their doctrine and their exemplification of faith: "For if you have ten thousands instructors in Christ, yet not many fathers. For in Christ Jesus, by the gospel, I have begotten you."[31] And again: "Let us now praise men of renown and our fathers in their generation."[32] However, let us praise them not in word only, but by imitating them; and we do this if nothing is found in us contrary to what we praise in them.

Our superiors in the Church are also called fathers; and they too are to be respected as the ministers of God: "Remember your prelates, . . . whose faith follow, considering the end of their conversation."[33] And again: "He that heareth you, heareth Me; and he that despiseth you, despiseth Me."[34] We honor them by showing them obedience: "Obey your prelates, and be subject to them."[35] And also by paying them tithes: "Honor the Lord with thy substance, and give Him of the first of thy fruits."[36]

Rulers and kings are called fathers: "Father, if the prophet had bid thee do some great thing, surely thou

---

[30] *Ibid.*, 11.
[31] I Cor., iv. 15.
[32] Ecclus., xliv. 1.
[33] Heb., xiii. 7.
[34] Luke, x. 16.
[35] Heb., xiii. 17.
[36] Prov. iii. 9.

shouldst have done it."[37] We call them fathers because their whole care is the good of their people. And we honor them by being subject to them: "Let every soul be subject to higher powers."[38] We should be subject to them not merely through fear, but through love; and not merely because it is reasonable, but because of the dictates of our conscience. Because "there is no power but from God."[39] And so to all such we must render what we owe them: "Tribute, to whom tribute is due; custom, to whom custom; fear, to whom fear; honor, to whom honor,"[40] And again: "My son, fear the Lord and the king."[41]

Our benefactors also are called fathers: "Be merciful to the fatherless as a father."[42] He, too, is like a father [who gives his bond] of whom it is said: "Forget not the kindness of thy surety."[43] On the other hand, the thankless shall receive a punishment such as is written: "The hope of the unthankful shall melt away as the winter's ice."[44] Old men also are called fathers: Ask thy father, and he will declare to thee; thy elders and they will tell thee."[45] And again: "Rise up before the hoary head, and honor the person of the aged man."[46] "In the company of great men take not upon thee to speak; and when the ancients are present, speak not much."[47] "Hear in silence, and for thy reverence good grace shall come to thee."[48] Now, all these fathers must be honored, because they all resemble to some degree our

---

[37] IV Kings, v. 13.
[38] Rom., xiii. 1.
[39] *Ibid.*, 7.
[40] *Ibid.*
[41] Prov., xxiv. 21.
[42] Ecclus., iv. 10.
[43] *Ibid.*, xxix. 19.
[44] Wis., xvi. 29.
[45] Deut., xxxii. 7.
[46] Lev., xix. 32.
[47] Ecclus., xxxii. 13.
[48] *Ibid.*, 9..

Father who is in heaven; and of all of them it is said: "He that despiseth you, despiseth Me."[49]

THE FIFTH COMMANDMENT:

"Thou Shalt Not Kill."

The Sin of Killing

In the divine law which tells us we must love God and our neighbor, it is commanded that we not only do good but also avoid evil. The greatest evil that can be done to one's neighbor is to take his life. This is prohibited in the Commandment: "Thou shalt not kill."[1]

Killing of Animals Is Lawful.—In connection with this Commandment there are three errors. Some have said that it is not permitted to kill even brute animals. But this is false. because it is not a sin to use that which is subordinate to the power of man. It is in the natural order that plants be the nourishment of animals, certain animals nourish others, and all for the nourishment of man: "Even the green herbs have I delivered them all to you."[2] The

[49] Luke x. 16.

[1] St. Thomas also treats of this Commandment in *Summa Theol.*, II-II, Q. lxix, art. 2, 3; Q. cxii, art. 6. "The Lord points out (Matt., v. 21) the twofold force of this Commandment. The one is prohibitory and forbids us to kill; the other is mandatory and com.ands us to cultivate charity, peace and friendship towards our enemies, to have peace with all men, and finally to suffer all things with patience" ("Roman Catechism," *Fifth Commandment*, 2).

[2] Gen. ix. 3.

Philosopher says that hunting is like a just war.[3] And St. Paul says: "Whatsoever is sold in the shambles eat; asking no questions for conscience' sake."[4] "Therefore, the sense of the Commandment is: "Thou shalt not kill men."

The Execution of Criminals.—Some have held that the killing of man is prohibited altogether. They believe that judges in the civil courts are murderers, who condemn men to death according to the laws. Against this St. Augustine says that God by this Commandment does not take away from Himself the right to kill. Thus, we read: "I will kill and I will make to live."[5] It is, therefore, lawful for a judge to kill according to a mandate from God, since in this God operates, and every law is a command of God: "By Me kings reign, and lawgivers decree just things."[6] And again: "For if thou dost that which is evil, fear; for he beareth not the sword in vain. Because he is God's minister."[7] To Moses also it was said: "Wizards thou shalt not suffer to live."[8] And thus that which is lawful to God is lawful for His ministers when they act by His mandate. It is evident that God who is the Author of laws, has every right to inflict death on account of sin. For "the wages of sin is death."[9] Neither does His minister sin in inflicting that punishment. The sense, therefore, of "Thou shalt not kill" is that one shall not kill by one's own authority.[10]

---

[3] Aristotle, "Politics," I.

[4] I Cor., x. 25.

[5] Deut., xxxii. 39.

[6] Prov., viii. 15.

[7] Rom., xiii. 4.

[8] Exod., xxii. 18.

[9] Rom., vi. 23.

[10] Killing in a just war and killing by accident are among the other exceptions to this Commandment. "The soldier is guiltless who in a just war takes the life of an enemy, provided that he is not actuated by motives of ambition or cruelty, but by a pure desire to serve the interests of his country. . . Again, death caused, not by intent or design, but by accident, is not murder" ("Roman Catechism." *loc. cit.*, 5-6).

Suicide is Prohibited — There are those who held that although this Commandment forbids one to kill another, yet it is lawful to kill oneself. Thus, there are the examples of **Samson** (Judges, xvi) and Cato and certain virgins who threw themselves into the flames, as St. Augustine relates in "The City of God."[11] But he also explains this in the words: "He who kills himself, certainly kills a man."[12] If it is not lawful to kill oneself except by the authority of God, then it is not lawful to kill oneself except either upon the authority of God or instructed by the Holy Spirit, as was the case of Samson. Therefore, "thou shalt not kill."[13]

Other Meanings of "To Kill."—It ought to be known that to kill a man may happen in several ways. Firstly, by one's own hand: "Your hands are full of blood."[14] This is not only against charity, which tells us to love our neighbor as ourself: "No murderer hath eternal life abiding in himself."[15] But also it is against nature, for "every beast loveth its like."[16] And so it is said: "He that striketh a man with a will to kill him, shall be put to death."[17] He who does this is more cruel than the wolf, of which Aristotle says that one wolf will not eat of the flesh of another wolf.[18]

Secondly, one kills another by word of mouth. This is done by giving counsel to anyone against another by provocation, accusation, or detraction: "The sons of men whose teeth are weapons and arrows, and their tongue a sharp sword."[19] Thirdly, by lending aid, as it is written: "My

---

[11] Book I, xxvii.

[12] *Ibid.*

[13] It is not lawful to take one's own life. No man possesses such power over his own life as to be free to put himself to death. We find that the Commandment does not say, 'Thou shalt not kill another,' but simply, 'Thou shalt not kill' " ("Roman Catechism," *loc. cit.*, 10).

[14] Isa., i. 15.

[15] I John, iii. 15.

[16] Ecclus., xiii. 19.

[17] Exod., xxi. 12.

[18] *De Animal.*, IV.

[19] Ps. lvi. 5.

son, walk not thou with them... for their teeth run to evil, and they make haste to shed blood."[20] Fourthly, by consent: "They are worthy of death, not only they that do them, but they also that consent to them that do them ."[21] Lastly, one kills another by giving a partial consent when the act could be completely prevented: "Deliver them that are led to death;"[22] or, if one can prevent it, yet does not do so through negligence or avarice. Thus, St. Ambrose says: "Give food to him that is dying of hunger; if you do not, you are his murderer.

We have already considered the killing of the body, but some kill the soul also by drawing it away from the life of grace, namely, by inducing it to commit mortal sin: "He was a murderer from the beginning,"[23] that is, in so far as he drew men into sin. Others, however, slay both body and soul. This is possible in two ways: First, by the murder of one with child, whereby the child is killed both in body and soul; and, secondly, by commiting suicide.

The Sin of Anger

Why We Are Forbidden to Be Angry.—In the Gospel of St. Matthew (chapter V) Christ taught that our justice should be greater than the justice of the Old Law. This means that Christians should observe the Commandments of the law more perfectly than the Jews observed them. The reason is that greater effort deserves a better reward: "He who soweth sparingly, shall also reap sparingly."[24] The Old Law promised a temporary and earthly reward: "If you be willing

---

[20] Prov., i. 15-16.
[21] Rom., i. 32.
[22] Prov., xxiv. 11.
[23] John, viii. 44.
[24] II Cor., ix. 6.

and will hearken to Me, you shall eat the good things of the land."[25] But in the New Law heavenly and eternal things are promised. Therefore, justice, which is the observance of the Commandments, should be more generous because a greater reward is expected.

The Lord mentioned this Commandment in particular among the others when He said: "You have heard that it was said to them of old: Thou shalt not kill. . . . But I say to you that anyone who is angry with his brother, shall be in danger of the judgment."[26] By this is meant the penalty which the law prescribes: "If any man kill his neighbor on set purpose, and by lying in wait for him; thou shalt take him away from My altar, that he may die."[27]

Ways of Avoiding Anger.—Now, there are five ways to avoid being angry. The first is that one be not quickly provoked to anger: "Let every man be swift to hear, but slow to speak and slow to anger."[28] The first reason is that anger is a sin; and is punished by God. But is all anger contrary to virtue? There are two opinions about this. The Stoics said that the wise man is free from all passions; even more, they maintained that true virtue consisted in perfect quiet of soul. The Peripatetics, on the other hand, held that the wise man is subject to anger, but in a moderate degree. This is the more accurate opinion. It is proved firstly by

---

[25] Isa., i. 19.

[26] Matt., v. 21-22.

[27] Exod., xxi. 14. "The Gospel has taught us that it is unlawful even to be angry with anyone. . . From these words (of Christ, cited above) it clearly follows that he who is angry with his brother is not free from sin, even though he does not display his wrath. So also he who gives indication of his anger sins grievously; and he who treats another with great harshness and hurls insults at him, sins even more grievously. This, however, is to be understood of cases in which no just cause of anger exists. God and His laws permit us to be angry when we correct the faults of those who are subject to us. But even in these cases the anger of a Christian should spring from stern duty and not from the impulse of passion, for we are temples of the Holy Spirit in which Jesus Christ may dwell" ("Roman Catechism," *loc. cit.*, 12).

[28] James, i. 19.

authority, in that the Gospel shows us that these passions were attributed to Christ, in whom was the full fountainhead of wisdom. Then, secondly, it is proved from reason. If all the passions were opposed to virtue, then there would be some powers of the soul which would be without good purpose; indeed, they would be positively harmful to man, since they would have no acts in keeping with them. Thus, the irascible and concupiscible powers would be given to man to no purpose. It must, therefore, be concluded that sometimes anger is virtuous, and sometimes it is not.

Three Considerations of Anger.—We see this if we consider anger in three different ways. First, as it exists solely in the judgment of reason, without any perturbation of soul; and this is more properly not anger but judgment. Thus, the Lord punishing the wicked is said to be angry: "I will bear the wrath of the Lord because I have sinned against Him."[29]

Secondly, anger is considered as a passion. This is in the sensitive appetite, and is twofold. Sometimes it is ordered by reason or it is restrained within proper limits by reason, as when one is angry because it is justly fitting to be angry and within proper limits. This is an act of virtue and is called righteous anger. Thus, the Philosopher says that meekness is in no way opposed to anger. This kind of anger then is not a sin.

There is a third kind of anger which overthrows the judgment of reason and is always sinful, sometimes mortally and sometimes venially. And whether it is one or the other will depend on that object to which the anger incites, which is sometimes mortal, sometimes venial. This may be mortal in two ways: either in its *genus* or by reason of the circumstances. For example, murder would seem to be a mortal sin in its *genus*, because it is directly opposite to a divine Commandment. Thus, consent to murder is a mortal

---

[29] Mic., vii. 9.

sin in its *genus*, because if the act is a mortal sin, then the consent to the act will be also a mortal sin. Sometimes, however, the act itself is mortal in its *genus*, but, nevertheless, the impulse is not mortal, because it is without consent. This is the same as if one is moved by the impulse of concupiscence to fornication, and yet does not consent; one does not commit a sin. The same holds true of anger. For anger is really the impulse to avenge an injury which one has suffered. Now, if this impulse of the passion is so great that reason is weakened, then it is a mortal sin; if, however, reason is not so perverted by the passion as to give its full consent, then it will be a venial sin. On the other hand, if up to the moment of consent, the reason is not perverted by the passion, and consent is given without this perversion of reason, then there is no mortal sin. "Whosoever is angry with his brother, shall be in danger of the judgment," must be understood of that impulse of passion tending to do injury to the extent that reason is perverted—and this impulse, inasmuch as it is consented to, is a mortal sin.

Why We Should Not Get Angry Easily.—The second reason why we should not be easily provoked to anger is because every man loves liberty and hates restraint. But he who is filled with anger is not master of himself: "Who can bear the violence of one provoked?"[30] And again: "A stone is heavy, and sand weighty, but the anger of a fool is heavier than both."[31]

The second is to take care that one does not remain angry over long: "Be ye angry, and sin not."[32] And: "Let not the sun go down upon your anger."[33] The reason for this is given in the Gospel by Our Lord: "Be at agreement with thy adversary betimes whilst thou art in the way with him; lest

[30] Prov., xxvii. 4.
[31] *Ibid.*, 3.
[32] Ps. iv. 5.
[33] Eph., iv. 26.

perhaps the adversary deliver thee to the judge, and the judge deliver thee to the officer, and thou be cast into prison. Amen, I say to thee, thou shalt not go out from hence till thou repay the last farthing."[34]

The third is to beware lest our anger grow in intensity, having its beginning in the heart, and finally leading on to hatred. For there is this difference between anger and hatred, that anger is sudden, but hatred is long lived and, thus is a mortal sin: "Whosoever hateth his brother is a murderer."[35] And the reason is because he kills both himself (by destroying charity) and another. Thus, St. Augustine in his "Rule" says: "Let there be no quarrels among you; or if they do arise, then let them end quickly, lest anger should grow into hatred, the mote becomes a beam, and the soul becomes a murderer."[36] Again: "A passionate man stirreth up strifes."[37] "Cursed be their fury, because it was stubborn, and their wrath, because it was cruel."[38]

The fourth is to take care lest our wrath explode in angry words: "A fool immediately showeth his anger."[39] Now, angry words are two-fold in effect; either they injure another, or they express one's own pride in oneself. Our Lord has reference to the first when He said: "And whosoever shall say to his brother: 'Thou fool,' shall be in danger of hell fire."[40] And He has reference to the latter in the words: "And he that shall say: 'Raca, shall be in danger of the council."[41] Moreover: "A mild answer breaketh wrath, but a harsh word stirreth up fury."[42]

[34] Matt., v. 25, 26.
[35] I John, iii. 15.
[36] *Epist.*, cxi.
[37] Prov., xv. 18.
[38] Gen., xlix. 7.
[39] Prov., xii. 16.
[40] Matt., v. 22.
[41] *Ibid.*
[42] Prov., xv. 1.

The last is to beware lest anger provoke us to deeds. In all our dealings we should observe two virtues, namely, justice and mercy; but anger hinders us in both: "For the anger of a man worketh not the justice of God."[43] For such a one may indeed be willing but his anger prevents him. A certain philosopher once said to a man who had offended him: "I would punish you, were I not angry." "Anger hath no mercy, nor fury when it breaketh forth."[44] And: "In their fury they slew a man."[45]

It is for all this that Christ taught us not only to beware of murder but also of anger. The good physician removes the external symptoms of a malady; and, furthermore, he even removes the very root of the illness, so that there will be no relapse. So also the Lord wishes us to avoid the beginnings of sins; and anger is thus to be avoided because it is the beginning of murder.

THE SIXTH COMMANDMENT:

"Thou Shalt Not Commit Adultery."

After the prohibition of murder, adultery is forbidden. This is fitting, since husband and wife are as one body. "They shall be," says the Lord, "two in one flesh."[1] Therefore, after an injury inflicted upon a man in his own person,

---

[43] James, i. 20.
[44] Prov., xxvii. 4.
[45] Gen., xlix. 6.

[1] Gen., ii. 24.

none is so grave as that which is inflicted upon a person with whom one is joined.[2]

Adultery is forbidden both to the wife and the husband. We shall first consider the adultery of the wife, since in this seems to lie the greater sin, for a wife who commits adultery is guilty of three grave sins, which are implied in the following words: "So every woman that leaveth her husband... first, she hath been unfaithful to the law of the Most High; and secondly, she hath offended against her husband; thirdly, she hath fornicated in adultery, and hath gotten her children of another man."[3]

First, therefore, she has sinned by lack of faith, since she is unfaithful to the law wherein God has forbidden adultery. Moreover, she has spurned the ordinance of God: "What therefore God has joined together, let no man put asunder."[4] And also she has sinned against the institution or Sacrament. Because marriage is contracted before the eyes of the Church, and thereupon God is called, as it were, to witness a bond of fidelity which must be kept: "The Lord hath been witness between thee and the wife of thy youth whom thou hast despised."[5] Therefore, she has sinned against the law of God, against a precept of the Church and against a Sacrament of God.

Secondly, she sins by infidelity because she has betrayed her husband: "The wife hath not power of her own

---

[2] "The bond between husband and wife is one of the strictest union, and nothing can be more gratifying to both than to realize that they are objects of mutual and undivided affection. On the other hand, nothing inflicts greater anguish than to feel that the legitimate love which they owe to each other has been transferred elsewhere. This Commandment which prohibits adultery follows properly and in order that which protects human life against the hand of the murderer" ("Roman Catechism," *Sixth Commandment*, 1). St. Thomas treats of this Commandment also in the *Summa Theol.*, II-II, Q. cxxii, art. 6; Q. cliv.

[3] Ecclus., xxiii. 32, 33.

[4] Matt., xix. 6.

[5] Mal., ii. 14.

body: but the husband."[6] In fact, without the consent of the husband she cannot observe chastity. If adultery is committed, then, an act of treachery is perpetrated in that the wife gives herself to another, just as if a servant gave himself to another master: "She forsaketh the guide of her youth, and hath forgotten the covenant of her God."[7]

Thirdly, the adulteress commits the sin of theft in that she brings forth children from a man not her husband; and this is a most grave theft in that she expends her heredity upon children not her husband's. Let it be noted that such a one should encourage her children to enter religion, or upon such a walk of life that they do not succeed in the property of her husband. Therefore, an adulteress is guilty of sacrilege, treachery and theft.

Husbands, however, do not sin any less than wives, although they sometimes, may salve themselves to the contrary. This is clear for three reasons. First, because of the equality which holds between husband and wife, for "the husband also hath not power of his own body, but the wife."[8] Therefore, as far as the rights of matrimony are concerned, one cannot act without the consent of the other. As an indication of this, God did not form woman from the foot or from the head, but from the rib of the man. Now, marriage was at no time a perfect state until the law of Christ came, because the Jew could have many wives, but a wife could not have many husbands; hence, equality did not exist.

The second reason is because strength is a special quality of the man, while the passion proper to the woman is concupiscence: "Ye husbands, likewise dwelling with them according to knowledge, giving honor to the female as to the weaker vessel."[9] Therefore, if you ask from your

---

[6] I Cor., vii. 4.
[7] Prov., ii 17-18.
[8] I Cor., vii. 4.
[9] I Peter, iii. 7.

wife what you do not keep yourself, then you are unfaithful. The third reason is from the authority of the husband. For the husband is head of the wife, and as it is said: "Women may not speak in the church... if they would learn anything, let them ask their husbands at home."[10] The husband is the teacher of his wife, and God, therefore, gave the Commandment to the husband. Now, as regards fulfillment of their duties, a priest who fails is more guilty than a layman, and a bishop more than a priest, because it is especially incumbent upon them to teach others. In like manner, the husband that commits adultery breaks faith by not obeying that which he ought.

Why Adultery and Fornication Must Be Avoided

Thus, God forbids adultery both to men and women. Now, it must be known that, although some believe that adultery is a sin, yet they do not believe that simple fornication is a mortal sin. Against them stand the words of St. Paul: "For fornicators and adulterers God will judge."[11] And: "Do not err: neither fornicators, ... nor adulterers, nor the effeminate, nor liers with mankind shall possess the kingdom of God."[12] But one is not excluded from the kingdom of God except by mortal sin; therefore, fornication is a mortal sin.

But one might say that there is no reason why fornication should be a mortal sin, since the body of the wife is not given, as in adultery. I say, however, if the body of the wife is not given, nevertheless, there is given the body of Christ which was given to the husband when he was sanctified in Baptism. If, then, one must not betray his wife, with

[10] I Cor., xiv. 34-35.
[11] Heb., xiii. 4.
[12] I Cor., vi. 9.

much more reason must he not be unfaithful to Christ: "Know you not that your bodies are the members of Christ? Shall I then take the members of Christ and make them the members of a harlot? God forbid!"[13] It is heretical to say that fornication is not a mortal 'sin.

Moreover, it must be known that the Commandment "Thou shalt not commit adultery," not only forbids adultery but also every form of immodesty and impurity.[14] There are some who say that intercourse between married persons is not devoid of sin. But this is heretical, for the Apostle says: "Let marriage be honorable in all and the bed undefiled."[15] Not only is it devoid of sin, but for those in the state of grace it is meritorious for eternal life. Sometimes, however, it may be a venial sin, sometimes a mortal sin. When it is had with the intention of bringing forth offspring, it is an act of virtue. When it is had with the intent of rendering mutual comfort, it is an act of justice. When it is a cause of exciting lust, although within the limits of marriage, it is a venial sin; and when it goes beyond these limits, so as to intend intercourse with another if possible, it would be a mortal sin.

Adultery and fornication are forbidden for a number of reasons. First of all, because they destroy the soul: "He that is an adulterer, for the folly of his heart shall destroy his own soul."[16] It says: "for the folly of his heart," which is whenever the flesh dominates the spirit. Secondly, they deprive one of life; for one guilty of such should die accord-

[13] I Cor., vi. 15.
[14] "By the prohibition of adultery, every kind of impurity and immodesty by which the body is defiled is also forbidden. Nay more, even every inward thought against chastity is forbidden by this Commandment. . . 'You have heard that it was said to them of old: Thou shalt not commit adultery. But I say to you, that whosoever shall look on a woman to lust after her, hath already committed adultery with her in his heart' " ("Roman Catechism," loc. cit., 5).
[15] Heb., xiii. 4.
[16] Prov., vi. 32.

ing to the Law, as we read in Leviticus (xx 10) and Deuter-
onomy (xxii. 22). Sometimes the guilty one is not punished
now bodily, which is to his disadvantage since punishment
of the body may be borne with patience and is conducive to
the remission of sins; but nevertheless he shall be
punished in the future life. Thirdly, these sins consume his
substance, just as happened to the prodigal son in that "he
wasted his substance living riotously."[17] "Give not thy soul
to harlots in any point; lest thou destroy thyself and thy
inheritance."[18] Fourthly, they defile the offspring: "The children of adulterers shall not come to perfection, and the
seed of the unlawful bed shall be rooted out. And if they
live long they shall be nothing regarded, and their last old
age shall be without honor."[19] And again: "Otherwise your
children should be unclean; but now they are holy."[20] Thus,
they are never honored in the Church, but if they be clerics
their dishonor, may go without shame. Fifthly, these sins
take away one's honor, and this especially is applicable to
women: "Every woman that is a harlot shall be trodden
upon as dung in the way."[21] And of the husband it is said:
"He gathereth to himself shame and dishonor, and his
reproach shall not be blotted out."[22]

St. Gregory says that sins of the flesh are more shameful in spite of being less blameful than those of the spirit,
and the reason is because they are common to the beasts:
"Man when he was in honor did not understand; and he
hath been compared to senseless beasts, and made like to
them."[23]

---

[17]Luke, xv. 13.
[18] Ecclus., ix. 6.
[19] Wis., iii. 16-17.
[20] I Cor., vii. 14.
[21] Ecclus. ix. 10.
[22] Prov., vi. 33.
[23] Ps. xlviii. 21. "If the occasions of sin which we have just enumerated
[viz., idleness, intemperance in eating and drinking, indulgence of the eyes,
immodest dress, immodest conversation and reading] be carefully avoided,

THE SEVENTH COMMANDMENT:

"Thou Shalt Not Steal."

The Lord specifically forbids injury to our neighbor in the Commandments. Thus, "Thou shalt not kill" forbids us to injure our neighbor in his own person; "Thou shalt not commit adultery" forbids injury to the person to whom one is bound in marriage; and now the Commandment, "Thou shalt not steal," forbids us to injure our neighbor in his goods. This Commandment forbids any worldly good whatsoever to be taken away wrongfully.[1]

Theft is committed in a number of ways. First, by taking stealthily: "If the good man of the house knew at what hour the thief would come."[2] This is an act wholly blameworthy because it is a form of treachery. "Confusion... is upon the thief."[3]

Secondly, by taking with violence, and this is an even greater injury: "They have violently robbed the fatherless."[4] Among such that do such things are wicked kings and rulers: "Her princes are in the midst of her as roaring lions; her judges are evening wolves, they left nothing for the morning."[5] They act contrary to God's will who wishes a rule according to justice: "By Me kings reign and lawgivers decree just things."[6] Sometimes they do such things steal-

---

almost every excitement to lust will be removed. But the most efficacious means to subdue its violence are frequent use of confession and reception of the Holy Eucharist. Unceasing and devout prayer to God, accompanied by fasting and giving of alms, has the same salutary effect. Chastity is a gift of God. To those who ask it aright, He does not deny it; nor does He allow us to be tempted beyond our strength" ("Roman Catechism," *loc. cit.*, 12).

[1] St. Thomas also treats of this Commandment in the *Summa Theol.*, II-II Q. cxxii, Art. 6.
[2] Matt., xxiv. 43.
[3] Ecclus., v. 17.
[4] Job, xxiv. 9.
[5] Soph., iii. 3.
[6] Prov., viii. 15.

thily and sometimes with violence: "Thy princes are faithless companions of thieves, they all love bribes, they run after rewards."[7] At times they steal by enacting laws and enforcing them for profit only: "Woe to them that make wicked laws."[8] And St. Augustine says that every wrongful usurpation is theft when he asks: "What are thrones but forms of thievery?"[9]

Thirdly, theft is committed by not paying wages that are due: "The wages of him that hath been hired by thee shall not abide by thee until the morning."[10] This means that a man must pay every one his due, whether he be prince, prelate, or cleric, etc.: "Render therefore to all men their dues. Tribute, to whom tribute is due, custom, to whom custom."[11] Hence, we are bound to give a return to rulers who guard our safety.

The fourth kind of theft is fraud in buying and selling: "Thou shalt not have diverse weights in thy bag, a greater and a less."[12] And again: "Do not any unjust thing in judgment, in rule, in weight, or in measure."[13] All this is directed against the keepers of wine-shops who mix water with the wine. Usury is also forbidden: "Who shall dwell in

[7] Isa., i. 23.

[8] *Ibid.*, x. 1.

[9] "The City of God," IV, 4. "It must be seen that the word 'steal' is understood not only of the taking away of anything from its rightful owner privately and without his consent, but also the possession of that which belongs to another, contrary to his will, although not without his knowledge. Otherwise we would say that he who forbids theft does not also forbid robbery, which is accomplished by violence and injustice. . . So robbery is a greater sin than theft, inasmuch as it not only deprives another of his property, but also offers violence and insult to him. Nor can it be a matter of surprise that the Commandment is expressed in the lighter word, 'steal', instead of 'rob.' A good reason for this is that theft is more general and of wider extent than robbery" ("Roman Catechism," *Seventh Commandment, 3-4*).

[10] Lev., xix. 13.

[11] Rom., xiii. 7.

[12] Deut., xxv. 13.

[13] Lev., xix. 35-36.

Thy tabernacle, or who shall rest in Thy holy hill?. . . He that hath not put his money out to usury."[14] This is also against money-changers who commit many frauds, and against the sellers of cloth and other goods.

Fifthly, theft is committed by those who buy promotions to positions of temporal or spiritual honor. "The riches which he hath swallowed, he shall vomit up, and God shall draw them out of his belly,"[15] has reference to temporal position. Thus, all tyrants who hold a kingdom or province or land by force are thieves, and are held to restitution. Concerning spiritual dignities: "Amen, amen, I say to you, he that entereth not by the door into the sheepfold but climbeth up another way is a thief and a robber."[16] Therefore, they who commit simony are thieves.

Why Stealing Must Be Avoided

"Thou shalt not steal." This Commandment, as has been said, forbids taking things wrongfully, and we can bring forth many reasons why it is given. The first is because of the gravity of this sin, which is likened to murder: "The bread of the needy is the life of the poor; he that defraudeth them thereof is a man of blood."[17] And again: "He that sheddeth blood and he that defraudeth the laborer of his hire are brothers."[18]

The second reason is the peculiar danger involved in theft, for no sin is so dangerous. After committing other sins a person may quickly repent, for instance, of murder

---

[14] Ps. xiv. 1, 5.
[15] Job, xx. 15.
[16] John, x. 1.
[17] Ecclus., xxxiv. 25.
[18] *Ibid.*, 27.

when his anger cools, or of fornication when his passion subsides, and so on for others; but even if one repents of this sin, one does not easily make the necessary satisfaction for it. This is owing to the obligation of restitution and the duty to make up for what loss is incurred by the rightful owner. And all this is above and beyond the obligation to repent for the sin itself: "Woe to him that heapeth together that which is not his own, how long doth he load himself with thick clay!"[19] For thick clay is that from which one cannot easily extricate himself.[20]

The third reason is the uselessness of stolen goods in that they are of no spiritual value: "Treasures of wickedness shall profit nothing."[21] Wealth can indeed be useful for almsgiving and offering of sacrifices, for "the ransom of a man's life are his riches."[22] But it is said of stolen goods: "I am the Lord that loves judgment, and hates robbery in a holocaust."[23] And again: "He that offereth sacrifice of the goods of the poor is as one that sacrificeth the son in the presence of his father."[24]

The fourth reason is that the results of theft are peculiarly harmful to the thief in that they lead to his loss of other goods. It is not unlike the mixture of fire and straw: "fire shall devour their tabernacles, who love to take bribes."[25] And it ought to be known that a thief may lose not only his own soul, but also the souls of his children, since they are bound to make restitution.

---

[19] Hab., ii. 6.

[20] "The possession of other men's property is called 'thick clay' by the prophet because it is difficult to emerge and disengage oneself from (ill-gotten goods). . . What shall we say of the obligation imposed by God on all of satisfying for the injury done? 'Without restitution,' says St. Augustine, 'the sin is not forgiven' " ("Roman Catechism," *loc. cit.,* 8).

[21] Prov., x. 2.

[22] *Ibid.,* xiii. 8.

[23] Isa., lxi. 8.

[24] Ecclus, xxxiv. 24.

[25] Job, xv. 34.

THE EIGHTH COMMANDMENT:

"Thou Shalt Not Bear False Witness Against Thy Neighbor."

The Lord has forbidden anyone to injure his neighbor by deed; now he forbids us to injure him by word. "Thou shalt not bear false witness against thy neighbor."[1] This may occur in two ways, either in a court of justice or in ordinary conversation.

In the court of justice it may happen in three ways, according to the three persons who may violate this Commandment in court.[2] The first person is the plaintiff who makes a false accusation: "Thou shalt not be a detractor nor a whisperer among the people."[3] And note well that it is not only wrong to speak falsely, but also to conceal the truth: "If thy brother shall offend against thee, go and rebuke him."[4]

The second person is the witness who testifies by lying: "A false witness shall not be unpunished."[5] For this Commandment includes all the preceding ones, inasmuch as the false witness may himself be the murderer or the thief, etc. And such should be punished according to the law. "When after most diligent inquisition, they shall find that the false witness hath told a lie against his brother,

---

[1] St. Thomas also treats of this Commandment in the *Summa Theol.*, II-II, Q. cxxii, art. 6.

[2] "The Commandment specially prohibits that species of *false testimony* which is given on oath in a court of justice. The witness swears by the Deity and thus pledges God's holy name for the truth of what he says, and this has very great weight and constitutes the strongest claim for credit. Such testimony, therefore, because it is dangerous, is particularly prohibited. When no legal exceptions can be taken against a sworn witness, and when he cannot be convicted of open dishonesty and malice, even the judge himself cannot reject his testimony. This is especially true since it is commanded by divine authority that 'in the mouth of two or three witnesses every word shall stand' " ("Roman Catechism," *Eighth Commandment*, 3).

[3] Lev., xix. 16.

[4] Matt., xviii. 15.

[5] Prov., xix. 5.

they shall render to him as he meant to do to his brother. . . Thou shalt not pity him, but shalt require life for life, eye for eye, tooth for tooth, hand for hand, foot for foot."[6] And again: "A man that beareth false witness against his neighbor is like a dart and a sword and a sharp arrow."[7] The third person is the judge who sins by giving an unjust sentence: "Thou shalt not. . . judge unjustly. Respect not the person of the poor, nor honor the countenance of the mighty. But judge thy neighbor according to justice."[8]

Ways of Violating This Commandment

In ordinary conversation one may violate this Commandment in five ways. The first is by detraction: "Detractors, hateful to God."[9] "Hateful to God" here indicates that nothing is so dear to a man as his good name: "A good name is better than great riches."[10] But detractors take away this good name: "If a serpent bite in silence, he is no better that backbiteth secretly."[11] Therefore, if detractors do not restore this reputation, they cannot be saved.

Secondly, one may break this precept by listening to detractors willingly: "Hedge in thy ears with thorns, hear not a wicked tongue, and make doors and bars to thy mouth."[12] One should not listen deliberately to such things, but ought to turn away, showing a sad and stern

---

[6] Deut., xix. 18-21.

[7] Prov., xxv. 18.

[8] Lev., xix. 15. "This Commandment prohibits deceit, lying, and perjury on the part of witnesses. The same prohibition also applies to plaintiffs, defendants, promoters, representatives, procurators, and advocates; in a word, all who take any part in lawsuits. . . Finally, God forbids all testimony which may injure others or do them injustice, whether it be a matter of legal evidence or not" ("Roman Catechism," *loc. cit.*, 6).

[9] Rom., i. 30.

[10] Prov., xxii. 1.

[11] Eccles., x. 11.

[12] Ecclus., xxviii. 28.

countenance: "The north wind driveth away rain as doth a sad countenance a backbiting tongue."[13]

Thirdly, gossipers break this precept when they repeat whatever they hear: "Six things there are which the Lord hateth, and the seventh His soul detesteth... him that soweth discord among brethren."[14] Fourthly, those who speak honied words, the flatterers. "The sinner is praised in the desires of his soul, and the unjust man is blessed."[15] And again: "O My people, they that call thee blessed, the same shall deceive thee."[16]

Special Effects of Telling Lies

The prohibition of this Commandment includes every form of falsehood: "Be not willing to make any manner of lie; for the custom thereof is no good."[17] There are four reasons for this. The first is that lying likens one to the devil, because a liar is as the son of the devil. Now, we know that a man's speech betrays from what region and country he comes from, thus: "Even thy speech doth discover thee."[18] Even so, some men are of the devil's kind,

---

[13] Prov., xxv. 23. "This Commandment not only forbids false testimony, but also the abominable sin of detraction. This is a moral pestilence which is the poisoned source of many and calamitous evils. . . That we may see the nature of the sin of detraction more clearly, we must know that reputation is injured not only by calumniating the character, but also by exaggerating the faults of others. He who makes known the secret sin of any man at any time or place unnecessarily, or before persons who have no right to know, is also rightly regarded as a detractor and evil-speaker, if his revelation seriously injures the other's reputation" ("Roman Catechism," *loc. cit.,* 9).

[14] Prov., vi. 16, 19.

[15] Ps. ix. 24.

[16] Isa., iii. 12. "Flatterers and sycophants are among those who violate this Commandment, for by fawning and insincere praise they gain the hearing and good will of those whose favor, money, and honors they seek" ("Roman Catechism," *loc. cit.,* 11).

[17] Ecclus., vii. 14.

[18] Matt., xxvi. 73.

and are called sons of the devil because they are liars, since the devil is "a liar and the father of lies."[19] Thus, when the devil said, "No, you shall not die the death,"[20] he lied. But, on the contrary, others are the children of God, who is Truth, and they are those who speak the truth.

The second reason is that lying induces the ruin of society. Men live together in society, and this is soon rendered impossible if they do not speak the truth to one another. "Wherefore putting away lying, speak ye the truth, every man with his neighbor; for we are members one of another."[21]

The third reason is that the liar loses his reputation for the truth. He who is accustomed to telling lies is not believed even when he speaks the truth: "What can be made clean by the unclean? And what truth can come from that which is false?"[22]

The fourth reason is because a liar kills his soul, for "the mouth that belieth killeth the soul."[23] And again: "Thou wilt destroy all that speak a lie."[24] Accordingly, it is clear that lying is a mortal sin; although it must be known that some lies may be venial.

It is a mortal sin, for instance, to lie in matters of faith. This concerns professors, prelates and preachers, and is the gravest of all other kinds of lies: "There shall be among you lying teachers, who shall bring in sects of perdition."[25] Then there are those who lie to wrong their neighbor: "Lie not to one another."[26] These two kinds of lies, therefore, are mortal sins.

[19] John, viii. 44.
[10] Gen., iii. 4.
[21] Eph., iv. 25
[22] Ecclus., xxxiv. 4.
[23] Wis., i. 11.
[24] Ps. v. 7.
[25] II Peter, ii. 1.
[26] Col., iii. 9.

There are some who lie for their own advantage, and this in a variety of ways. Sometimes it is out of humility This may be the case in confession, about which St. Augustine says: "Just as one must avoid concealing what he has committed, so also he must not mention what he has not committed." "Hath God any need of your lie?"[27] And again: "There is one that humbleth himself wickedly, and his interior is full of deceit; and there is one that humbleth himself exceedingly with a great lowness."[28]

There are others who tell lies out of shame, namely, when one tells a falsehood believing that he is telling the truth, and on becoming aware of it he is ashamed to retract: "In no wise speak against the truth, but be ashamed of the lie of thy ignorance."[29] Others lie for desired results as when they wish to gain or avoid something: "We have placed our hope in lies, and by falsehood we are protected."[30] And again: "He that trusteth in lies feedeth the winds."[31]

Finally, there are some who lie to benefit another, that is, when they wish to free someone from death, or danger, or some other loss. This must be avoided, as St. Augustine tells us: "Accept no person against thy own person, nor against thy soul a lie."[32] But others lie only out of vanity, and this, too, must never be done, lest the habit of such lead us to mortal sin: "For the bewitching of vanity obscureth good things."[33]

[27] Job, xiii. 7.
[28] Ecclus., xix. 23-24.
[29] *Ibid.*, iv. 30.
[30] Isa., xxviii. 15.
[31] Prov., x. 4.
[32] Ecclus., iv. 26.
[33] Wis., iv. 12.

THE NINTH (TENTH) COMMANDMENT:

"Thou Shalt Not Covet Thy Neighbor s Goods."

"Thou shalt not covet thy neighbor's goods."[1] There is this difference between the divine and the human laws that human law judges only deeds and words, whereas the divine law judges also thoughts. The reason is because human laws are made by men who see things only exteriorly, but the divine law is from God, who sees both external things and the very interior of men. "Thou art the God of my heart."[2] And again. "Man seeth those things that appear, but the Lord beholdeth the heart."[3] Therefore, having considered those Commandments which concern words and deeds, we now treat of the Commandments about thoughts. For with God the intention is taken for the deed, and thus the words, "Thou shalt not covet," mean to include not only the taking by act, but also the intention to take. Therefore, it says: "Thou shalt not covet thy neighbor's goods." There are a number of reasons for this.

The first reason for the Commandment is that man's desire has no limits, because desire itself is boundless. But he who is wise will aim at some particular end, for no one should have aimless desires: "A covetous man shall not be satisfied with money."[4] But the desires of man are never satisfied, because the heart of man is made for God. Thus,

---

[1] St. Thomas places the Tenth Commandment (in the present traditional enumeration) before the Ninth. The Tenth Commandment is wider in extension than the Ninth, which is specific. The "Roman Catechism" (*Ninth and Tenth Commandments*, 1) treats both the Ninth and Tenth Commandments together, and remarks that "what is commanded in these two precepts amounts to this, that to observe the preceding Commandments we must be particularly careful not to covet. For he who does not covet, being content with what he has, will not desire what belongs to others, but will rejoice in their prosperity, giving glory to God."

[2] Ps. lxxii. 26.

[3] I Kings, xvi. 7.

[4] Eccles., v. 9.

says St. Augustine: "Thou hast made us for Thee, O Lord, and our heart is restless until it rests in Thee."[5] Nothing, therefore, less than God can satisfy the human heart: "Who satisfieth thy desire with good things."[6]

The second reason is that covetousness destroys peace of heart, which is indeed highly delightful. The covetous man is ever solicitous to acquire what he lacks, and to hold that which he has: "The fullness of the rich will not suffer him to sleep."[7] "For where thy treasure is, there is thy heart also."[8] It was for this, says St Gregory, that Christ compared riches to thorns.[9]

Thirdly, covetousness in a man of wealth renders his riches useless both to himself and to others, because he desires only to hold on to them: "Riches are not comely for a covetous man and a niggard."[10] The fourth reason is that it destroys the equality of justice: "Neither shalt thou take bribes, which even blind the wise, and pervert the words of the just."[11] And again: "He that loveth gold shall not be justified."[12] The fifth reason is that it destroys the love of God and neighbor, for, says St. Augustine: "The more one loves, the less one covets," and also the more one covets, the less one loves. "Nor despise thy dear brother for the sake of gold."[13] And just as "No man can serve two masters," so neither can he serve "God and mammon."[14]

Finally, covetousness produces all kinds of wickedness. It is the root of all evil," says St. Paul, and when this root is implanted in the heart it brings forth murder and

[5] "Confessions," I.
[6] Ps. cii. 5.
[7] Eccles., v. 11.
[8] Vi. vi. 21.
[9] Luk. iii. 14.
[10] Ecclus., xiv. 3.
[11] Exod., xxiii. 8.
[12] Ecclus., xxxi. 5.
[13] *Ibid.*, vii. 20.
[14] Matt., vi. 24.

theft and all kinds of evil. "They that will become rich, fall into temptation, and into the snare of the devil, and into many unprofitable and hurtful desires which drown men in destruction and perdition. For the desire of money is the root of all evil."[15] And note, furthermore, that covetousness is a mortal sin when one covets one's neighbor's goods without reason: and even if there be a reason, it is a venial sin"[16]

THE TENTH (NINTH) COMMANDMENT:

"Thou Shalt Not Covet Thy Neighbor's Wife"

St. John says in his first Epistle that "all that is in the world is the concupiscence of the flesh, the concupiscence of the eyes, and the pride of life."[1] Now, all that is desirable

---

[15] I Tim., vi. 9, 10.

[16] "Another reason for these two Commandments is that they clearly and in definite terms forbid some things not expressly prohibited in the Sixth and Seventh Commandments. The Seventh Commandment, for instance, forbids an unjust desire to take what belongs to another; but the Tenth Commandment further prohibits even to covet it in any way, even though it could be acquired justly and lawfully—if we foresee that by such acquisition our neighbor would suffer some loss. . . Another reason why this sort of vicious desire is condemned is that it has for its object that which belongs to another, such as a house, maidservant, field, wife, ox, ass, and many other things, all of which the law of God forbids us to covet, simply because they belong to another. The desire for such things, when consented to. is criminal, and is numbered among the most grievous sins. When the mind, yielding to the impulse of evil desires, is pleased with evil or does not resist it, sin is necessarily committed" ("Roman Catechism," loc. cit., 11).

[1] John, ii. 16.

is included in these three, two of which are forbidden by the precept: "Thou shalt not covet thy neighbor's house."[2] Here "house," signifying height, refers to avarice, for "glory and wealth shall be in his house."[3] This means that he who desires the house, desires honors and riches. And thus, after the precept forbidding desire of the house of one's neighbor comes the Commandment prohibiting concupiscence of the flesh: "Thou shalt not covet thy neighbor's wife."[4]

Because of the corruption which resulted from the Fall, none has been free from concupiscence except Christ and the glorious Virgin. And wherever there is concupiscence there is either venial or mortal sin, provided that it is allowed to dominate the reason."[5] Hence the precept is not, let sin not be; for it is written: "I know that there dwelleth not in me [that is to say, in my flesh] that which is good."[6]

First of all, sin rules in the flesh when, by giving consent to it, concupiscence reigns in the heart. And, therefore, St. Paul adds "so as to obey the lusts thereof" to the words: "Let not sin reign in your mortal body."[7] Accordingly the Lord says: "Whosoever shall look on a woman to lust

---

[2] The text of Exodus, xx. 17, which contains the Ninth and Tenth Commandments, reads as follows: "Thou shalt not covet thy neighbor's house: neither shalt thou desire his wife, nor his servant, nor his hand-maid, nor his ox, nor his ass, nor anything that is his."

[3] Ps. cxi. 3.

[4] "He [the pastor] will show how these two Commandments are dissimilar; how one covetousness looks only to utility and interest (the tenth), the other to unlawful desire and criminal pleasure (the ninth). If one covets a field or house, he acts out of desire for gain or utility, while he who covets another man's wife yields to a desire for criminal pleasure rather than monetary gain" ("Roman Catechism," *loc. cit.*, 2).

[5] "Concupiscence, the fuel of sin, which originated in sin, is always present in our fallen nature; from it we know that we are born in sin, and, therefore, we suppliantly fly to Him who alone can efface the sordid stains of sin" ("Roman Catechism," *loc. cit.*, 5).

[6] Rom., vii. 18.

[7] *Ibid.*, vi. 12.

after her, hath already committed adultery with her in his heart."[8] For with God the intention is taken for the act.

Secondly, sin rules in the flesh when the concupiscence of our heart is expressed in words: "Out of the abundance of the heart the mouth speaketh."[9] And again: "Let no evil speech proceed from your mouth."[10] Therefore, one is not without sin who composes frivolous songs. Even the philosophers so thought, and poets who wrote amatory verses were sent into exile. Lastly, sin rules in the flesh when at the behest of desire the members are made to serve iniquity: "As you have yielded your members to serve uncleanness and iniquity unto iniquity."[11] These, therefore, are the progressive steps of concupiscence.

Ways to Overcome Concupiscence

We must realize that the avoidance of concupiscence demands much labor, for it is based on something within us. It is as hard as trying to capture an enemy in one's own household. However, this desire can be overcome in four ways.

Firstly, by fleeing the external occasions such as, for instance, bad company; and in fact whatever may be an occasion for this sin: "Gaze not upon a maiden lest her beauty be a stumbling block to thee... Look not around about thee in the ways of the city, nor wander up and down in the streets thereof. Turn away thy face from a woman dressed up, and gaze not about upon another's beauty. For many have perished by the beauty of a woman, and hereby lust is enkindled as a fire."[12] And again: "Can a man hide

---

[8] Matt., v. 28.
[9] Matt., xii. 34.
[10] Eph., iv. 29.
[11] Rom., vi. 19.
[12] Ecclus., ix. 5-9.

me in his bosom, and his garments not burn?"[13] And thus Lot was commanded to flee, "neither stay thou in all the country about."[14]

The second way is by not giving an opening to thoughts which of themselves are the occasion of lustful desires. And this must be done by mortification of the flesh: "I chastise my body, and bring it into subjection."[15] The third way is perseverance in prayer: "Unless the Lord build the house, they labor in vain who build it."[16] And also: "I knew that I could not otherwise be continent, except God gave it."[17] Again: "This kind is not cast out save by prayer and fasting."[18] All this is not unlike to a fight between two persons, one of whom you desire to win, the other to lose. You must sustain the one and withdraw all support from the other. So also between the spirit and the flesh there is a continual combat. Now, if you wish the spirit to win, you must assist it by prayer, and likewise you must resist the flesh by such means as fasting; for by fasting the flesh is weakened.

The fourth way is to keep oneself busy with wholesome occupations: "Idleness hath taught much evil."[19] Again: "This was the iniquity of Sodom thy sister, pride, fullness of bread, and abundance, and the idleness of her."[20] St. Jerôme says: "Be always busy in doing something good, so that the devil may find you ever occupied." Now, study of the Scriptures is the best of all occupations, as St. Jerome tells us: "Love to study the Scriptures and you will not love the vices of the flesh."[21]

[13] Prov., vi. 27.
[14] Gen., xix. 17.
[15] I Cor., ix. 27.
[16] Ps., cxxvi. 1.
[17] Wis., viii. 21.
[18] Matt., xvii. 20.
[19] Ecclus., xxxiii. 29.
[20] Ezech., xvi. 49.
[21] *Ad Paulin.*

Summary of the Ten Commandments

These are the ten precepts to which Our Lord referred when He said: "if thou wilt enter into life, keep the commandments" (Matt., xix. 17). There are two main principles of all the Commandments, namely, love of God and love of neighbor. The man that loves God must necessarily do three things: (1) he must have no other God. And in support of this is the Commandment: "Thou shalt not have strange gods"; (2) he must give God all honor. And so it is commanded: "Thou shalt not take the name of God in vain"; (3) he must freely take his rest in God. Hence: "Remember that thou keep holy the Sabbath day."

But to love God worthily, one must first of all love one's neighbor. And so: "Honor thy father and mother." Then, one must avoid doing harm to one's neighbor in act. "Thou shalt not kill" refers to our neighbor's person; "Thou shalt not commit adultery" refers to the person united in marriage to our neighbor; "Thou shalt not steal" refers to our neighbor's external goods. We must also avoid injury to our neighbor both by word. "Thou shalt not bear false witness," and by thought, "Thou shalt not covet thy neighbor's goods" and "Thou shalt not covet thy neighbor's wife."

The baptism of Jesus by the River Jordan. Inset, the rites for the sacrament of Baptism.

EXPLANATION OF THE SACRAMENTS

The Sacraments of the Church

We shall now consider the Sacraments of the Church. We shall treat them under one heading, since they all pertain to the effect of grace. First of all, that must be known which St. Augustine wrote in the tenth book of "The City of God": "a Sacrament is a sacred thing" or "the sign of a sacred thing."[1] Even in the Old Law there were certain sacraments, that is, signs of a sacred thing for example, the paschal lamb and other legal sacred signs or "sacraments" which, however, did not *cause* grace but only signified or indicated the grace of Christ. The Apostle calls these "sacraments" *weak and needy elements.*[2] They were *needy* because they did not contain grace, and they were *weak* because they could not confer grace. In them, as St. Augustine says, the merits of Christ brought about salvation in a more hidden manner under the cover of visible things. The Sacraments of the New Law, on the other hand, both contain grace and confer it. A Sacrament of the New Law is a visible form of invisible grace. Thus, the exterior washing which takes place when the water is poured in Baptism represents that interior cleansing which takes away sin by virtue of the Sacrament of Baptism.[3]

---

[1] *Sacramentum est sacrum signum.* This is slightly different in the passage quoted in "The City of God," Book X, chapter x. See also *Epist. ii.* The "Roman Catechism" (*The Sacraments in General* Chapter 1, 4,) seemingly follows St. Thomas here.

[2] Gal., iv. 9.

[3] "A Sacrament, therefore, is clearly understood to be numbered amongst those things which have been instituted as signs. It makes known to us by a certain appearance and resemblance that which God, by His invisible power, accomplishes in our souls. . . In order to explain more fully the nature of a Sacrament, it should be taught that it is a thing subject to the senses which possesses, by divine institution, the power not only of signifying holiness and

There are seven Sacraments of the New Law: Baptism, Confirmation, the Eucharist, Penance, Extreme Unction, Orders, and Matrimony. The first five of these Sacraments are intended to bring about the perfection of the individual man in himself; whereas the other two, Orders and Matrimony, are so constituted that they perfect and multiply the entire Church.

The Spiritual and the Physical Life: An Analogy

The spiritual life conforms to the physical life. In the physical life man is perfected in three chief ways: First, by generation, in that he is born into this world; secondly, by growth, through which he is brought up into stature and perfect strength; thirdly, by food which sustains man's life and powers. This would suffice were it not that man is attacked by illnesses, and hence, fourthly, he needs something which will bring him back to health.

This also holds true in the spiritual life. First, man needs regeneration or re-birth which is brought through the Sacrament of Baptism: "Unless a man be born again of water and the Holy Spirit he cannot enter into the kingdom of God."[4] Secondly, it is necessary that man develop perfect strength, which is, as it were, a spiritual growth, and this indeed comes to him in the Sacrament of Confirmation. This is like the strenthening which the Apostles received when the Holy Spirit came upon them and confirmed them.

---

justice, but also to impart both to the recipient. Hence, it is easy to see that the images of the Saints, crosses, and the like, although they are signs of sacred things, cannot be called Sacraments. Thus, the solemn ablution of the body [in Baptism] not only signifies, but also has the power to effect a sacred thing which is worked interiorly in the soul by the invisible operation of the Holy Spirit" ("Roman Catechism," *Sacraments in General*, Chapter 1, 6, and 11).

[4] John., iii. 5.

The Lord had said to them: "But stay you in the city of Jerusalem till you be endued with power from on high."[5] The third similarity is that man must be fed with spiritual food: "Unless you eat the flesh of the Son of Man, and drink His blood, you shall not have life in you."[6] Fourthly, man must be healed spiritually through the Sacrament of Penance: "Heal, O Lord, my soul, for I have sinned against Thee."[7] Lastly, one is healed both in soul and in body in the Sacrament of Extreme Unction: "Is any man sick among you? Let him bring in the priests of the church, and let them pray over him, anointing him with oil in the name of the Lord. And the prayer of faith shall save the sick man, and the Lord shall raise him up, and if he be in sin, they shall be forgiven him."[8] Two of the Sacraments, Orders and Matrimony, are instituted for the common good of the Church. Through the Sacrament of Orders the Church is ruled and is spiritually multiplied; and through Matrimony it is increased physically in numbers.[9]

The Seven Sacraments in General

The seven Sacraments have some things which they all hold in common, and some things which are proper to each one. That which is common to all the Sacraments is that they confer grace. It is also common to all the Sacraments that a Sacrament is made up of words and physical acts. And so also Christ, who is the Author of the Sacraments, is

[5] Luke, xxiv. 49.
[6] John, vi. 54.
[7] Ps. xl. 5.
[8] James, v. 14.
[9] "Why there are neither more nor less [than seven Sacraments] may be shown at least with some degree of probability from the analogy that exists between the spiritual and the physical life" ("Roman Catechism," *loc. cit.*, 20).

the Word made flesh. And just as the flesh of Christ was sanctified, and has the power of sanctifying because of the Word united to itself, so also the Sacraments are made holy and have the power of sanctifying through the words which accompany the action. Thus, St. Augustine says: "The word is joined to the element, and the Sacrament is made."[10] Now, the words by which the Sacraments are sanctified are called the *form* of the Sacraments; and the things which are sanctified are called the *matter* of the Sacraments. Water, for example, is the *matter* of Baptism, and the holy chrism is the *matter* of Confirmation.

In each Sacrament there is required a *minister*, who confers the Sacrament with the intention of doing that which the Church intends. If any one of these three requirements is lacking, the Sacrament is not brought into being, viz., if there is lacking the due *form* of the words, or if the *matter* is not present, or if the *minister* does not intend to confer the Sacrament.[11]

The effect of the Sacrament is likewise impeded through the fault of the recipient, for example, if one feigns to receive it and with a heart unprepared to receive worthily. Such a one, although he actually receives the Sacrament, does not receive the effect of the Sacrament, that is,

---

[10] *In Joan.*, Tract LXXX, 3.

[11] "It should be explained that the pastor will inform the faithful that the 'sensible thing' which enters into the definition of a Sacrament as already given, although constituting but one sign, is of a twofold nature. Every Sacrament consists of two things: 'matter' which is called the element, and 'form' which is commonly called the word. . . In order to make the meaning of the rite that is being performed easier and clearer, words had to be added to the matter. Water, for example, has the quality of cooling as well as of making clean, and may be symbolic of either. In Baptism, therefore, unless the words were added, it would not be certain which meaning of the sign was intended. When the words are added, we immediately understand that the Sacrament possesses and signifies the power of cleansing. . . Although God is the author and dispenser of the Sacraments, He nevertheless willed that they should be administered by men in His Church, not by Angels. The ministers of the Sacraments, in performing their duties, do not act in their own persons but in that they represent Christ, and hence, be they good or bad, they validly

the grace of the Holy Spirit. "For the Holy Spirit of discipline will flee from the deceitful."[12] On the other hand, however, there are some who never even receive sacramentally, yet who receive the effect of the Sacrament because of their devotion towards the Sacrament, which they may have in desire or in a vow.

There are some things which are characteristic of each individual Sacrament. Certain ones impress a *character* on the soul which is a certain spiritual sign distinct from the other Sacraments. Such are the Sacraments of Orders, Baptism, and Confirmation. The Sacraments which give a character are never repeated in the same person who has once received it. Thus, he who is baptized need never again receive this Sacrament; neither can he who has been confirmed receive Confirmation again; and one who has been ordained need never repeat his ordination. The reason is that the character which each of these Sacraments impresses is indelible.

In the other Sacraments, however, a character is not impressed on the recipient, and hence they can be repeated as far as the person is concerned, not however as far as the matter is concerned. Thus, one can frequently receive Penance, frequently receive the Eucharist, and can be anointed more than once with Extreme Unction, and likewise he can be married more than once. Yet, regarding the matter the same Host cannot be frequently consecrated, nor ought the oil of the sick be frequently blessed."[13]

---

confer the Sacraments as long as they make use of the matter and the form always observed in the Catholic Church according to the institution of Christ, and intend to do what the Church does in the administration of the Sacraments" ("Roman Catechism," *loc. cit.*, 16 and 24).

[12] Wis., i. 5.

[13] "This character has a twofold effect. It qualifies us to receive or perfom a sacred act, and distinguishes us by some mark one from another. This is seen, for example, in Baptism, whose character first renders one qualified to receive the other Sacraments, and, secondly, by it the Christian is distinguished from those who do not profess the faith" ("Roman Catechism," *loc. cit.*, 31).

BAPTISM

Having considered the Sacraments in general, it is now necessary to say something about each one in particular. First, we consider Baptism, of which it must be known that the *matter* of this Sacrament is natural water, and it makes no difference whether it is cold or warm. In artificial waters, however, such as rose water, one cannot baptize. The *form* of Baptism is: "I baptize thee in the name of the Father and of the Son and of the Holy Spirit." The minister of Baptism ordinarily is the priest, whose office it is to baptize. In case of necessity, however, not only a deacon but also any lay person, even a pagan or a heretic, can baptize as long as he observes the *form* specified by the Church, and intends to act according to the intention of the Church. If a person is baptized by these not in a case of necessity, he received the Sacrament and must not again be baptized; but the grace of the Sacrament is not received, because such persons are not truly deputed to baptize outside of cases of necessity, and, hence, they act contrary to the law of the Church regulating reception of the Sacraments.[14]

The Effect of Baptism

The effect of Baptism is to remit both original and actual sin as well as all guilt and punishment which they

[14] The priest is the ordinary minister of Baptism. In case of necessity, however, anyone who observes the proper form and intention can baptize validly and licitly. If it is not a case of necessity, a layman who baptizes acts validly but not licitly; and an adult who permits himself to be baptized without necessity by a layman would be acting illicitly, but the baptism is valid. For such conduct places an *obex* (obstacle or hindrance) to the reception of grace. The grace of the Sacrament is revived (*reviviscilur*) with at least contrition, and probably attrition, or simply by an act of perfect contrition.

incur. No kind of punishment must be enjoined for past sins upon those just newly baptized. Hence, those who die immediately after Baptism are admitted to the glory of God without delay. The effect, therefore, of Baptism is the opening of the gates of paradise.

Errors Concerning Baptism

There have been certain errors concerning this Sacrament. The first was that of the Solentiani, who received a baptism not of water but of the spirit. Against them the Lord says: "Unless a man be born again of water and the Holy Spirit, he cannot enter into the kingdom of God."[15] The second error was that of the Donatists, who re-baptized those who had been baptized by the Catholics. Against them it is written: "One faith, one baptism."[16] They also err in holding that a man in the state of sin cannot baptize. Against them it is said: "He upon whom thou shalt see the Spirit descending, and remaining upon Him, He it is that baptizeth."[17] It is thus seen that a minister who is himself evil does not invalidate either this or any of the other Sacraments, because it is Christ who, by the merits of His passion, gives to each Sacrament its efficacy; and He is good. The fourth error is that of the Pelagians who say that children must be baptized because by their regeneration they, as adopted children of God, are admitted into the kingdom, but by this regeneration they are not freed from original sin.

[15] John, iii. 5.
[16] Eph., iv. 5.
[17] John, i. 33.

CONFIRMATION

The second Sacrament is Confirmation. The *matter* of this Sacrament is chrism made from oil, which signifies the bright lustre of conscience, and from balsam, which signifies the odor of a good name; both of which are blessed by the bishop. The *form* of this Sacrament is: "I sign thee with the sign of the cross, and I confirm thee with the chrism of salvation, in the name of the Father, and of the Son, and of the Holy Spirit. Amen."[18] The minister of this Sacrament is solely the bishop.[19] It is not licit for a priest to anoint on the forehead with chrism those who are to be confirmed.[20]

The Effect of Confirmation

The effect of Confirmation is that the Holy Spirit is imparted to give strength, just as He was given to the Apostles on the day of Pentecost. Thus, the Christian must boldly confess the name of Christ. The one who is confirmed is anointed on the forehead wherein is the seat of fear; so that he will not blush to confess either the name of Christ or especially the cross of Christ, which to the Jews was a scandal and to the pagans foolishness. For this reason he is signed with the sign of the cross.

---

[18] "Amen" is omitted in the Roman Pontifical.

[19] The ordinary minister of Confirmation in the Latin Church is the bishop. In virtue of Canon 782, & 3, only Abbots, Prelates Nullius, Vicars and Prefects Apostolic can confer this Sacrament validly and only within the confines of their own territory and during their term of office. Cardinals can confirm validly anywhere.

[20] A priest of the Latin Rite who has a special indult granted by the Holy See may confirm Catholics of his own rite only, unless it is otherwise stated (Canon 782, & 4).

Errors Concerning Confirmation

Certain of the Greeks erred concerning this Sacrament in saying that it could be administered by one who is only a priest. Against this it is said that the Apostles sent the Apostles Peter and John to impose hands upon those who had been baptized by Philip the Deacon, and they received the Holy Spirit. Now, the bishops of the Church are in the places of the Apostles, and in their place also do they impose hands when the Sacrament of Confirmation is administered.

THE HOLY EUCHARIST

The third Sacrament is the Holy Eucharist. Its *matter* is wheaten bread and wine from the grape mixed with a little water so that the water becomes part of the wine. The water signifies the faithful who are incorporated into Christ. Other than wheaten bread and wine from the grape cannot be the *matter* for this Sacrament. The *form* of this Sacrament is the very words of Christ, "This is My Body," and "This is the chalice of My Blood of the new and eternal testament; the mystery of faith, which shall be shed for you and for many, to the remission of sins." These words spoken by the priest in the person of Christ brings into being this Sacrament. The minister of this Sacrament is the priest; and no one else can consecrate this matter into the Body of Christ.

The Effect of the Eucharist

The effect of this Sacrament is twofold: first, in the very consecration of the Sacrament, since in virtue of the above words bread is changed into the Body of Christ, and wine into His Blood; so that Christ is entirely contained under the appearances of bread which remain without a subject; and Christ is entirely contained under the appearances of wine. And, moreover, under each part of the consecrated Host and of the consecrated wine, Christ is totally present even after the separation is made.[21] The second effect of this Sacrament brought about in the soul of one who worthily receives is the union of man with Christ, as He himself says: "He that eateth My flesh, and drinketh My Blood, abideth in Me, and I in him."[22] And since man is incorporated with Christ and united to His members through grace, it follows that through this Sacrament grace is increased in those who receive it worthily. Thus, therefore, in this Sacrament there is that which is the Sacrament alone (*sacramentum tantum*), that is, the species of bread and

---

[21] "Hence it also follows that Christ is so contained, whole and entire, under either species that, as under the species of bread are contained not only the body but also the blood and Christ entire, so in like manner under the species of wine are truly contained not only the blood, but also the body and Christ entire. These are matters on which the faithful cannot entertain a doubt. Wisely, however, was it ordained that two distinct consecrations should take place. They represent in a more lively manner the Passion of Our Lord, in which His blood was separated from His body; and hence in the form of consecration we commemorate the shedding of His blood. Again, since the Sacrament is to be used by us as the food and nourishment of our souls, it was most appropriate that it should be instituted as food and drink, two things which obviously constitute the complete sustenance of man.

"Nor should it be forgotten that Christ is, whole and entire, contained not only under either species, but also in each particle of either species. 'Each,' says St. Augustine, 'receives Christ the Lord, and He is entire in each portion. He is not diminished by being given to many, but gives Himself whole and entire to each' (cited in Gratian, 'De consecratione,' dist. 2). This is also an obvious inference from the narrative of the Evangelists. It is not to be supposed that Our Lord consecrated the bread used at the Last Supper in separate parts, applying the form particularly to each, but that all the bread then used for the sacred mysteries was consecrated at the same time and with the same form, and in a quantity sufficient for all the Apostles. That the consecration of the chalice was performed in this manner, is clear from these words of the Saviour: 'Take and divide it among you' (Luke, xxii, 17)" ("Roman Catechism;" *The Eucharist*, 35-36).

[22] John. vi. 57.

wine; and that which is known as the *res et sacramentum*, that is, the true Body of Christ; and that which is the *res tantum*, that is the unity of the Mystical Body, that is, the Church which this Sacrament both signifies and causes.[23]

Errors Concerning the Eucharist

There have been many errors regarding this Sacrament. The first error is of those who say that in this Sacrament is not the true Body of Christ but only a sign of it. The author of this error is said to be Berengarius against whom it is written: "For My flesh is meat indeed; and My Blood is drink indeed."[24] The second is the error of the Arrodinici, who offer in their sacrament bread and cheese because they say men at first made offerings of the fruits of the earth and of their flocks. Against this, however, stands the fact that the Lord who is the institutor of this Sacrament ·gave to His disciples bread and wine. The third is the error of the Cataphrygae and the Praeputiati, who drew the blood of an infant from tiny punctures in its body, and mixing this with flour made a bread of it; and thus asserted that they consecrated the sacrament. This is more like the sacrifices of demons than that of Christ: "And they shed innocent blood ... which they sacrificed to the idols of Chanaan."[25] The fourth is the error of the Aquarii, who offer water only in their sacrifices. But against this are the words

---

[23] "Those who receive this Sacrament piously and fervently must, without any doubt, so receive the Son of God into their souls as to be united as living members to His Body. For it is written, 'he that eateth Me, the same also shall live by me.' And again: 'The bread which I will give is My flesh for the life of the world' (John, vi. 58).
. . . For the Eucharist is the end of all the Sacraments, and the symbol of unity and brotherhood in the Church" ("Roman Catechism," *loc. cit.*, 49).

[24] John, vi. 56.

[25] Ps. cv. 39.

from the mouth of Wisdom, which is Christ: "Drink the wine which I have mingled for you."[26] Another error is that of the Poor People of Lyons who hold that any just man can consecrate this Sacrament. Against such errors is the fact that the Lord gave to the Apostles the power to celebrate this Sacrament; and hence only those who receive this power in a certain succession from the Apostles can consecrate this Sacrament.

PENANCE

The fourth Sacrament is Penance. The matter,[27] as it were, of this Sacrament is the acts of the penitent, which are called the three parts of Penance. The first part is a heart-felt *contrition*, by which one is sorry for the sins one has committed, and determines not to sin again. The second part is *confession*, which consists in this that the sinner confesses all the sins of which he is mindful to the priest; and all of them at one time to one priest, not dividing them to a number of priests. The third part is *satisfaction*, which is enjoined according to the judgment of the priest; and consists especially in fasting and prayer and almsgiving.

[26] Prov., ix. 5.

[27] St. Thomas uses here the words: *quasi materia*. The "Roman Catechism" (*Penance*, 13) follows this teaching. "The faithful should be especially informed on the *matter* of this Sacrament. That it differs from the other Sacraments in that for them the *matter* is something, whether natural or artificial; the *matter* as it were (*quasi-materia*) of Penance is the acts of the penitent, i. e., contrition, confession, and satisfaction. This has thus been defined by the Council of Trent. . . It is not because they are not the real matter that they are called by the Council *the matter as it were*, but because they are not of that sort of matter which is applied externally, such, for instance, as water in Baptism and chrism in Confirmation."

The *form* of this Sacrament is the words of absolution which the priest speaks when he says: "I absolve thee" (E*go te absolvo*). The minister of this Sacrament is the priest having authority to absolve, which is either ordinary or by commission of his superior. The effect of this Sacrament is absolution from sin.[28]

Concerning this Sacrament is the error of the Novati, who say that any one who has sinned after having been baptized cannot receive pardon through the Sacrament of Penance. Against this are the words: "Be mindful therefore from whence thou art fallen; and do penance, and do the first works."[29]

EXTREME UNCTION

The fifth Sacrament is Extreme Unction. Its *matter* is olive oil blessed by the bishop. This Sacrament should not only be received by those who are in danger of death through sickness. They are to be anointed in the places of the five senses: that is, on the eyes, because it is the organ

---

[28] "A knowledge of it [the *form* of Penance] will excite the faithful to receive the grace of this Sacrament with the greatest possible devotion. The *form* is: 'I absolve thee,' as may be inferred not only from the words: 'Wha soever you shall bind upon earth shall be bound also in heaven' (Matt., xviii. 18), but also from the teaching of Christ our Lord, handed down to us by the Apostles. . . The minister of the Sacrament of Penance must be a priest possessing ordinary or delegated jurisdiction, as is evident in the law of the Church. Whoever performs this sacred duty must be invested not only with the powers of orders, but also with that of jurisdiction. We have greatest proof of this ministry in the words of Our Lord: 'Whose sins you shall forgive, they are forgiven them; and whose sins you shall retain, they are retained' (John, xx. 23). These words were not addressed to all, but only to the Apostles, who are succeeded in this ministry by priests" ("Roman Catechism," *loc. cit.*, 54).

[29] Apoc., ii. 5.

of the sense of sight; on the ears, because of hearing; on the nostrils, because of smell; on the lips, because of taste or speech; and on the hands because of touch, and on the feet because of walking.[30] The *form* of this Sacrament is this: "Through this anointing and through His most divine mercy, may the Lord forgive thee whatever thou hast committed through sight" (and so on for the other senses). The minister of this Sacrament is the priest. The effect of this Sacrament is a medicine for both mind and body.[31]

Concerning this Sacrament is the error of the Elaeonitae, who are said to anoint their dying with oil and balsam and water and to accompany the anointing with invocations in Hebrew pronounced over the head of the sick. This is, however, contrary to the form handed down by St. James, as given above.

HOLY ORDERS

The sixth Sacrament is Holy Orders. There are seven orders: priesthood, deaconate, subdeaconate, acolyte, exorcist, lector, and porter. Tonsure (clerk-ship, *clericatus*) is not an order, but a formal profession of giving one's life to the divine ministry. The episcopate is rather a dignity than an order.[32] The *matter* of this Sacrament is that matter

---

[30] Anointing of the feet may now be omitted (Canon 947).

[31] "This Sacrament imparts grace which remits sins, especially lighter sins or venial sins; for mortal sins are removed by the Sacrament of Penance. Extreme Unction was not instituted primarily for the remission of grave offenses; only Baptism and Penance accomplish this directly. . . Finally, the recovery of health, if indeed advantageous, is another effect of the Sacrament" ("Roman Catechism," *Extreme Unction,* 14-16).

[32] "That the number of ministers was wisely established, is proved by considering the various offices that are necessary for the celebration of the Holy Sacrifice of the Mass and the administration of the Blessed Sacrament.

which is handed over to the candidate at the conferring of the order. Thus, priesthood is conferred by the handing over of the chalice, and so each order is conferred by the handing over of that matter which in a special way pertains to the ministry of that particular order. The *form* of this Sacrament is this: "Receive the power to offer sacrifice in the Church for the living and the dead." And similarly power is conferred in the other orders. The minister of this Sacrament is the bishop who confers the orders. The effect of this Sacrament is an increase of grace for the performance of the duties of a worthy minister of Christ.

Concerning this Sacrament was the error of Arius, who taught that the priesthood could not be distinguished from the episcopate.

MATRIMONY

Matrimony is the seventh Sacrament. It is a sign of the union between Christ and the Church. The efficient cause of Matrimony is the mutual consent expressed in words effective in the present by the parties.[33]

This is the chief scope of their institution. They are divided into major or sacred orders (priesthood, deaconship, subdeaconship) and minor orders. . . The bishops are placed over the various dioceses to govern, not only the other ministers of the Church, but also the faithful, and to promote their salvation with supreme care and diligence" ("Roman Catechism," *Holy Orders,* 26). It is the common opinion today that the episcopate is an order.

[33] "This means that the consent is the effective cause of marriage. . . because without the consent and the contract, the obligation and the bond cannot exist. . . God Himself instituted marriage, and, as the Council of Trent declares, He made it perpetual and indissoluble. 'What God hath joined together, let no man put asunder,' said Our Lord (Matt., xix. 6). It belongs to marriage as a natural contract to be indissoluble; but, above all, its indissolubility arises from its nature as a Sacrament. This sacramental character raises marriage to the highest perfection. Moreover, dissolubility of mar-

Matrimony has a threefold good. The first is the birth of children and the educating of them to the worship of God. The second is that fidelity which one must render to the other; and the third is that it is a Sacrament, or, in other words, the indivisibility of Matrimony which shows forth the indivisible union of Christ and His Church.

Concerning Matrimony there are a number of errors. The first is that of Tatian, who condemned marriage, and against such it is written: "If thou take a wife, thou hast not sinned."[34] The second error is that of Jovinian, who made marriage equal to virginity. The third is that of the Nicolaitae, who mutually exchange their wives. There were also many other heretics who taught and worked impurities, and against which are the words of St. Paul: "Marriage honorable in all, and the bed undefiled."[35]

Seven Gifts of Eternal Glory

By the reception of these Sacraments, man is led to future eternal glory which consists in seven gifts, three of the soul and four of the body. The first gift given to the *soul* is the *vision of God* in His essence, according to the words: "We shall see Him as He is."[36] The second gift is *comprehension*, or that understanding of God as the reward of our merits: "So run that you may obtain."[37] The third is *perfect enjoyment*, wherein we shall have full happiness in God: "Then shalt thou abound in delights of the Almighty, and shalt lift up thy face to God."[38]

riage is immediately contrary to the proper education of children and to the other advantages of marriage. Holy Scripture frequently proposes to us the divine union of Christ and His Church under the figure of marriage" ("Roman Catechism," *Matrimony*, 11-15).

[34] Cor., vii. 28.
[35] Heb., xiii. 4.
[36] I John, iii. 2.
[37] I Cor., ix. 24.
[38] Job, xxii. 26.

The first gift which shall be enjoyed by the *body* is that of *impassibility*,[39] for "this corruptible must put on incorruption."[40] The second gift is *brilliancy*: "Then shall the just shine as the sun, in the kingdom of their Father."[41] The third is *agility*, through which they can instantly be present wheresoever they wish: "They shall run to and fro like sparks among the reeds."[42] The fourth is the gift of *subtility*, whereby they can penetrate wherever they desire: "It is sown a natural body, it shall rise a spiritual body."[43] To all of which may He lead us, who liveth and reigneth forever and ever! Amen.

---

[39] For another description of these gifts, see above, p. 71.
[40] I Cor., xv. 53.
[41] Matt., xiii. 43.
[42] Wis., iii. 7.
[43] I Cor., xv. 14.

The institution of the Holy Eucharist at Our Lord's Last Supper. Inset, Holy Communion during Holy Mass.

EXPLANATION OF THE LORD'S PRAYER

Five Qualities of Prayer

"Our Father who art in heaven." Among all other prayers, the Lord's Prayer holds the chief place. It has five excellent qualities which are required in all prayer. A prayer must be *confident, ordered, suitable, devout* and *humble*.

It must be *confident*: "Let us, therefore, go with confidence to the throne of grace."[1] It must not be wanting in faith, as it is said: "But let him ask in faith, nothing wavering."[2] That this is a most trustworthy prayer is reasonable, since it was formed by Him who is our Advocate and the most wise Petitioner for us: "In whom are hid all the treasures of wisdom and knowledge;"[3] and of whom it is said: "For we have an advocate with the Father, Jesus Christ the just one."[4] Hence, St. Cyprian says: "Since we have Christ as our Advocate with the Father for our sins, when we pray on account of our faults, we use the very words of our Advocate."[5]

Furthermore, this prayer is even more worthy of confidence in that He who taught us how to pray, graciously hears our prayer together with the Father, as it is said in the Psalm: "He shall cry to Me, and I will hear him."[6] Thus writes St. Cyprian: "It is a friendly, familiar, and devout prayer to ask of the Lord in His own words."[7] And so no one

[1] Heb., iv. 16.
[2] James, i. 6.
[3] Col., ii. 3.
[4] I John, ii. 1.
[5] *De oratione dominica.*
[6] Ps. xc. 15.
[7] *Ibid.*

goes away from this prayer without fruit. St.Augustine says that through it our venial sins are remitted.[8]

Moreover, our prayer must be *suitable*, so that a person asks of God in prayer what is good for him. St.John Damascene says: "Prayer is the asking of what is right and fitting from God."[9] Many times our prayer is not heard because we seek that which is not good for us: "You ask and you do not receive, because you ask amiss."[10] To know, indeed, what one ought to pray for is most difficult; for it is not easy to know what one ought to desire. Those things which we rightly seek in prayer are rightly desired; hence, the Apostle says: "For we know not what we should pray for as we ought."[11] Christ Himself is our Teacher; it is He who teaches us what we ought to pray for, and it was to Him that the disciples said: "Lord, teach us to pray."[12] Those things, therefore, which He has taught us to pray for, we most properly ask for. "Whatsoever words we use in prayer," says St.Augustine, "we cannot but utter that which is contained in our Lord's Prayer, if we pray in a suitable and worthy manner."[13]

Our prayer ought also to be *ordered* as our desires should be ordered, for prayer is but the expression of desire. Now, it is the correct order that we prefer spiritual to bodily things, and heavenly things to those merely earthly. This is according to what is written: "Seek ye first therefore the kingdom of God and His justice, and all these things shall be added unto you."[14] Here Our Lord shows that heavenly things must be sought first, and then things material.

---

[8] *Enchir.*, lxxviii.
[9] *De fide orthodoxa*, III, c. 24.
[10] James, iv. 3.
[11] Rom., viii 26.
[12] Luke, xi. 1.
[13] *Ad Probam*, Epist. cxxx.
[14] Matt., vi. 33.

Our prayer must be *devout*, because a rich measure of piety makes the sacrifice of prayer acceptable to God: "In Thy name I will lift up my hands. Let my soul be filled with marrow and fatness."[15] Many times because of the length of our prayers our devotion grows cool; hence Our Lord taught us to avoid wordiness in our prayers: "When you are praying, speak not much."[16] And St. Augustine says: "Let much talking be absent from prayer; but as long as fervor continues, let prayer likewise go on."[17] For this reason the Lord made His Prayer short. Devotion in prayer rises from charity which is our love of God and neighbor, both of which are evident in this prayer. Our love for God is seen in that we call God "our Father;" and our love for our neighbor when we say: "Our Father . . . forgive us our trespasses," and this leads us to love of neighbor.

Prayer ought to be *humble*: "He hath had regard for the prayer of the humble."[18] This is seen in the parable of the Pharisee and the Publican (Luke, xviii. 9-15), and also in the words of Judith: "The prayer of the humble and the meek hath always pleased Thee."[19] This same humility is observed in this prayer, for true humility is bad when a person does not presume upon his own powers, but from the divine strength expects all that he asks for.

It must be noted that prayer brings about three good effects. First, prayer is an efficacious and useful remedy against evils. Thus, it delivers us from the sins we have committed: "Thou hast forgiven the wickedness of my sin. For this shall every one that is holy pray to Thee in a seasonable time."[20] The thief on the Cross prayed and

---

[15] Ps. lxii. 5.
[16] Matt., vi. 7.
[17] *Loc. cit.*
[18] Ps. ci. 18.
[19] Jud., ix. 16.
[20] Ps. xxxi. 5.

received forgiveness: "This day thou shalt be with Me in paradise."[21] Thus also prayed the Publican, and "went down to his home justified."[22] Prayer, also, frees one from the fear of future sin, and from trials and sadness of soul: "Is any one of you sad? Let him pray."[23] Again it delivers one from persecutors and enemies: "Instead of making me a return of love, they detracted me, but I gave myself to prayer."[24]

In the second place, prayer is efficacious and useful to obtain all that one desires: "All things whatsoever you ask when you pray, believe that you shall receive."[25] When our prayers are not heard, either we do not persevere in prayer, whereas "we ought always to pray, and not to faint,"[26] or we do not ask for that which is more conducive to our salvation. "Our good Lord often does not give us what we wish," says St. Augustine, "because it would really be what we do not wish for." St. Paul gives us an example of this in that he thrice prayed that the sting of his flesh be removed from him, and his prayer was not heard.[27] Thirdly, prayer is profitable because it makes us friends of God: "Let my prayer be directed as incense in Thy sight."[28]

---

[21] Luke, xxiii. 43.
[22] *Ibid.*, xviii. 14.
[23] James, v. 13.
[24] Ps. xviii. 4.
[25] Mark, xi. 24.
[26] Luke, xviii. 1.
[27] II Cor., xii. 7.
[28] Ps. cxl. 2.

THE OPENING WORDS OF THE LORD'S PRAYER

Preparation for the Petitions

Our FATHER.—Note here two things, namely, that God is our Father, and what we owe to Him because He is our Father. God is our Father by reason of our special creation, in that He created us in His image and likeness, and did not so create all inferior creatures: "Is not He thy Father, that made thee, and created thee?"[1] Likewise God is our Father in that He governs us, yet treats us as masters, and not servants, as is the case with all other things. "For Thy providence, Father, governeth all things;"[2] and "with great favor disposest of us."[3] God is our Father also by reason of adoption. To other creatures He has given but a small gift, but to us an heredity—indeed, "if sons, heirs also."[4] "For you have not received the spirit of bondage again in fear; but you have received the spirit of adoption of sons, whereby we cry, Abba (Father)."[5]

We owe God, our Father, four things. First, honor: "If then I be a Father, where is My honor?"[6] Now, honor consists in three qualities. (1) It consists in giving praise to

---

[1] Deut., xxxii. 6. "The first word which, by the command and institution of Our Lord, we say in this prayer is 'Father.' The Saviour could, indeed, have begun this prayer with some other word more expressive of His majesty, such as 'Creator' or 'Lord.' Yet, He omitted all such expressions as they might be associated with fear, and instead of them He has chosen a word which inspires love and confidence. What name is more tender than that of *Father?* It is a name which expresses both indulgence and love" ("Roman Catechism," *Lord's Prayer*, Chapter IX, 1).

[2] Wis., xiv. 3.

[3] *Ibid.*, xii. 18.

[4] Rom., viii. 17.

[5] *Ibid.*, 15.

[6] Mal., i. 6.

God: "The sacrifice of praise shall glorify Me."[7] This ought not merely come from the lips, but also from the heart, for: "This people draw near Me with their mouth, and with their lips glorify Me, but their heart is far from Me."[8] (2) Honor, again, consists in purity of body towards oneself: "Glorify and bear God in your body."[9] (3) Honor also consists in just estimate of one's neighbor, for: "The king's honor loveth judgment."[10]

Secondly, since God is our Father, we ought to imitate Him: "Thou shalt call Me Father, and shalt not cease to walk after Me."[11] This imitation of our Father consists of three things. (1) It consists in love: "Be ye therefore followers of God, as most dear children; and walk in love."[12] This love of God must be from the heart. (2) It consists in mercy: "Be ye merciful."[13] This mercy must likewise come from the heart, and it must be in deed. (3) Finally, imitation of God consists in being perfect, since love and mercy should be perfect: "Be ye therefore perfect, as also your Heavenly Father is perfect."[14]

Thirdly, we owe God obedience: "Shall we not much more obey the Father of spirits?"[15] We must obey God for three reasons. First, because He is our Lord: "All things that the Lord has spoken we will do, we will be obedient."[16] Secondly, because He has given us the example of obedience, for the true Son of God "became obedient to His Father even unto death."[17] Thirdly, because it is for our

[7] Ps. xxix. 13.
[8] Isa., xxix. 13.
[9] I Cor., vi. 20.
[10] Ps. xcviii. 3.
[11] Jerem., iii. 19.
[12] Eph., v. 1.
[13] Luke, vi. 36.
[14] Matt., v. 48.
[15] Heb., xii. 9.
[16] Exod., xxiv. 7.
[17] Phil., ii. 8.

good: "I will play before the Lord who hath chosen me."[18]
Fourthly, we owe God patience when we are chastised by
Him: "Reject not the correction of the Lord; and do not
faint when thou art chastised by Him. For whom the Lord
loveth He chastises; and as a father in the son He pleaseth
Himself."[19]

OUR *Father*. From this we see that we owe our neighbor
both love and reverence. We must love our neighbor because we are all brothers, and all men are sons of God, our
Father: "For he that loveth not his brother whom he seeth
how can he love God whom he seeth not?[20] We owe reverence to our neighbor because he is also a child of God:
"Have we not all one Father? Hath not one God created us?
Why then does everyone of us despise his brother?"[21] And
again: "With honor preventing one another."[22] We do this
because of the fruit we receive, for "He became to all that
obey the cause of eternal salvation."[23]

The Preeminence of God

Who Art in Heaven.—Among all that is necessary for one
who prays, faith is above all important: "Let him ask in
faith, nothing wavering."[24] Hence, the Lord, teaching us to

---

[18] II Kings, vi. 21.

[19] Prov., iii 11-12.

[20] I John, iv. 20. "When we call upon the Father, invoking Him as our
Father, we are to understand it as a necessary consequence of the gift and
right of divine adoption, and that we are all brethren, and should love one
another as brothers. 'You are all brethren,' says Our Lord, 'for one is your
Father, He that is in heaven' (Matt., xxiii. 8). For this reason the Apostles in
their Epistles call the faithful, "brethren" ("Roman Catechism," *loc. cit.*,
14).

[21] Mal., ii. 10.

[22] Rom., xii. 10.

[23] Heb., v. 9.

[24] James, i. 6.

pray, first mentions that which causes faith to spring up, namely, the kindness of a father. So, He says "Our Father," in the meaning which is had in the following: "If you then being evil know how to give good gifts to your children, how much more will your Father from heaven give the good Spirit to them that ask him!"[25] Then, He says "Who art in heaven" because of the greatness of His power: "To Thee have I lifted up my eyes, who dwellest in heaven."[26]

The words, "who art in heaven," signify three things. In the first place, it serves as a preparation for him who utters the prayer, for, as it is said: "Before prayer prepare thy soul."[27] Thus, "in heaven" is understood for the glory of heaven: "For your reward is very great in heaven."[28] And this preparation ought to be in the form of an imitation of heavenly things, since the son ought to imitate his father: "Therefore, as we have borne the image of the earthly, let us bear also the image of the heavenly."[29] So also this preparation ought to be through contemplation of heavenly things, because men are wont to direct their thoughts to where they have a Father and others whom they love, as it is written: "For where thy treasure is, there is thy heart also."[30] The Apostle wrote: "Our conversation is in heaven."[31] Likewise, we prepare through attention to heavenly things, so that we may then seek only spiritual things from Him who is in heaven: "Seek things that are above, where Christ is."[32]

"Who art in heaven" can also pertain to Him who hears us, who is nearest to us; and then the "in heaven" is understood to mean "in devout persons" in whom God

---

[25] Luke, ii. 13.
[26] Ps. cxxii. 1.
[27] Ecclus., xviii. 23.
[28] Matt., v. 12.
[29] I Cor., xv. 49.
[30] Matt., vi. 21.
[31] Phil., iii. 20
[32] Col., iii. 1.

dwells, as it is written: "Thou, O Lord, art among us."[33] For holy persons are called "the heavens" in the Psalm: "The heavens show forth the glory of God."[34] God dwells in the devout through faith. "That Christ may dwell by faith in your hearts."[35] God also dwells in us through love: "He that abideth in charity, abideth in God and God in him."[36] And also through the keeping of the commandments: "If any one love Me, he will keep My word, and My Father will love him, and We will come to him, and will make Our abode with him."[37]

In the third place, "who art in heaven" can pertain to Him who is in heaven, He who cannot be included in the physical heavens, for "the heaven and the heaven of heavens cannot contain Thee."[38] And so it can mean that God is all seeing in His survey of us, in that He sees us from above, that is, from heaven: "Because He hath looked forth from His high sanctuary; from heaven the Lord hath looked upon the earth."[39] It also signifies how sublime is God in His power: "The Lord hath prepared His throne in heaven",[40] and that He lives without change through eternity: "But Thou, O Lord, endurest forever."[41] And again: "Thy years shall not fail."[42] And so of Christ was it written: "His throne as the days of heaven."[43]

The Philosopher says that on account of the incorruptibility of the heavens all have considered them as the abode of spirits.[44] And so "who art in heaven" tends to give

[33] Jerem., xiv. 9.
[34] Ps. xvii. 2.
[35] Eph., iii. 17.
[36] I John, iii. 16.
[37] John, xiv. 23. "And. . . with him" in Vives ed., omitted in Parma ed.
[38] III Kings, viii. 27.
[39] Ps. ci. 20.
[40] Ps. cii. 19.
[41] Ps. ci. 13.
[42] *Ibid.*, 28.
[43] Ps. lxxxviii. 30.
[44] Aristotle, *De Coelo*, 1.

us confidence in our prayer which arises from a threefold consideration: of God's power, of our familiarity with Him and of the fitness of our requests.

The power of Him to whom we pray is implied if we consider "heaven" as the corporeal heavens. God is not limited by any physical bounds: "Do not I fill heaven and earth? saith the Lord."[45] Nevertheless, He is said to be in the corporeal heavens to indicate two things: the extent of His power and the greatness of His nature. The form of these attributes is contrary to the view that all things happen out of necessity, by a fate regulated by the celestial bodies; and thus all prayer would be vain and useless. But such is absurd, since God dwells in the heavens as their Lord: "The Lord has prepared His throne in heaven."[46] The latter attribute, viz., His sublime nature, is against those who in praying propose or build up any corporeal images of God. Therefore, God is stated to be "in heaven" in that He exceeds corporeal things, and even the desires and intellects of men; so that whatsoever man thinks or desires is far less than God. Thus, it is said: "Behold, God is great, exceeding our knowledge."[47] And again: "The Lord is high above all nations."[48] And finally: "To whom then have you likened God? Or what image will you make for Him?"[49]

Familiar intercourse with God is shown through this "in heaven." Some indeed have said that because of His great distance from us God does not care for men, and they cite these words: "He walketh about the poles of heaven, and He doth not consider our things."[50] Against this is the fact that God is nearer to us than we are to ourselves. This brings confidence to one who prays. First, because of the

---

[45] Jerem., xxiii. 24.
[46] Ps. cii. 19.
[47] Job, xxxvi. 26.
[48] Ps. cxii. 4.
[49] Isa., xl. 18.
[50] Job, xxii. 14.

nearness of God: "The Lord is nigh unto all them that call upon Him."[51] Hence, it is written: "But thou when thou shalt pray, enter into thy chamber,[52] that is, into thy heart. Second, because of the intercession of all the Saints among whom God dwells; for from this arises faith to ask through their merits for what we desire: "Turn to some of the Saints,"[53] and, "Pray one for another, that you may be saved."[54]

This part of the prayer—that is, "in heaven"—is appropriate and fitting also, if "in heaven" is taken to mean that spiritual and eternal good in which true happiness consists. Because of it our desires are lifted up towards heavenly things; since our desires ought to tend towards where we have our Father, because there is our true home: "Seek the things that are above."[55] And again: "Unto an inheritance incorruptible, and undefiled, and that cannot fade, reserved in heaven for you."[56] Moreover, from it we are told that, if our life is to be in heaven, then we ought to be conformed to our Heavenly Father: "Such as is the heavenly, such also are they that are heavenly."[57] From all this the words "in heaven" are most appropriate in prayer in that they signify both a heavenly desire and heavenly life.

[51] Ps. cxliv. 18.
[52] Matt., vi. 6.
[53] Job, v. 1.
[54] James, v. 16.
[55] Col., iii. 1.
[56] I Pet., i. 4.
[57] I Cor., xv. 48.

THE FIRST PETITION:

"Hallowed Be Thy Name."

This is the first petition, and in it we ask that God's name be manifested and declared in us. The name of God, first of all, is wonderful because it works wonders in all creatures. Thus said Our Lord: "In My name they shall cast out devils, they shall speak new tongues. They shall take up serpents; and if they shall drink any deadly thing, it shall not hurt them."[1]

God's Name is Lovable

This name is lovable: "There is no other name under heaven given to men, whereby we must be saved."[2] We all should desire to be saved. We have an example in Blessed Ignatius, who had such great love for the name of Christ that, when Trajan ordered him to deny it, he affirmed that it could not be dragged from his mouth. Then, the emperor threatened to have him beheaded, and thus take the name of Christ out of the mouth of the Saint. But Ignatius replied: "Even though you take it from my mouth, you will never snatch it from my heart. I have this name written in my heart and there I never cease to invoke it." Trajan heard this and wished to put it to the test. He had the servant of God beheaded and then commanded that his heart be taken out, and there upon the heart was found the name of Christ inscribed in letters of gold. This name had been engraved on the heart as a seal.

[1] Mark, xvi. 17-18
[2] Acts, iv. 12.

God's Name is Venerable

The name of God is venerable: "In the name of Jesus every knee should bow, of those that are in heaven, on earth, and under the earth."[3] "Those that are in heaven" refers to the Angels and the blessed; "those that are on earth" to people living in this world, who do so for love of heaven which they wish to gain; "those under the earth" to the damned, who do so out of fear.

God's Name is Ineffable

This name is ineffable, for in the telling of it every tongue is wholly inadequate. Accordingly, it is sometimes compared to created things as, for instance, it is likened to a rock because of its firmness: "Upon this rock I will build My Church."[4] It is likened to a fire because of its purifying power; for as fire purifies metal, so does God purify the hearts of sinners: "My God is a consuming fire."[5] It is compared to light because of its power of enlightening; for as light illumines the darkness, so does the name of God overcome the darkness of the mind: "O my God, enlighten my darkness."[6]

Meaning of "Hallowed"

We pray that this name may be manifested in us, that it be known and revered as holy. Now "holy" (or hallowed) may have a threefold meaning. First, it is the same as firm. Thus, those who are firmly established in eternal happiness

---

[3] Phil., ii. 10.
[4] Matt., xvi. 18.
[5] Deut., iv. 24.
[6] Ps. xvii. 29.

are all the blessed in heaven, the Saints. In this sense, none is a "Saint" on earth because here all is continually changeable. As St. Augustine says: "I sank away from Thee, O Lord, and I wandered too much astray from Thee who art my *firm* support."[7]

Secondly, "holy" may be understood as "unearthly." The holy ones who are in heaven have naught earthly about them: "I count (all things) . . . but as dung, that I may gain Christ."[8] Earth may signify sinners. This would arise as reference to production. For if the earth is not cultivated, it will produce thorns and thistles. Similarly, if the soul of the sinner is not cultivated by grace, it will produce only thistles and thorns of sins: "Thorns and thistles shall it bring forth to thee."[9] Again, earth may signify sinners as regards its darkness. The earth is dark and opaque; and so also is the sinner dark and obstructive to light: "Darkness was on the face of the deep."[10] And, finally, earth is a dry element which will fall to pieces unless it is mixed with the moisture of water. So God placed earth just above water: "Who established the earth above the waters."[11] So also the soul of the sinner is dry and without moisture as it is said: "My soul is as earth without water unto Thee."[12]

"Holy" may, finally, be understood as "laved in blood," since the Saints in heaven are called Saints because they have been washed in blood: "These are they who are come out of great tribulation, and have washed their robes, and have made them white in the blood of the Lamb."[13] And again: "He hath washed us from our sins in His blood."[14]

[7] "Confessions," II, x.
[8] 'Phil., iii. 8.
[9] Gen., iii. 18.
[10] Gen., i. 2.
[11] Ps. cxxxv. 6.
[12] Ps. cxlii. 6.
[13] Apoc., vii. 14.
[14] *Ibid.*, i. 5.

THE SECOND PETITION:

"Thy Kingdom Come."

The Holy Spirit makes us love, desire and pray rightly; and instills in us, first of all, a fear whereby we ask that the name of God be sanctified. He gives us another gift, that of piety. This is a devout and loving affection for our Father and for all men who are in trouble. Now, since God is our Father, we ought not only reverence and fear Him, but also have towards Him a sweet and pious affection. This love makes us pray that the kingdom of God may come: "We should live soberly and justly in this world, looking for the blessed hope and coming of the glory of the great God."[1]

It may be asked of us: "Why, since the kingdom of God always was, do we then ask that it may come?" This, however, can be understood in three ways. First, a king sometimes has only the right to a kingdom or dominion, and yet his rule has not been declared because the men in his kingdom are not as yet subject to him. His rule or dominion will come only when the men of his kingdom are his subjects. Now, God is by His very essence and nature the Lord of all things; and Christ being God and Man is the Lord over all things: "And He gave Him power and glory and a kingdom."[2] It is, therefore, necessary that all things be subject to Him. This is not yet the case, but will be so at the end of the world: "For He must reign, until He hath put all His enemies under His feet."[3] Hence it is for this we pray when we say: "Thy kingdom come."

---

[1] Tit., ii. 12.
[2] Dan., vii. 14.
[3] I Cor., xv. 25.

Why We Pray Thus

In so doing we pray for a threefold purpose: that the just may be strengthened, that sinners may be punished, and that death be destroyed. Now, the reason is that men are subject to Christ in two ways either willingly or unwillingly. Again, the will of God is so efficacious that it must be fully complied with; and God does wish that all things be subject to Christ. Hence, two things are necessary: either man will do the will of God by subjecting himself to His commands, as do the just; or God shall exert His will and punish those who are sinners and His enemies; and this will take place at the end of the world: "Until I make Thy enemies Thy footstool."[4]

It is enjoined upon the faithful to pray that the kingdom of God may come, namely, that they subject themselves completely to Him. But it is a terrible thing for sinners, because for them to ask the coming of God's kingdom is nothing else than to ask that they be subjected to punishment: "Woe to them that desire the day of the Lord!"[5] By this prayer, too, we ask that death be destroyed. Since Christ is life, death cannot exist in His kingdom,[6] because death is the opposite of life: "And the enemy, death, shall be destroyed last."[7] "He shall cast death down headlong forever."[8] And this shall take place at the last resurrection: "Who will reform the body of our lowness, made like to the body of His glory."[9]

In a second sense, the kingdom of heaven signifies the glory of paradise. Nor is this to be wondered at, for a kingdom (*regnum*) is nothing other than a government (*reg-*

---

[4] Ps. cix. 1.
[5] Amos, v. 18.
[6] "Since. . . Kingdom" in Vives edition; not in Parma.
[7] I Cor., xv. 26.
[8] Isa., xxv. 8. This is in Vives edition; not in Parma.
[9] Phil., iii. 21.

imen). That will be the best government where nothing is found contrary to the will of the governor. Now, the will of God is the very salvation of men, for He "will have all men to be saved";[10] and this especially shall come to pass in paradise where there will be nothing contrary to man's salvation. "They shall gather out of His kingdom all scandals."[11] In this world, however, there are many things contrary to the salvation of men. Hence, when we pray, "Thy kingdom come," we pray that we might participate in the heavenly kingdom and in the glory of paradise.

Why We Desire This Kingdom

This kingdom is greatly to be desired for three reasons. (1) It is to be greatly desired because of the perfect justice that obtains there: "Thy people shall be all just."[12] In this world the bad are mingled with the good, but in heaven there will be no wicked and no sinners. (2) The heavenly kingdom is to be desired because of its perfect liberty. Here below there is no liberty, although all men naturally desire it; but above there will be perfect liberty without any form of oppression: "Because the creature also shall be delivered from the servitude of corruption."[13] Not only will men then be free, but indeed they will all be kings: "And Thou hast made us to our God a kingdom."[14] This is because all shall be of one will with God, and God shall will what the Saints will, and the Saints shall will whatsoever God wills; hence, in the will of God shall their will be done. All, therefore, shall reign, because the will of all shall be done, and the Lord shall be their crown: "In that day, the

---

[10] I Tim., ii. 4.
[11] Matt., xiii. 41.
[12] Isa., lx. 21.
[13] Rom., viii. 21.
[14] Apoc., v. 10.

Lord of hosts shall be a crown of glory and a garland of joy to the residue of His people."[15] (3) The kingdom of God is to be desired because of the marvellous riches of heaven: "The eye hath not seen, O God, besides Thee, what things Thou hast prepared for them that wait for Thee."[16] And also: "Who satisfieth thy desire with good things."[17]

Note that man will find everything that he seeks for in this world more excellently and more perfectly in God alone. Thus, if it is pleasure you seek, then in God you will find the highest pleasure: "You shall see and your heart shall rejoice."[18] "And everlasting joy shall be upon their heads."[19] If it is riches, there you will find it in abundance: "When the soul strays from Thee, she looks for things apart from Thee, but she finds all things impure and useless until she returns to Thee," says St Augustine.[20]

Lastly, "Thy kingdom come" is understood in another sense because sometimes sin reigns in this world. This occurs when man is so disposed that he follows at once the enticement of sin. "Let not sin reign in your mortal body,"[21] but let God reign in your heart, and this will be when thou art prepared to obey God and keep all His Commandments. Therefore, when we pray to God that His kingdom may come, we pray that God and not sin may reign in us.

May we through this petition arrive at that happiness of which the Lord speaks: "Blessed are the meek!"[22] Now, according to what we have first explained above, viz., that man desires that God be the Lord of all things, then let him not avenge injuries that are done him, but let him leave

[15] Isa., xxviii. 5.
[16] *Ibid.*, lxiv. 4.
[17] Ps. cii. 5.
[18] Isa., lxvi. 14.
[19] *Ibid.*, xxxv. 10. These two citations in Vives edition are omitted in Parma.
[20] "Confessions," II, 6.
[21] Rom., vi. 12.
[22] Matt., v. 4.

that for the Lord. If you avenge yourself, you do not really desire that the kingdom of God may come. According to our second explanation (i.e., regarding the glory of paradise), if you await the coming of this kingdom which is the glory of paradise, you need not worry about losing earthly things. Likewise, if according to the third explanation, you pray that God may reign within you, then you must be humble, for He is Himself most humble: "Learn of Me because I am meek and humble of heart."[23]

THE THIRD PETITION:

"Thy Will Be Done on Earth as It Is in Heaven."

The third gift which the Holy Spirit works in us is called the gift of knowledge. The Holy Spirit not only gives us the gift of fear and the gift of piety (which is a sweet affection for God, as we have said); but He also makes man wise. It was this for which David prayed: "Teach me goodness and discipline and knowledge."[1] This knowledge which the Holy Spirit teaches us is that whereby man lives justly. Among all that goes to make up knowledge and wisdom in man, the principal wisdom is that man should not depend solely upon his own opinion: "Lean not upon thy own prudence."[2] Those who put all their trust in their own judgment so that they do not trust others, but only themselves, are always found to be stupid and are so

---

[23] *Ibid.*, xi. 29. "Finally, we pray that God alone may live, alone may reign, within us, that death no longer may exist, but may be absorbed by the victory won by Christ our Lord, who, having broken and scattered the power of all His enemies, may, in His might, subject all things to His dominion. . . Let us, therefore, earnestly implore. . . that His commands may be observed, that there be found no traitor, no deserter, and that all may so act that they may come with joy into the presence of God their King: and may reach the possession of the heavenly kingdom prepared for them from all eternity" ("Roman Catechism," *Lord's Prayer*, Chapter xi. 14, 19).

[1] Ps. cxviii. 66.
[2] Prov., iii. 5.

adjudged by others: "Hast thou seen a man wise in his own conceit? There shall be more hope of a fool than of him."[3]

The Will of God

Out of humility one does not trust one's own knowledge: "Where humility is there is also wisdom."[4] The proud trust only themselves. Now, the Holy Spirit, through the gift of wisdom, teaches us that we do not have our own will but the will of God. It is through this gift that we pray to God that His "will be done on earth as it is in heaven." And in this is seen the gift of knowledge. Thus, one says to God "let Thy will be done," in the same way as one who is sick desires something from the physician; and his will is not precisely his own, because it is the will of the physician. Otherwise, if his desire were purely from his own will, he would be indeed foolish. So we ought not to pray other than that in us God's will may be done; that is, that His will be accomplished in us. The heart of man is only right when it is in accord with the will of God. This did Christ: "Because I came down from heaven, not to do My own will but the will of Him that sent Me."[5] Christ, as God, has the same will with the Father; but as a Man He has a distinct will from the Father's and it was according to this that He says He does not do His will but the Father's. Hence, He teaches us to pray and to ask: "Thy will be done."[6]

[3] *Ibid.*, xxvi. 12.
[4] *Ibid.*, xi. 2.
[5] John, vi. 38.
[6] "Now, this is what we implore when we address these words to God: 'Thy will be done.' We have fallen into this state of misery by disobeying and despising the divine will. Now, God deigns to propose to us, as the sole corrective of all our evils, a conformity to His will which by our sins we despised. He commands us to regulate all our thoughts and actions by this standard. And to be able to accomplish this is our aim when we humbly say this prayer to God: 'Thy will be done' " ("Roman Catechism," *Lord's Prayer*, Chapter xii. 8).

What Does God Will?

But what is this that is asked? Does not the Psalm say: "Whatsoever the Lord pleased [has willed], He hath done?"[7] Now, if He has done all that He has willed both in heaven and on earth, what then is the meaning of this: "Thy will be done on earth as it is in heaven?" To understand this we must know that God wills of us three things, and we pray that these be accomplished. The first thing that God wills is that we may have eternal life. Whoever makes something for a certain purpose, has a will regarding it which is in accord with the purpose for which he made it. In like manner, God made man, but it was not for no purpose, as it is written: "Remember what my substance is; for hast Thou made all the children of men in vain?"[8]

Hence, God made men for a purpose; but this purpose was not for their mere pleasures, for also the brutes have these, but it was that they might have eternal life. The Lord, therefore, wills that men have eternal life. Now, when that for which a thing is made is accomplished, it is said to be saved; and when this is not accomplished, it is said to be lost. So when man gains eternal life, he is said to be saved, and it is this that the Lord wills: "Now, this is the will of My Father that sent Me, that every one who seeth the Son and believeth in Him may have life everlasting."[9] This will of God is already fulfilled for the Angels and for the Saints in the Fatherland, for they see God and know and enjoy Him. We, however, desire that, as the will of God is done for the blessed who are in heaven, it likewise be done for us who are on earth. For this we pray when we say "Thy will be done" for us who are on earth, as it is for the Saints who are in heaven.

---

[7] Ps. cxxxiv. 6.
[8] Ps. lxxxviii. 48.
[9] John, vi. 10.

The Commandments: God's Will

In the second place, the will of God for us is that we keep His Commandments. When a person desires something, he not only wills that which he desires, but also everything which will bring that about. Thus, in order to bring about a healthy condition which he desires, a physician also wills to put into effect diet, medicine, and other needs. We arrive at eternal life through observance of the Commandments, and, accordingly, God wills that we observe them: "But if thou wilt enter into life, keep the Commandments."[10] "Your reasonable service . . . that you may prove what is the good and the acceptable and the perfect will of God."[11] That is, good because it is profitable: "I am the Lord thy God that teach thee profitable things."[12] And acceptable, that is, pleasing: "Light is risen to the just; and joy to the right heart."[13] And perfect, because noble: "Be you therefore perfect, as your Heavenly Father is perfect."[14] When we say "Thy will be done," we pray that we may fulfil the Commandments of God. This will of God is done by the just, but it is not yet done by sinners. "In heaven" here signifies the just; while "on earth" refers to sinners. We, therefore, pray that the will of God may be done "on earth," that is, by sinners, "as it is in heaven," that is, by the just.[15]

---

[10] Matt., xix. 17.

[11] Rom., xii. 1-2.

[12] Isa., xlviii. 17.

[13] Ps., xcvi. 11.

[14] Matt., v. 48.

[15] "When, therefore, we pray, 'Thy will be done,' we first of all ask our Heavenly Father to enable us to obey His divine commands, and to serve Him all the days of our lives in holiness and justice. Likewise that we do all things in accord with His will and pleasure, that we perform all the duties prescribed for us in the sacred writings, and thus, guided and assisted by Him, so conduct ourselves in all things as becomes those 'who are born, not of the will of flesh but of God' " ("Roman Catechism," *loc. cit.*, 12).

Let Thy Will Be Done

It must be noted that the very words used in this petition teach us a lesson. It does not say "Do" or "Let us do," but it says, "[Let] Thy will be done," because two things are necessary for eternal life: the grace of God and the will of man. Although God has made man without man. He cannot save man without his cooperation. Thus, says St Augustine: "Who created thee without thyself, cannot save thee without thyself,"[16] because God wills that man cooperate with Him or at least put no obstacle in His way: "Turn ye to Me, saith the Lord of hosts, and I will turn to you."[17] "By the grace of God, I am what I am. And His grace in me hath not been void."[18] Do not, therefore, presume on your own strength, but trust in God's grace; and be not negligent, but use the zeal you have. It does not say, therefore, "Let us do," lest it would seem that the grace of God were left out; nor does it say, "Do," lest it would appear that our will and our zeal do not matter. He does say "Let it be done" through the grace of God at the same time using our desire and our own efforts.

Thirdly, the will of God in our regard is that men be restored to that state and dignity in which the first man was created. This was a condition in which the spirit and soul felt no resistance from sensuality and the flesh. As long as the soul was subject to God, the flesh was in such subjection to the spirit that no corruption of death, or weakness, or any of the passions were felt. When, however, the spirit and the soul, which were between God and the flesh, rebelled against God by sin, then the body rebelled against the soul. From that time death and weaknesses began to be felt together with continual rebellion of sensuality against

---

[16] *Super Verbum Apost.*, XV.
[17] Zach., i. 3.
[18] I Cor., xv. 10.

the spirit: "I see another law in my members, fighting against the law of my mind."[19] "The flesh lusteth against the spirit, and the spirit against the flesh."[20]

Thus, there is an endless strife between the flesh and the spirit, and man is continually being brought lower by sin. The will of God, therefore, is that man be restored to his primal state so that no more would the flesh rebel against the spirit: "For this is the will of God, your sanctification."[21] Now, this will of God cannot be fulfilled in this life, but it will be fulfilled in the resurrection of the just, when glorified bodies shall arise incorrupt and most perfect: "It is sown a natural body; it shall rise a spiritual body."[22] In the just the will of God is fulfilled relative to the spirit, which abides in justice and knowledge and perfect life. Therefore, when we say "Thy will be done," let us pray that His will also may be done regarding the flesh. Thus, the sense of "Thy will be done *on earth*" is that it may be done "for our flesh," and "as it is *in heaven*" means in our spirit. Thus, we take "in heaven" for our spirit, and "on earth" as our flesh.[23]

By means of this petition we arrive at the happiness of those who mourn, as it is written: "Blessed are they that mourn; for they shall be comforted."[24] This can be applied to each of the threefold explanations we have given above. According to the first we desire eternal life. And in this very desire we are brought to a mourning of soul: "Woe is me,

[19] Rom., vii. 23.

[20] Gal., v. 17.

[21] I Thess., iv. 3.

[22] I Cor., xv. 44.

[23] "When we say, Thy will be done,' we expressly detest the works of the flesh, of which the Apostle writes: 'The works of the flesh are manifest, which are fornication, uncleanness, immodesty, lust, etc'. (Gal., v. 19); 'if you live according to the flesh you shall die' (Rom. viii. 13). We also pray God not to permit us to yield to the suggestions of sensual appetite, of our lusts, of our infirmities, but to govern our will by His will" ("Roman Catechism," *loc. cit.*, 14).

[24] Matt., v. 5.

that my sojourning is prolonged:"[25] This desire in the Saints is so vehement that because of it they wish for death, which in itself is something naturally to be avoided: "But we are confident and have a good will to be absent rather from the body and to be present with the Lord."[26] Likewise, according to our second explanation—viz., that we will to keep the Commandments—they who do so are in sorrow. For although such be sweet for the soul, it is bitter indeed for the flesh which is continually kept in discipline. "Going, they went and wept," which refers to the flesh. "But coming they shall come with joyfulness," which pertains to the soul.[27] Again, from our third explanation (that is, concerning the struggle which is ever going on between the flesh and the spirit), we see that this too causes sorrow. For it cannot but happen that the soul be wounded by the venial faults of the flesh; and so in expiating for these the soul is in mourning. "Every night," that is, the darkness of sin, "I will wash my bed [that is, my conscience] with my tears."[28] Those who thus sorrow will arrive at the Fatherland, where may God bring us also!

THE FOURTH PETITION:

"Give Us This Day Our Daily Bread."

Sometimes it happens that one of great learning and wisdom becomes fearful and timid; and, therefore, it is necessary that he have fortitude of heart lest he lack necessities: "It is He that giveth strength to the weary, and

---

[25] Ps. cxix. 5.
[26] II Cor., v. 8.
[27] Ps. cxxv. 6.
[28] Ps. vi. 7.

increaseth force and might to them that are not."[1] The Holy
Spirit gives this fortitude: "And the Spirit entered into me, .
. . and He set me upon my feet."[2] This fortitude which is
given by the Holy Spirit so strengthens the heart of man
that he does not fear for the things that are necessary for
him, but he trusts that God will provide for all his needs.
The Holy Spirit who gives us this strength teaches us to
pray to God: "Give us this day our daily bread." And thus
He is called the Spirit of fortitude.

It must be noted that in the first three petitions of this
prayer only things spiritual are asked for—those which
indeed begin to be in this world but are only brought to
fruition in the life eternal. Thus, when we pray that the
name of God be hallowed, we really ask that the name of
God be known; when we pray that the kingdom of God may
come, we ask that we may participate in God's kingdom;
and when we pray that the will of God be done, we ask that
His will be accomplished in us. All these things, however,
although they have their beginning here on earth, cannot
be had in their fullness except in heaven. Hence, it is
necessary to pray for certain necessaries which can be
completely had in this life. The Holy Spirit, then, taught us
to ask for the requirements of this present life which are
here obtainable in their fullness, and at the same time He
shows that our *temporal* wants are provided us by God. It is
this that is meant when we say: "Give us this day our daily
bread."[3]

---

[1] Isa., xl. 29.

[2] Ezech., ii. 2.

[3] "The fourth and following petitions, in which we particularly and
expressly pray for the necessary wants of soul and body, are subordinate to
those which have preceded. According to the order of the Lord's Prayer, we
ask for what regards the body and its preservation only after we have prayed
for the things that pertain to God" ("Roman Catechism," *Lord's Prayer*,
Chapter xiii. 1).

In these very words the Holy Spirit teaches us to avoid five sins which are usually committed out of the desire for temporal things. The first sin is that man, because of an inordinate desire, seeks those things which go beyond his state and condition of life. He is not satisfied with what befits him. Thus, if he be a soldier and desires clothes, he will not have them suitable for a soldier, but rather for a knight; or if he be a cleric, clothes fit for a bishop. This vicious habit withdraws man from spiritual things, in that it makes his desires cleave to transitory things. The Lord taught us to avoid this vice by instructing us to ask for the temporal necessities of this present life as they are in accord with the position of each one of us. All this is understood under the name of "bread." And so He does not teach us to pray for that which is luxurious, nor for variety, nor for what is over-refined, but for bread which is common to all and without which man's life could not be sustained: "The chief thing for man's life is water and bread."[4] And: "Having food and wherewith to be covered, with these we are content."[5]

The second sin is that some in acquiring temporal goods burden others and defraud them. This vicious practice is dangerous, because goods thus taken away can be restored only with difficulty. For, as St. Augustine says: "The sin is not forgiven until that which is taken away is restored."[6] "They eat the bread of wickedness."[7] The Lord teaches us to avoid this sin, and to pray for our own bread,

---

[4] Ecclus., xxix. 27.

[5] I Tim., vi. 8. "We also ask 'our daily bread,' that is, necessary sustenance, and under the name of bread we understand whatever is necessary for food and raiment. . . To comprehend fully the meaning of this petition, it is also to be noted that by this word 'bread' ought not to be understood an abundance of exquisite food and of rich clothing, but what is necessary and simple" ("Roman Catechism," *loc. cit.*, 10).

[6] *Epistle* cliii, in Migne, *P.L.*, XXXIII, 662.

[7] Prov., iv. 17.

not that of another. Robbers do not eat their own bread, but the bread of their neighbor.

The third sin is unnecessary solicitude. There are some who are never content with what they have, but always want more. This is wholly immoderate, because one's desire must always be measured by his need: "Give me neither beggary nor riches, but give me only the necessaries of life."[8] We are taught to avoid this sin in the words, "our daily bread," that is, bread of one day or for one time.[9]

The fourth sin is inordinate voracity. There are those who in one day would consume what would be enough for many days. Such pray not for bread for one day, but for ten days. And because they spend too much, it happens that they spend all their substance. "They that give themselves to drinking and that club together shall be consumed.[10] And: "A workman that is a drunkard shall not be rich."[11]

The fifth sin is ingratitude. A person grows proud in his riches, and does not realize that what he has comes from God. This is a grave fault, for all things that we have, be they spiritual or temporal, are from God: "All things are Thine; and we have given Thee what we received of Thy hand."[12] Therefore, to take away this vice, the prayer has, "Give us" even "our daily bread," that we may know that all things come from God.

From all this we draw one great lesson. Sometimes one who has great riches makes no use of them, but suffers spiritual and temporal harm; for some because of riches

---

[8] *Ibid.*, xxx. 8.

[9] "We also call it 'our daily bread,' because we use it to regain the vital energy that is daily consumed. . . Finally, the word 'daily' implies the necessity of continually praying to God, in order to be kept in the habit of loving and serving Him, and that we may be thoroughly convinced of the fact that upon Him we depend for life and salvation" ("Roman Catechism," *loc cit.*, 12).

[10] Prov., xxiii. 21.

[11] Ecclus., xix. 1.

[12] I Paral., xxix. 14.

have perished. "There is also another evil which I have seen under the sun, and that frequent among men. A man to whom God hath given riches and substance and honor, and his soul wanteth nothing of all that he desireth; yet God doth not give him power to eat thereof, but a stranger shall eat it up."[13] And again: "Riches kept to the hurt of the owner."[14] We ought, therefore, pray that our riches will be of use to us; and it is this we seek for when we say, "Give us our bread," that is, make our riches be of use to us. "His bread in his belly shall be turned into the gall of asps within him. The riches which he hath swallowed, he shall vomit up; and God shall draw them out of his belly."[15]

Another great vice is concerned with the things of this world, viz., excessive solicitude for them. For there are some who daily are anxious about temporal goods which are enough for them for an entire year; and they who are thus troubled will never have rest: "Be not solicitous therefore, saying: "What shall we eat, or What shall we drink, or Wherewith shall we be clothed?"[16] The Lord, therefore, teaches us to pray that *today* our bread will be given us, that is, those things which will be needful for us for the present time.

One may also see in this bread another twofold meaning, viz., Sacramental Bread and the Bread of the Word of God. Thus, in the first meaning, we pray for our Sacramental Bread which is consecrated daily in the Church, so that we receive it in the Sacrament, and thus it profits us unto salvation: "I am the living bread which came down from heaven."[17] And: "He that eateth and drinketh unworthily, eateth and drinketh judgment to himself."[18]

---

[13] Eccles., vi. 1-2.
[14] *Ibid.*, v. 12.
[15] Job, xx. 14-15.
[16] Matt., vi. 31.
[17] John, vi. 51.
[18] I Cor., xi. 29. "But Christ our Lord, substantially present in the Sacrament of the Eucharist, is preëminently this bread. This ineffable pledge

In the second meaning this bread is the Word of God: "Not in bread alone doth man live, but in every word that proceedeth from the mouth of God."[19] We pray, therefore, that He give us bread, that is, His Word.[20] From this man derives that happiness which is a hunger for justice. For after spiritual things are considered, they are all the more desired; and this desire arouses a hunger, and from this hunger follows the fullness of life everlasting.

THE FIFTH PETITION:

And Forgive Us Our Trespasses As We Forgive Those Who Trespass Against Us."

There are some men of great wisdom and fortitude who, because they trust too much in their own strength, do not wisely carry out what they attempt, and they do not bring to completion that which they have in mind. "Designs are strengthened by counsels."[1] It must be known that the Holy Spirit who gives fortitude also gives counsel. Every

---

of His love He gave us when about to return to His Father, and of it He said: 'He that eateth My flesh and drinketh My blood, abideth in Me, and I in him' (John, vi. 57). 'Take ye and eat: this is My body' (Matt., xxvi. 26). . . This Bread is called 'our bread,' because it is the spiritual food of the faithful only, that is, of those who, uniting charity to faith, wash away sin from their souls in the Sacrament of Penance, and mindful that they are the children of God, receive and adore this divine mystery with all the holiness and veneration to which they can arouse themselves" ("Roman Catechism," *loc. cit.,* 20).

[19] Matt., iv. 4.

[20] "It remains to speak of that spiritual bread which also is the object of this petition of the Lord's Prayer, which takes in everything that is necessary for the health and safety of the spirit and soul. Just as the food by which the body is nourished is of various sorts, so is the food which preserves the life of the spirit and soul not of one kind. Thus, the word of God is the food of the soul" ("Roman Catechism,' *loc. cit.,* 18).

[1] Prov., xx. 18.

good counsel concerning the salvation of man is from the Holy Spirit. Thus, counsel is necessary for man when he is in difficulty, just as is the counsel of physicians when one is ill. When man falls into spiritual illness through sin, he must look for counsel in order to be healed. This necessity for counsel on the part of the sinner is shown in these words: "Wherefore, O king, let my counsel be acceptable to thee, and redeem thou thy sins with alms."[2] The best counsel, therefore, against sin is alms and mercy. Hence, the Holy Spirit teaches sinners to seek and to pray: "Forgive us our trespasses."[3]

We owe God that which we have taken away from His sole right; and this right of God is that we do His will in preference to our own will. Now, we take away from God's right when we prefer our will to God's will, and this is a sin. Sins, therefore, are our trespasses.[4] And it is the counsel of the Holy Spirit that we ask God pardon for our sins, and so we say: "Forgive us our trespasses."

We can consider these words in three ways: (1) Why do we make this petition? (2) How may it be fulfilled? (3) What is required on our part?

---

[2] Dan., iv. 24.

[3] "In this petition we find a new manner of prayer. In the other petitions we asked of God not only eternal and spiritual goods, but also transient and temporal advantages. But now we ask to be liberated from the evils of the soul and of the body, of this life and of the life to come" ("Roman Catechism," *Lord's Prayer,* Chapter XIV, 1).

[4] Literally, our debts; that is, the difference between what we ought to give God and actually do not give Him. "The type of offense requiring expiation, a sin" (Oxford English Dictionary). "What we pray for is that God may deliver us from sin. This is the interpretation of St. Luke, who, instead of 'debts,' uses the word 'sins,' because through our sins we become guilty before God and incur a debt of punishment which we must pay either by satisfaction or by suffering. . . With regard to serious sins, however, this petition cannot procure forgiveness unless it derive that efficacy from the Sacrament of Penance, received, as we have already said, either actually or at least in desire" ("Romam Catechism," *loc. cit.,* 15).

Why Do We Make This Petition?

It must be known that from this petition we can draw two things that are necessary for us in this life. One is that we be ever in a state of salutary fear and humility. There have been some, indeed, so presumptuous as to say that man could live in this world and by his own unaided strength avoid sin. But this condition has been given to no one except Christ, who had the Spirit beyond all measure, and to the Blessed Virgin, who was full of grace and in whom there was no sin. "And concerning whom," that is, the Virgin, "when it is a question of sin I wish to make no mention," says St. Augustine.[5] But for all the other Saints it was never granted them that they should not incur at least venial sin: "If we say that we have no sin, we deceive ourselves and the truth is not in us."[6] And, moreover, this very petition proves this; for it is evident that all Saints and all men say the "Our Father" in which is contained "Forgive us our trespasses." Hence, all admit and confess that they are sinners or trespassers. If, therefore, you are a sinner, you ought to fear and humble yourself.

Another reason for this petition is that we should ever live in hope. Although we be sinners, nevertheless we must not give up hope, lest our despair drive us into greater and different kinds of sins. As the Apostle says: "Who despairing, have given themselves up to lasciviousness, unto the working of all uncleanness."[7] It is, therefore, of great help that we be ever hopeful; for in the measure that man is a sinner, he ought to hope that God will forgive him if he be perfectly sorry for sin and be converted. This hope is strengthened in us when we say: "Forgive us our trespasses."

---

[5] *De Natura et gratia*, XXXVI.
[6] I John, i. 8.
[7] Eph., iv. 19.

The Novatiani destroyed this hope, saying that one who has sinned but once after Baptism can never look for mercy. But this is not true, if Christ spoke truly when He said: "I forgave thee all the debt, because thou besoughtest Me."[8] In whatsoever day, therefore, you ask, you can receive mercy if with sorrow for sin you make your prayer. Both fear and hope arise from this petition. For all sinners who are contrite and confess their guilt, receive mercy. Hence, this petition is necessary.

The Fulfillment of this Petition

Concerning the second consideration of this petition (viz., how it may be fulfilled), it must be known that there are two factors in sin: the fault by which God is offended, and the punishment which is due because of this fault. But the sin is taken away in contrition which goes with the purpose to confess and make satisfaction: "I said: I will confess against myself my injustice to the Lord. And Thou hast forgiven the wickedness of my sin."[9] One has no need to fear then, because for the remission of a fault, contrition with a purpose to confess is sufficient.[10]

But one might say: "If sin is thus taken away when a man is contrite, of what necessity is the priest?" To this it must be said that God does forgive the sin in contrition, and eternal punishment is changed to temporal, but nevertheless the debt of temporal punishment remains. If one

---

[8] Matt., xviii. 32.

[9] Ps. xxxi. 5.

[10] See Editor's Note in English Translation of "Summa Theologica Supplement," Q. xviii, art. 1, which says: "St. Thomas here follows the opinion of Peter Lombard. . . Later in life he altered his opinion. Cfr. P. III, Q, lxvii, art. 1; Q. lxiv. art. 1; Q. lxxxvi, art. 6." See footnote below.

should die without confession, not out of contempt for it but prevented from it, one would go to purgatory, where the punishment, as St. Augustine says, is very great. When you confess, the priest absolves you of this punishment in virtue of the keys to which you subject yourself in confession.[11] When, therefore, one has confessed, something of this punishment is taken away; and similarly when he has again confessed, and it could be that after he has confessed many times, all would be remitted.

The successors of the Apostles found another mode of remission of this punishment, namely, the good use of indulgences, which have their force for one living in the state of grace, to the extent that is claimed for them and as indicated by the grantor. That the Pope can bring this about, is sufficiently evident. Many holy men have accomplished much good, and they have not greatly sinned, at least not mortally; and these good deeds were done for the common use of the Church. Likewise the merits of Christ and the Blessed Virgin are, as it were, in a treasury; and from it the Supreme Pontiff and they who are by him permitted can dispense these merits where it is necessary. Thus, therefore, sins are taken away not only as regards

[11] The effects of the Sacrament of Penance are: (1) sanctifying grace is imparted whereby the guilt of mortal sin is taken away and at the same time the guilt of eternal punishment; (2) the guilt of temporal punishment is more or less remitted according to the dispositions of the penitent, "and the disposition can be such that in virtue of contrition the entire punishment is removed," says St. Thomas (IV *Sent.*, Dist., xviii, art. 3, sol. 2, ad. 4). The Council of Trent (Session XIV, cap. 2) teaches that this *entire* remission of punishment, which is obtained through Baptism, is not obtained through the Sacrament of Penance "without much tears and labors" (*magnis nostris fletibus et laboribus*). For other effects of this Sacrament, such as the bestowal of sacramental grace and the revival of the merits of former good works, see the Manuals of Moral Theology (e.g., Aertnys-Damen, II, lib. VI, tract. v, n. 272).

their guilt by contrition,[12] but also as regards punishment for them in confession and through indulgences.[13]

What Must We Do?

Concerning the third consideration of this petition, it must be known that on our part we are required to forgive our neighbor the offenses which he commits against us. Thus, we say: "As we forgive those who trespass against us." Otherwise God would not forgive us: "Man to man reserveth anger: and doth he seek remedy of God?"[14] "Forgive and you shall be forgiven."[15] Therefore, only in this petition is there a condition when it says: "As we forgive those who trespass against us." If you do not forgive, you shall not be forgiven.

But you may think, "I shall say what goes first in the petition, namely, 'forgive us,' but that 'As we forgive those who trespass against us,' I shall not say." Would you seek to deceive Christ? You certainly do not deceive Him. For Christ who made this prayer remembers it well and cannot be deceived. If therefore, you say it with the lips, let the heart fulfil it.

---

[12] See footnote above.

[13] An indulgence is a remission of that temporal punishment which, even after the sin is forgiven, we have yet to undergo either here or in purgatory. Indulgences derive their value and efficacy from the spiritual treasury of the Church, which consists of the superabundant merits of Christ, His Blessed Mother, and the Saints. This treasury is to be considered as the common property of the faithful, committed to the administration of the Church. In virtue of the Communion of Saints, by which we are united as members of one body, the abundance of some supplies for the want of others. The Council of Trent (Session XXV) points out to all the faithful that the use of indulgences is very salutary.

[14] Ecclus., xxviii. 3.

[15] Luke, vi. 37.

But one may ask whether he who does not intend to forgive his neighbor ought to say: "As we forgive those who trespass against us." It seems not, for such is a lie. But actually it must be said that he does not lie, because he prays not in his own person, but in that of the Church which is not deceived, and, therefore the petition itself is in the plural number.[16] And it must also be known that forgiveness is twofold. One applies to the perfect, where the one offended seeks out the offender: "Seek after peace."[17] The other is common to all, and to it all are equally bound, that one offended grant pardon to the one who seeks it: "Forgive thy neighbor if he hath hurt thee; and then shall thy sins be forgiven to thee when thou prayest."[18] And from this follows that other beatitude: "Blessed are the merciful." For mercy causes us to have pity on our neighbor.

THE SIXTH PETITION:

"And Lead Us Not Into Temptation."

There are those who have sinned and desire forgiveness for their sins. They confess their sins and repent. Yet, they do not strive as much as they should in order that they may not fall into sin again. In this indeed they are not consistent. For, on the one hand, they deplore their sins by being sorry for them; and, on the other hand, they sin again and again and have them again to deplore. Thus it is

---

[16] "Nor do we say 'forgive me,' but 'forgive us,' because the brotherly relationship and charity which subsist between all men demand of each of us that, being solicitous for the salvation of our neighbor, we pray also for them while offering prayers for ourselves" ("Roman Catechism," *loc. cit.*, 16).

[17] Ps. xxxiii. 15.

[18] Ecclus., xxviii. 2.

written: "Wash yourselves, be clean. Take away the evil of your devices from my eyes. Cease to do perversely."[1]

We have seen in the petition above that Christ taught us to seek forgiveness for our sins. In this petition, He teaches us to pray that we might avoid sin—that is, that we may not be led into temptation, and thus fall into sin. "And lead us not into temptation."[2]

Three questions are now considered: (1) What is temptation? (2) In what ways is one tempted and by whom? (3) How is one freed from temptation?

What Is Temptation?

Regarding the first, it must be known that to tempt is nothing other than to test or to prove. To tempt a man is to test or try his virtue. This is done in two ways just as a man's virtue requires two things. One requirement is to do good, the other is to avoid evil: "Turn away from evil and do good."[3] Sometimes a man's virtue is tried in doing good, and sometimes it is tested in avoiding evil. Thus, regarding the first, a person is tried in his readiness to do good, for example, to fast and such like. Then is thy virtue great when thou art quick to do good. In this way does God sometimes try one's virtue, not, however, because such virtue is hidden from Him, but in order that all might know it, and it would be an example to all. God tempted Abraham in this way, and Job also.[4] For this reason God frequently sends trials to the just, who in sustaining them with all patience make

---

[1] Isa., i. 16.
[2] "We should implore the divine assistance in general under all temptations, and especially when we are assailed by any particular temptation ("Roman Catechism," *Lord's Prayer*, Chapter XV, 15).
[3] Ps. xxxiii. 15.
[4] Gen., xxii; Job, i.

manifest their virtue and themselves increase in virtue: "The Lord your God trieth you, that it may appear whether you love Him with all your heart and with all your soul, or not.[5] Thus does God tempt man by inciting him to good deeds.

As to the second, the virtue of man is tried by solicitation to evil. If he truly resists and does not give his consent, then his virtue is great. If, however, he falls before the temptation, he is devoid of virtue. God tempts no man in this way, for it is written: "God is not a tempter of evils, and He tempteth no man."[6]

How Is One Tempted?

The Temptations of the Flesh.—Man is tempted by his own flesh, by the devil and by the world. He is tempted by the flesh in two ways. First, the flesh incites one to evil. It always seeks its own pleasures, namely, carnal pleasures, in which often is sin. He who indulges in carnal pleasures neglects spiritual things: "Every man is tempted by his own concupiscence."[7]

Secondly, the flesh tempts man by enticing him away from good. For the spirit on its part would delight always in spiritual things, but the flesh asserting itself puts obstacles in the way of the spirit: "The corruptible body is a load upon the soul."[8] "For I am delighted with the law of God, according to the inward man. But I see another law in my members, fighting against the law of my mind, and captivating me in the law of sin, that is in my members."[9] This

[5] Deut., xiii. 3.
[6] James, i. 13.
[7] *Ibid.*, i. 14.
[8] Wis., ix. 15.
[9] Rom., vii. 22-23.

temptation which comes from the flesh is most severe, because our enemy, the flesh, is united to us; and as Böethius says: "There is no plague more dangerous than an enemy in the family circle." We must, therefore, be ever on our guard against this enemy: "Watch and pray that ye enter not into temptation."[10]

The Temptations of the Devil.—The devil tempts us with extreme force. Even when the flesh is subdued, another tempter arises, namely, the devil against whom we have a heavy struggle. Of this the Apostle says: "Our wrestling is not against flesh and blood, but against principalities and powers, against the rulers of the world of this darkness, against the spirits of wickedness in high places."[11] For this reason he is very aptly called the tempter: "Lest perhaps he that tempteth should have tempted you."[12]

The devil proceeds most cunningly in tempting us. He operates like a skillful general when about to attack a fortified city. He looks for the weak places in the object of his assault, and in that part where a man is most weak, he tempts him. He tempts man in those sins to which, after subduing his flesh, he is most inclined. Such, for instance, are anger, pride and the other spiritual sins. "Your adversary the devil, as a roaring lion, goeth about seeking whom he may devour."[13]

How the Devil Tempts Us.—The devil does two things when he tempts us. Thus, he does not at once suggest something that appears to us as evil, but something that has a semblance of good. Thereby he would, at least in the beginning, turn a man from his chief purpose, and then afterwards it will be easier to induce him to sin, once he

[10] Matt., xxvi. 41.
[11] Eph., vi. 12.
[12] I Thess., iii. 5.
[13] I Peter, v. 8.

has been turned away ever so little. "Satan himself transformeth himself into an angel of light."[14] Then when he has once led man into sin, he so enchains him as to prevent his rising up out of his sin. The devil, therefore, does two things: he deceives a man first, and then after betraying him, enthralls him in his sin.

Temptations of the World.—The world has two ways of tempting man. The first is excessive and intemperate desire for the goods of this life: "The desire of money is the root of all evil."[15] The second way is the fears engendered by persecutors and tyrants. "We are wrapped up in darkness."[16] "All that will live godly in Christ Jesus shall suffer persecution."[17] And again: "Fear not those that slay the body."[18]

How Is One Freed from Temptation?—Now we have seen what temptation is, and also in what way and by whom one is tempted. But how is one freed from temptation? In this we must notice that Christ teaches us to pray, not that we may not be tempted, but that we may not be led into temptation. For it is when one overcomes temptation that one deserves the reward. Thus it is said: "Count it all joy when you shall fall into divers temptations."[19] And again: "Son, when thou comest to the service of God, . . prepare thy soul for temptation."[20] Again: "Blessed is the man that endureth temptation; for when he hath been proved, he shall receive the crown of life."[21] Our Lord, therefore, teaches us to pray that we be not led into temptation, by

---

[14] II Cor., xi. 14.
[15] I Tim., vi. 10.
[16] Job, xxxvii. 19.
[17] II Tim., iii. 12.
[18] Matt., x. 28.
[19] James, i. 2.
[20] Ecclus., ii. 1.
[21] James, i. 12.

giving our consent to it: "Let no temptation take hold on you, but such as is human."[22] The reason is that it is human to be tempted, but to give consent is devilish.

But does God lead one to evil, that he should pray: "Lead us not into temptation"? I reply that God is said to lead a person into evil by permitting him to the extent that, because of his many sins, He withdraws His grace from man, and as a result of this withdrawal man does fall into sin. Therefore, we sing in the Psalm: "When my strength shall fail, do not Thou forsake me."[23] God, however, directs man by the fervor of charity that he be not led into temptation. For charity even in its smallest degree is able to resist any kind of sin: "Many waters cannot quench charity."[24] He also guides man by the light of his intellect in which he teaches him what he should do. For as the Philosopher says: "Every one who sins is ignorant."[25] "I will give thee understanding and I will instruct thee."[26] It was for this last that David prayed, saying: "Enlighten my eyes that I never sleep in death; lest at any time my enemy say: I have prevailed against him."[27] We have this through the gift of understanding. Therefore, when we refuse to consent to temptation, we keep our hearts pure: "Blessed are the clean of heart, for they shall see God."[28] And it follows from this petition that we are led up to the sight of God, and to it may God lead us all!

[22] I Cor., x. 13.
[23] Ps. lxx. 9.
[24] Cant., viii. 7.
[25] Aristotle, "Ethics," III, 1.
[26] Ps. xxxi. 8.
[27] Ps. xii. 4-5.
[28] Matt., v. 8.

THE SEVENTH PETITION:

"But Deliver Us From Evil. Amen."

The Lord has already taught us to pray for forgiveness of our sins, and how to avoid temptations. In this petition, He teaches us to pray to be preserved from evil, and indeed from all evil in general, such as sin, illness, affliction and all others, as St. Augustine explains it.[1] But since we have already mentioned sin and temptation, we now must consider other evils, such as adversity and all afflictions of this world. From these God preserves us in a fourfold manner.

First, He preserves us from affliction itself; but this is very rare because it is the lot of the just in this world to suffer, for it is written: "All that will live godly in Christ Jesus shall suffer persecution."[2] Once in a while, however, God does prevent a man from being afflicted by some evil; this is when He knows such a one to be weak and unable to bear it. Just so a physician does not prescribe violent medicines to a weak patient. "Behold, I have given before thee a door opened, which no man can shut; because thou hast little strength."[3] In heaven this will be a general thing, for there no one shall be afflicted. "In six troubles," those, namely, of this present life which is divided into six periods, "He shall deliver thee, and in the seventh evil shall not touch thee."[4] "They shall no more hunger nor thirst."[5]

---

[1] "Our Lord Himself made use of this petition when on the eve of His passion He prayed to God His Father for the salvation of all mankind. He said, 'I pray that Thou keep them from evil' (John, xvii. 15). In this form of prayer He, as it were, summarized the force and efficacy of the other petitions; and He delivered it by way of precept and confirmed it by example" ("Roman Catechism," *loc. cit.,* Chapter XVI, 1).

[2] II Tim., iii. 12.

[3] Apoc., iii. 8.

[4] Job, v. 19.

[5] Apoc., vii. 16.

Second, God delivers us from afflictions when He consoles us in them; for unless He console us, we could not long persevere: "We were pressed out of measure above our strength so that we were weary even of life."[6] "But God, who comforteth the humble, comforted us."[7] "According to the multitude of my sorrows in my heart, Thy comforts have given joy to my soul."[8]

Third, God bestows so many good things upon those who are afflicted that their evils are forgotten: "After the storm Thou makest a calm."[9] The afflictions and trials of this world, therefore, are not to be feared, both because consolations accompany them and because they are of short duration: "For that which is at present momentary and light of our tribulation, worketh for us above measure exceedingly an eternal weight of glory."[10]

Fourth, we are preserved from afflictions in this way that all temptations and trials are conducive to our own good. We do not pray, "Deliver us from tribulation," but "from evil." This is because tribulations bring a crown to the just, and for that reason the Saints rejoiced in their sufferings: "We glory also in tribulations, knowing that tribulation worketh patience."[11] "In time of tribulation Thou forgivest sins."[12]

The Value of Patience

God, therefore, delivers man from evil and from affliction by converting them to his good. This is a sign of

---

[6] II Cor., i. 8.
[7] *Ibid.*, vii. 6.
[8] Ps. xciii. 19.
[9] Tob., iii. 22.
[10] II Cor., iv. 17.
[11] Rom., v. 3.
[12] Tob., iii. 13.

supreme wisdom to divert evil to good. And patience in bearing trials is a result of this. The other virtues operate by good things, but patience operates in evil things, and, indeed, it is very necessary in evil things, namely, in adversity: "The learning of a man is known by his patience."[13]

The Holy Spirit through the gift of wisdom has us use this prayer, and by it we arrive at supreme happiness which is the reward of peace. For it is by patience we obtain peace, whether in time of prosperity or of adversity. For this reason the peacemakers are called the children of God, because they are like to God in this, that nothing can hurt God and nothing can hurt them, whether it be prosperity or adversity: "Blessed are the peacemakers, for they shall be called the children of God."[14]

"Amen." This is general ratification of all the petitions.[15]

A Short Explanation of the Whole Prayer

By way of brief summary, it should be known that the Lord's Prayer contains all that we ought to desire and all that we ought to avoid. Now, of all desirable things, that must be most desired which is most loved, and that is God.

Therefore, you seek, first of all, the glory of God when you say: "Hallowed be Thy name." You should desire three

---

[13] Prov., xix. 11.

[14] Matt., v. 9.

[15] "The word 'Amen' which brings the Lord's Prayer to a close, contains, as it were, the germs of many of those thoughts and considerations which we have just treated. Indeed, so frequent was this Hebrew word in the mouth of Our Lord that it pleased the Holy Spirit to have it retained in the Church of God. The meaning of it may be said to be: 'Know that thy prayers are heard.' It has the force of a response, as if God answers the prayer of the suppliant, and graciously dismisses him after He has kindly heard his prayers" ("Roman Catechism," *loc. cit.*, Chapter xvii, 4).

things from God, and they concern yourself. The first is that you may arrive at eternal life. And you pray for this when you say: "Thy kingdom come." The second is that you will do the will of God and His justice. You pray for this in the words: "Thy will be done on earth as it is in heaven." The third is that you may have the necessaries of life. And thus you pray: "Give us this day our daily bread." Concerning all these things the Lord says: "Seek ye first the kingdom of God," which complies with the second, "and all these things shall be added unto you,"[16] as in accord with the third.

We must avoid and flee from all things which are opposed to the good. For, as we have seen, good is above all things to be desired. This good is fourfold. First, there is the glory of God, and no evil is contrary to this: "If thou sin, what shalt thou hurt Him? And if thou do justly, what shall thou give Him?"[17] Whether it be the evil inasmuch as God punishes it, or whether it be the good in that God rewards it—all redound to His glory.

The second good is eternal life, to which sin is contrary: because eternal life is lost by sin. And so to remove this evil we pray: "Forgive us our trespasses as we forgive those who trespass against us." The third good is justice and good works, and temptation is contrary to this, because temptation hinders us from doing good. We pray, therefore, to have this evil taken away in the words: "Lead us not into temptation." The fourth good is all the necessaries of life, and opposed to this are troubles and adversities. And we seek to remove them when we pray: "But deliver us from evil. Amen."

[16] Matt., vi. 33.
[17] Job, xxxv. 6, 7.

JE VOUS SALUE MARIE

...RACES

LE SEIGNEUR EST AVEC...

VOUS ETES BENIE ENTRE TOUTES LES FEMMES

DE VOS ENTRAILLES

...UIT

EST BENI...

SAINTE M... DE DIEU

Maison de la Bonne Presse, 5, rue Bayard, Paris-VIII'

EXPLANATION OF THE HAIL MARY

THE ANGELIC SALUTATION

This salutation has three parts. The Angel gave one part, namely: "Hail, full of grace, the Lord is with thee, blessed art thou among women."[1] The other part was given by Elizabeth, the mother of John the Baptist, namely: "Blessed is the fruit of thy womb."[2] The Church adds the third part, that is, "Mary," because the Angel did not say, "Hail, Mary," but "Hail, full of grace." But, as we shall see, this name, "Mary," according to its meaning agrees with the words of the Angels.[3]

"HAIL, MARY"

We must now consider concerning the first part of this prayer that in ancient times it was no small event when Angels appeared to men; and that man should show them reverence was especially praiseworthy. Thus, it is written to the praise of Abraham that he received the Angels with all courtesy and showed them reverence. But that an Angel should show reverence to a man was never heard of until the Angel reverently greeted the Blessed Virgin saying: "Hail."

[1] Luke, i. 28.
[2] *Ibid.*, 42.
[3] The Hail Mary or Angelical Salutation or Ave Maria in the time of St. Thomas consisted only of the present first part of the prayer. The words, "Mary" and "Jesus," were added by the Church to the first part, and the second part—"Holy Mary, Mother of God, etc."—was also added by the Church later. "Most fittingly has the Holy Church of God added to this thanksgiving [i.e., the Hail Mary] a petition also and an invocation to the most holy Mother of God. This is to impress upon us the need to have recourse to her in order that by her intercession she may reconcile God with us sinners, and obtain for us the blessings necessary for this life and for life eternal" ("Roman Catechism," *On Prayer,* Chapter V. 8).

The Angel's Dignity

In olden times an Angel would not show reverence to a man, but a man would deeply revere an Angel. This is because Angels are greater than men, and indeed in three ways. First, they are greater than men in dignity. This is because the Angel is of a spiritual nature: "Who makest Thy Angels spirits."[4] But, on the other hand, man is of a corruptible nature, for Abraham said: "I will speak to my Lord, whereas I am dust and ashes."[5] It was not fitting, therefore, that a spiritual and incorruptible creature should show reverence to one that is corruptible as is a man. Secondly, an Angel is closer to God. The Angel, indeed, is of the family of God, and as it were stands ever by Him: "Thousands of thousands ministered to Him, and ten thousand times a hundred thousand stood before Him."[6] Man, on the other hand, is rather a stranger and afar off from God because of sin: "I have gone afar off."[7] Therefore, it is fitting that man should reverence an Angel who is an intimate and one of the household of the King.

Then, thirdly, the Angels far exceed men in the fullness of the splendor of divine grace. For Angels participate in the highest degree in the divine light: "Is there any numbering of His soldiers? And upon whom shall not His light arise?[8] Hence, the Angels always appear among men clothed in light, but men on the contrary, although they partake somewhat of the light of grace, nevertheless do so in a much slighter degree and with a certain obscurity. It was, therefore, not fitting that an Angel should show reverence to a man until it should come to pass that one would be found in human nature who exceeded the Angels in

---

[4] Ps. ciii. 4.
[5] Gen., xviii. 27.
[6] Dan., vii. 10.
[7] Ps. liv. 8.
[8] Job, xxv. 3.

these three points in which we have seen that they excel over men—and this was the Blessed Virgin. To show that she excelled the Angels in these, the Angel desired to show her reverence, and so he said: "Ave (Hail)."

"FULL OF GRACE"

The Blessed Virgin was superior to any of the Angels in the fullness of grace, and as an indication of this the Angel showed reverence to her by saying: "Full of grace." This is as if he said: "I show thee reverence because thou dost excel me in the fullness of grace."

The Blessed Virgin is said to be full of grace in three ways. First, as regards her soul she was full of grace. The grace of God is given for two chief purposes, namely, to do good and to avoid evil. The Blessed Virgin, then, received grace in the most perfect degree, because she had avoided every sin more than any other Saint after Christ. Thus it is said: "Thou art fair, My beloved, and there is not a spot in thee."[9] St. Augustine says: "If we could bring together all the Saints and ask them if they were entirely without sin, all of them, with the exception of the Blessed Virgin, would say with one voice: 'If we say that we have no sin, we deceive ourselves and the truth is not in us.'[10] ! except, however, this holy Virgin of whom, because of the honor of God, I wish to omit all mention of sin."[11] For we know that to her was granted grace to overcome every kind of sin by Him

[9] Cant., iv. 7.
[10] I John, i. 8.
[11] *De natura et gratia*, c xxxvi. Elsewhere St. Thomas says: "In the Angelic Salutation is shown forth the worthiness of the Blessed Virgin for this Conception when it says, 'Full of grace'; it expresses the Conception itself in the words, 'The Lord is with thee'; and it foretells the honor which will follow with the words, 'Blessed art thou among women' " (*Summa Theol.*, III, Q. xxx, art 4).

whom she merited to conceive and bring forth, and He certainly was wholly without sin.

Virtues of the Blessed Virgin

Christ excelled the Blessed Virgin in this, that He was conceived and born without original sin, while the Blessed Virgin was conceived in original sin, but was not born in it.[12] She exercised the works of all the virtues, whereas the Saints are conspicuous for the exercise of certain, special virtues. Thus, one excelled in humility, another in chastity, another in mercy, to the extent that they are the special exemplars of these virtues—as, for example, St Nicholas is an exemplar of the virtue of mercy. The Blessed Virgin is the exemplar of all the virtues.

In her is the fullness of the virtue of humility: "Behold the handmaid of the Lord."[13] And again: "He hath regarded the humility of his handmaid."[14] So she is also exemplar of the virtue of chastity: 'Because I know not man."[15] And thus it is with all the virtues, as is evident. Mary was full of grace not only in the performance of all good, but also in the avoidance of all evil. Again, the Blessed Virgin was full of grace in the overflowing effect of this grace upon her flesh

---

[12] St. Thomas wrote before the solemn definition of the Immaculate Conception by the Church and at a time when the subject was still a matter of controversy among theologians. In an earlier work, however, he pronounced in favor of the doctrine (*I Sent.*, c. 44, Q. i, ad. 3), although he seemingly concluded against it in the *Summa Theologica*. "Yet much discussion has arisen as to whether St. Thomas did or did not deny that the Blessed Virgin was immaculate at the instant of her animation" ("Catholic Encyclopedia," art. "Immaculate Conception"). On December 8, 1854, Pope Pius IX settled the question in the following definition: "Mary, ever blessed Virgin in the first instant of her conception, by a singular privilege and grace granted by God, in view of the merits of Jesus Christ, the Saviour of the human race, was preserved exempt from all stain of original sin."

[13] Luke, i. 38.

[14] *Ibid.*, 48.

[15] *Ibid.*, 34.

or body. For while it is a great thing in the Saints that the abundance of grace sanctified their souls, yet, moreover, the soul of the holy Virgin was so filled with grace that from her soul grace poured into her flesh from which was conceived the Son of God. Hugh of St Victor says of this: "Because the love of the Holy Spirit so inflamed her soul, He worked a wonder in her flesh, in that from it was born God made Man." "And therefore also the Holy which shall be born of thee shall be called the Son of God."[16]

Mary, Help of Christians

The plenitude of grace in Mary was such that its effects overflow upon all men. It is a great thing in a Saint when he has grace to bring about the salvation of many, but it is exceedingly wonderful when grace is of such abundance as to be sufficient for the salvation of all men in the world, and this is true of Christ and of the Blessed Virgin. Thus, "a thousand bucklers," that is, remedies against dangers, "hang therefrom."[17] Likewise, in every work of virtue one can have her as one's helper. Of her it was spoken: "In me is all grace of the way and of the truth, in me is all hope of life and of virtue."[18] Therefore, Mary is full of grace, exceeding the Angels in this fullness and very fittingly is she called "Mary" which means "in herself enlightened": "The Lord will fill thy soul with brightness."[19] And she will illumine others throughout the world, for which reason she is compared to the sun and to the moon.[20]

---

[16] *Ibid.*, 35.
[17] Cant., iv. 4.
[18] Ecclus., xxiv. 25
[19] Isa., lviii. 11.
[20] "The Blessed Virgin Mary obtained such a plenitude of grace that she was closest of all creatures to the Author of Grace; and thus she received in her womb Him who is full of grace, and by giving Him birth she is in a certain

"THE LORD IS WITH THEE"

The Blessed Virgin excels the Angels in her closeness to God. The Angel Gabriel indicated this when he said: "The Lord is with thee"—as if to say: "I reverence thee because thou art nearer to God than I, because *the Lord is with thee.*" By the Lord, he means the Father with the Son and the Holy Spirit, who in like manner are not with any Angel or any other spirit: "The Holy which shall be born of thee shall be called the Son of God."[21] God the Son was in her womb: "Rejoice and praise, O thou habitation of Sion: for great is He that is in the midst of thee, the Holy One of Israel."[22]

The Lord is not with the Angel in the same manner as with the Blessed Virgin; for with her He is as a Son, and with the Angel He is the Lord. The Lord, the Holy Spirit, is in her as in a temple, so that it is said: "The temple of the Lord, the sanctuary of the Holy Spirit,[23] because she conceived by the Holy Spirit. "The Holy Spirit shall come upon thee."[24] The Blessed Virgin is closer to God than is an Angel, because with her are the Lord the Father, the Lord the Son, and the Lord the Holy Spirit—in a word, the Holy Trinity. Indeed of her we sing: "Noble resting place of the Triune God."[25] "The Lord is with thee" are the most praise-laden words that the Angel could have uttered; and, hence, he so profoundly reverenced the Blessed Virgin because she is the Mother of the Lord and Our Lady. Accordingly

---

manner the source of grace for all men" (*Summa Theol.*, III, Q. xxvii, art. 5). St. Bernard says: "It is God's will that we should receive all graces through Mary" *Serm, de aquaductu*, n. vii). Mary is called the "Mediatrix of all Graces," and her mediation is immediate and universal, subordinate however to that of Jesus.

[21] Luke, i. 35.
[22] Isa., xii. 6.
[23] Antiphon from the Little Office of Blessed Virgin.
[24] Luke, i. 35.
[25] "*Totius Trinitatis nobile Triclinium.*"

she is very well named "Mary," which in the Syrian tongue means "Lady."

"BLESSED ART THOU AMONG WOMEN"

The Blessed Virgin exceeds the Angels in purity. She is not only pure, but she obtains purity for others. She is purity itself, wholly lacking in every guilt of sin, for she never incurred either mortal or venial sin. So, too, she was free from the penalties of sin. Sinful man, on the contrary, incurs a threefold curse on account of sin. The first fell upon woman who conceives in corruption, bears her child with difficulty, and brings it forth in pain. The Blessed Virgin was wholly free from this, since she conceived without corruption, bore her Child in comfort, and brought Him forth in joy: "It shall bud forth and blossom, and shall rejoice with joy and praise."[26]

The second penalty was inflicted upon man in that he shall earn his bread by the sweat of his brow. The Blessed Virgin was also immune from this because, as the Apostle says, virgins are free from the cares of this world and are occupied wholly with the things of the Lord.[27]

The third curse is common both to man and woman in that both shall one day return to dust. The Blessed Virgin was spared this penalty, for her body was raised up into heaven, and so we believe that after her death she was revived and transported into heaven: "Arise, O Lord, into Thy resting place, Thou and the ark which Thou hast sanctified."[28] Because the Blessed Virgin was immune from these punishments, she is "blessed among women." Moreover, she alone escaped the curse of sin, brought forth the Source of blessing, and opened the gate of heaven. It is

[26] Isa., xxxv. 2.
[27] I Cor., vii. 34.
[28] Ps. cxxxi. 8.

surely fitting that her name is "Mary," which is akin to the Star of the Sea (*Maria—maris stella*), for just as sailors are directed to port by the star of the sea, so also Christians are by Mary guided to glory.

"BLESSED IS THE FRUIT OF THY WOMB"

The sinner often seeks for something which he does not find; but to the just man it is given to find what he seeks: "The substance of the sinner is kept for the just."[29] Thus, Eve sought the fruit of the tree (of good and evil), but she did not find in it that which she sought. Everything Eve desired, however, was given to the Blessed Virgin.[30] Eve sought that which the devil falsely promised her, namely, that she and Adam would be as gods, knowing good and evil. "You shall be," says this liar, "as gods."[31] But he lied, because "he is a liar and the father of lies."[32] Eve was not made like God after having eaten of the fruit, but rather she was unlike God in that by her sin she withdrew from God and was driven out of paradise. The Blessed Virgin, however, and all Christians found in the Fruit of her womb Him whereby we are all united to God and are made like to Him: "When He shall appear, we shall be like to Him, because we shall see Him as He is."[33]

Eve looked for pleasure in the fruit of the tree because it was good to eat. But she did not find this pleasure in it, and, on the contrary, she at once discovered she was naked and was stricken with sorrow. In the Fruit of the Blessed

---

[29] Prov., xiii. 22.

[30] Here St. Thomas compares the fruit of the forbidden tree for Eve with the Fruit of Mary's womb for all Christians.

[31] Gen., iii. 5.

[32] John, viii. 44.

[33] I John, iii. 2.

Virgin we find sweetness and salvation: "He that eateth My flesh . . . hath eternal life."[34]

The fruit which Eve desired was beautiful to look upon, but that Fruit of the Blessed Virgin is far more beautiful, for the Angels desire to look upon Him: "Thou art beautiful above the sons of men."[35] He is the splendor of the glory of the Father. Eve, therefore, looked in vain for that which she sought in the fruit of the tree, just as the sinner is disappointed in his sins. We must seek in the Fruit of the womb of the Virgin Mary whatsoever we desire. This is He who is the Fruit blessed by God, who has filled Him with every grace, which in turn is poured out upon us who adore Him: "Blessed be God and the Father of our Lord Jesus Christ, who hath blessed us with spiritual blessings in Christ."[36] He, too, is revered by the Angels: "Benediction and glory and wisdom and thanksgiving, honor and power and strength, to our God."[37] And He is glorified by men: "Every tongue should confess that the Lord Jesus Christ is in the glory of God the Father."[38] The Blessed Virgin is indeed blessed, but far more blessed is the Fruit of her womb: "Blessed is He who cometh in the name of the Lord."[39]

[34] John, vi. 55.
[35] Ps. xliv. 3.
[36] Eph., i. 3.
[37] Apoc., vii. 12.
[38] Phil., ii. 11.
[39] Ps. cxvii. 26.

QUESTIONS FOR DISCUSSION

The Apostles' Creed

What is Faith?

1. What is the threefold division of the Apostles' Creed?
2. In what way is faith a union with God?
3. Explain these words: "Blessed are they that have not seen and have believed."
4. Explain the fourth effect of faith, viz., by it we overcome temptations.
5. Discuss these questions: Why do we believe that which we cannot see? Does all our knowledge come solely through our senses? Do we take nothing in the natural order on faith?
6. Explain St. Thomas' statement that the spread of Christianity was a great miracle.

The Existence of God

1. Either we believe in God or in chance. Develop, therefore, the argument: "All nature operates with a certain definite time and order, and is subject to the rule and foresight and orderly arrangement of someone."
2. How does the Providence of God account for the fact that the good often are afflicted, and that the wicked often prosper?
3. Give one reason why there can be only one God.
4. Discuss any one of the causes or motives which led men to believe in many gods (*polytheism*).
5. What is *astrology*, and what is wrong about it?
6. Discuss fortune-telling, palm-reading, etc.

One God, The Creator

1. St. Thomas here states the argument from causality or the First Cause for the existence of God. Can you restate it in your own words?
2. Note that the errors of which St. Thomas speaks are similar to certain views held today. Thus, the Manicheans and modern "reformers" who consider legitimate pleasures to be evil. Can you think of any errors today which correspond somewhat to the other errors mentioned in the text?
3. How does consideration of God as our Creator lead us to greater knowledge of God?
4. Gratitude, patience, and the right use of created things are taught us by our belief in the Creator. How?
5. Where does man belong in relation to the rest of God's creation?
6. Make personal the proof of the existence of God, the Creator: that He created me and is interested in me.

The Divinity of Christ

1. From the words of St. Peter how does the Transfiguration prove the Divinity of Our Lord?
2. Do you see a similarity between the beliefs of some men today and the error of Photinus?
3. Arianism was one of the great heresies which still exists today (only less philosophically) in the Unitarian religion. Discuss this.
4. Did not the great English poet, John Milton, hold views similar to Arianism?
5. The eternal generation of the Word or Son of God is likened by St. Thomas to the generation of the word in the mind of man—a thought conceived in the intellect. Can you explain this?

6. In what ways are we told to give adoration and honor to the Second Person of the Blessed Trinity, the Word of God?

The Incarnation

1. Explain the third article of the Creed by telling the story of the Annunciation by the Angel to the Blessed Virgin.
2. What do you mean by the Virgin Birth?
3. How is our faith strengthened by these considerations of the Incarnation?
4. What do you understand by the words of St. Thomas: "He [Christ] became man in order that He might make man divine"?
5. In what way does the thought of the Incarnation enkindle our charity?
6. Explain the words: "Christ our brother."

The Passion of Christ

1. Why is it that we cannot fully understand the tremendous fact of the passion and death of Christ?
2. "He [Christ] did not die as God, but as man." Explain these words of St. Thomas.
3. Why did the Son of God suffer and die for us?
4. Discuss the various effects of sin, and observe how the passion of Christ is a remedy against sin.
5. How can our consideration of the passion and death of Our Lord bring about a complete reformation of our lives?
6. What are some of the virtues of which Our Lord is the supreme Exemplar and Model?

The Descent into Hell

1. What are the three meanings of "hell" used by St. Thomas?
2. Where was Christ from the Death on the Cross until the Resurrection?
3. How does the descent of Christ into Limbo differ from that of the just men who died before the crucifixion of Our Lord?
4. Discuss a few of the reasons why Our Lord "descended into hell."
5. From a consideration of the descent of Christ into Limbo, hope, fear, and anxiety should be aroused in us. Explain.
6. How can we rescue the souls detained in purgatory?

The Resurrection

1. What does the Resurrection of Christ really mean?
2. In what ways did Our Lord's Resurrection differ from the resurrection of Lazarus?
3. What was the actual number of days from Good Friday to Easter Sunday?
4. St. Thomas says: "Let us endeavor to arise spiritually." Discuss this.
5. What is the relation of the Resurrection of Our Lord and our own future resurrection?
6. Does the Resurrection prove the Divinity of Christ?

The Ascension

1. Discuss the place, time, and other circumstances of Our Lord's Ascension into heaven as it is described by St. Luke in the Acts of the Apostles (chapter i).

What was the length of time between Easter Sunday and Ascension Thursday?

"And sitteth at the right hand of God." What does this mean?

Discuss the reasonableness of the Ascension of Our Lord.

What are the benefits to us of the Ascension?

If the other mysteries (incarnation, passion, death, etc.) of Our Lord manifest His humility and meekness, what is demonstrated by the Ascension into heaven?

The Last Judgment

Does St. Thomas speak here of the general judgment of all men on the last day, or of the particular judgment which all of us will undergo immediately after death?

"God decreed a general judgment in addition to the particular judgment to show forth His glory and also that of Christ and of the just, also to put the wicked to shame, and in order that man might receive, both in body and soul, the sentence of reward or punishment in the presence of all" (Cardinal Gasparri's Catechism, chap. iii, sect. ii, art 4). Discuss this.

3. Some do not hesitate to accuse God of injustice when they see the wicked prosper and the good suffer. Does not the last judgment show God's justice? Discuss this point.

4. What meaning do you attach to the phrases, "the living" and "the dead"?

5. Discuss the four classes of those to be judged.

6. What sentence will be pronounced at the last judgment? (See Matt., xxv, 34-41.)

7. Why should we have a wholesome fear of the judgment?

8. Note the remedies against fear of the judgment?

The Holy Spirit

1. Why is it necessary that there be will and love in God?
2. "The charity of God is poured forth in our hearts by the Holy Spirit who is given to us." In what way is this hearts of St. Paul a definition of the Holy Spirit.
3. What was the purpose of placing five articles on the Holy Spirit in the Nicene Creed?
4. Explain how each of these five articles indicates that the Holy Spirit is not a mere angelic minister but is truly God.
5. The Holy Spirit is love, and therefore He cleanses us from sin. Discuss this.
6. Name two ways in which the Holy Spirit aids the intellect or mind of man.
7. Discuss the role of the Holy Spirit in the attainment of our eternal salvation.

The Catholic Church

1. What is meant by the expression, "the Church"?
2. How do the theological virtues of faith, hope, and charity give unity to the Church? Would you say that another source of her unity or oneness is sanctifying grace?
3. St. Thomas says the faithful are sanctified (that is, made holy) in four ways. What is the Source of this holiness? Discuss this.
4. Show that the Catholic Church merits the title or mark of "catholic," despite the fact that there are non-Catholics.
5. St. Thomas classifies the elements which make up the mark, "apostolicity." Discuss how these elements are contained in the text of St. Matthew, xvi, 18 (see footnote 29).
6. Why is it necessary that the Church of Christ have marks?

Saints-Sacraments-Sins

1. Discuss the similarity between the natural body with its head and members, and the spiritual body, the Church, with its Head and members. Why is the Church called the Mystical Body of Christ?

2. The Communion of Saints means that between the members of the Church—in heaven, in purgatory, and on earth—there exists, by reason of their close union with one another under Christ their head, a mutual communication in spiritual riches or "good." Discuss this doctrine.

3. Why does St. Thomas give us a review of the seven Sacraments in treating of the Communion of Saints?

4. Trace the origin and growth of the life in the Mystical Body by its analogy with the life of the physical body in each of the Sacraments.

5. Discuss St. Thomas' answer to the objection: men cannot forgive sins committed against God.

6. Some day I shall be thanking people whom I never knew existed. Explain and discuss this.

Resurrection of the Body

1. Show that the Holy Spirit sanctifies (that is, makes holy) the whole man.

2. Discuss the practical effects of belief in the resurrection of the body.

3. How can a strong belief in the resurrection help us to attain salvation?

4. What will the body be like after it arises from the dead?

5. Discuss what St. Thomas calls the "perfect age" of thirty-three years.

6. Compare point for point the condition of the resurrected body of the blessed and that of the damned, showing in

what they are alike and in what they differ; and also point out that these diffferences conduce to the happiness of the saved and the misery of the damned.

Everlasting Life

1. Discuss how in this article of the Creed, the dignity and destiny of man are set forth and defended.
2. The true end of love is union with the beloved. Will this be realized in heaven? If so, how?
3. Show that in heaven there are no unfulfilled desires.
4. If there is no heaven, earth is a hell. Explain this.
5. In what will the punishment of the damned consist?

THE TEN COMMANDMENTS

The First Commandment

1. Recall in detail the circumstances when God gave the Ten Commandments to Moses; and also when Christ confirmed them (see Exodus, xx, 2-17; Matt., v. 17-18, xix. 17-20).
2. Discuss how all the Commandments are founded on the two precepts of love of God and love of neighbor.
3. Would you say that the Ten Commandments constitute the very foundation of society? In what way?
4. How was the first Commandment violated by the ancient peoples?
5. Discuss the dignity of God and the necessity of adoring Him only.
6. What are some of the ways of refusing to give due adoration to God?
7. Does the first Commandment forbid veneration to the Saints, their relics, pictures and statues? Explain and discuss this.

The Second Commandment

1. What is actually forbidden by the Second Commandment?
2. What is the positive side of this precept, i.e., what does it tell us to do?
3. Read the words from the "Roman Catechism" in footnote 1. Do you think it exaggerates conditions?
4. Discuss one or two of the meanings of "in vain."
5. Discuss the conditions of a lawful oath.

6. "There can be no lasting society unless men believe one another." Explain and discuss this statement.
7. What is the relation of the *Holy Name Society* to this Commandment?

The Third Commandment

1. Explain the first reason which St. Thomas gives for observance of the Sabbath or Sunday, i.e., to remind us of the creation of the world.
2. Why do we keep holy the Sunday and not Saturday? Explain this as though you were talking to a *Seventh Day Adventist*.
3. The third reason for the Third Commandment refers to "the promise of rest." Is rest for the body alone meant here?
4. What is the spiritual condition of men who do not keep one day "to praise and pray to the Lord"? Discuss this.
5. Just what does "holy" mean in this Commandment?
6. What is understood by "servile works," and when may one work on Sunday?
7. St. Thomas tells us not to work and not to be idle on Sunday. Do you think that he advocates a "blue Sunday"?
8. To assist at Holy Mass (see footnote 37) and to hear a sermon are the best ways to keep the Sunday in a proper way. Observe the references from the Scriptures in support of this.
9. There is also a "Spiritual Sabbath" for those who lead saintly lives (the "more perfect" of the text). This is a continual rest for the soul while it is still here on earth. Explain this.
10. What is meant by the "Heavenly Sabbath"?

The Fourth Commandment

1. Notice the difference as to object (God—neighbor) between the first three Commandments and the last series of seven Commandments.
2. Discuss some of the reasons which St. Thomas gives us to honor our parents, such as birth, nourishment and care, education.
3. Discuss a number of the references from the Scriptures which support this Commandment.
4. Although the obligation to honor our parents rests upon the natural law, yet observe the rewards which are promised those who keep this precept.
5. Our superiors in the Church, our temporal rulers, and our benefactors are called by the name "father." Discuss the obligation of giving them reverence and honor.
6. Parents also have an obligation to supervise the religious and moral education of their children; and if they find it insufficient in school, they must supply it. Discuss this teaching of the "Roman Catechism."

The Fifth Commandment

1. What does this precept forbid, and what positive virtue does it command?
2. What does St. Thomas say about killing of animals?
3. How do you justify the killing of criminals, killing in a just war, killing by accident?
4. "But to repel force by force against an *unjust aggressor*, while careful to preserve due moderation in a blameless *self-defense* is permitted by every law and right" (Gasparri's Catechism, chap. iv, sect. ii, art. 2). Discuss this principle.
5. Why is suicide prohibited?

6. What is the relation between killing and anger? (See footnote 27.)
7. What are some ways of avoiding anger?
8. What is the difference between righteous anger and anger that is sinful?
9. Discuss St. Thomas' reasons why we should not get angry easily.

The Seventh Commandment

1. How does St. Thomas distinguish between stealing and robbery?
2. Discuss the forms of theft enumerated by St. Thomas which today would be listed as: paying starvation wages; cheating; "graft."
3. Explain the obligation of restoring to the rightful owner what is stolen.

The Eighth Commandment

1. Perjury is defined in civil law as the crime of willfully uttering false evidence while one is under oath to tell the truth. Recall the references from the Scriptures which support this definition.
2. Since calumny refers to spreading what is untrue about our neighbor, and detraction refers to spreading what is true but otherwise unknown about him—which seems to be the greater evil?
3. St. Thomas says this precept is violated by detraction, by listening to detractors, and by gossipers. Discuss this.
4. Why is lying in all its forms forbidden by this Commandment?

5. Some will tell a falsehood for their own advantage, viz., out of humility, out of shame, to gain or to avoid something, or even to benefit some one else, and even out of vanity. Give examples of these points, and discuss the wrongfulness of all such motives.

Ninth and Tenth Commandments

1. Covetousness—wrongful desires and longings—destroys a man's peace of soul. Discuss this.
2. Notice the similarity between the Seventh and Tenth Commandments, and also between the Sixth and Ninth Commandments (see footnote 16).
3. Discuss the differences which St. Thomas gives between human laws and divine laws.
4. Observe the differences between the Ninth and Tenth Commandments (see footnote 4 under Tenth Commandment).
5. Explain how love of God and neighbor is the one principle or force underlying all the Commandments.

THE SACRAMENTS OF THE CHURCH

Sacraments in General

1. "A sacrament is a visible sign of invisible grace." Explain these words of St. Thomas and give some Sacraments as examples (see footnote 3).
2. One Sacrament pertains to society, another to the entire Church, and five Sacraments perfect the individual. Explain this.
3. Discuss the parallels between the physical and the spiritual life.
4. Discuss the three elements that go to make up a Sacrament: (1) certain things as the *matter*; (2) certain words as the *form*; (3) a *minister*.
5. What is common to all the Sacraments?
6. What is characteristic of each individual Sacrament?

The Sacraments. Part I

1. What is Baptism?
2. Discuss the matter and the minister of Baptism.
3. How would you administer Baptism in case of necessity?
4. Discuss the descent of the Holy Spirit upon the Apostles on Pentecost Sunday, and relate it to the Sacrament of Confirmation.
5. Discuss the matter and form of Confirmation.
6. Why must we be confirmed?
7. Discuss the matter and form of the Sacrament of the Holy Eucharist.

8. St. Thomas says the chief effects of the Holy Eucharist are: (1) the change of the bread and wine into the Body and Blood of Christ, and (2) the union of the soul of a communicant with Our Lord. Discuss these effects.
9. Discuss the Last Supper and the institution of the Blessed Sacrament. What is the relation of the Last Supper to the Holy Sacrifice of the Mass?
10. Explain the two separate consecrations, one of the bread and one of the wine, in the Mass (see footnote 21).

The Sacraments. Part II

1. Discuss the three parts of the Sacrament of Penance.
2. What is the form of the Sacrament of Penance?
3. Our Lord instituted this Sacrament when, after the Resurrection, He breathed upon the Apostles and said: "Receive you the Holy Spirit; whose sins you shall forgive they are forgiven, and whose sins you shall retain they are retained" (John, xx. 22-23; Matt., xvi. 19). Did Christ mean that this power would cease at the deaths of the Apostles?
4. Discuss the practical value of the Sacrament of Penance.
5. Discuss the words of St. James regarding the Sacrament of Extreme Unction, and point out in these words the different effects of this Sacrament.
6. Why does the priest anoint on "the places of the five senses"? What are they, and what does the priest say?
7. Discuss the view that the last anointing is a sure sign of death.

The Sacraments. Part III

1. Name and discuss the various orders according to their importance (see "Roman Catechism" for special treatment of each order).
2. Our Lord instituted the Sacrament of Holy Orders when He gave the Apostles and their successors in the priesthood the power to offer the Sacrifice of the Mass (at the Last Supper: "Do this for a commemoration of Me," Luke, xxi. 19), and when He breathed on the Apostles and gave them the power to remit or to retain sins (on the day of the Resurrection, John, xx. 23). From this discuss the power and dignity of the priest.
3. What is the effect of the Sacrament of Holy Orders?
4. How many years are required for the education of a priest?
5. The Sacrament of Matrimony is marriage validly entered upon between Christians, that is, all who are baptized. Does the Church legislate for marriage between non-baptized persons? Explain and discuss this.
6. Who are the ministers of the Sacrament of Matrimony, and what is its form?
7. Discuss the importance of consent in the Sacrament of Matrimony.
8. What is the threefold "good" or purpose of marriage?

THE LORD'S PRAYER

Prayer

1. Why should prayer be "confident" and "suitable"?
2. May we not pray for temporal things? Explain.
3. Discuss the connection between "fervor" and "brevity" in our prayers.

4. Discuss the qualities of the prayers made by the Publican and the Samaritan (Luke, xviii. 10-14).
5. Enlarge upon the three effects of prayer mentioned by St. Thomas.
6. Why is the Our Father called the "Lord's Prayer"?
7. How should we honor and imitate God our Father?
8. In the Lord's Prayer, why not say "my Father" instead of "our Father"?

Who Art in Heaven

1. "Who art in heaven" in general signifies heaven where God dwells, and also the good things of heaven. Explain how this is an incentive for us to use this prayer.
2. We are told that "in heaven" also refers to devout persons in whom God dwells by sanctifying grace. Explain this, and cite the references from the Scriptures in support of it.
3. St. Thomas says that the phrase "who art in heaven" gives us confidence in our prayer because of God's power, our familiarity with God, and because we feel our petitions are good for us. Explain this and discuss it.

Hallowed Be Thy Name

1. There are seven petitions in the Lord's Prayer. Can you think of other series (such as Seven Sacraments) which are seven in number?
2. God's name is: wonderful, venerable, ineffable. Explain this and observe the Scriptural references.
3. The word "hallow" comes from Anglo-Saxon, meaning "to honor as holy," and is preserved in "Hallowe'en," etc. Discuss the other meanings of the word "hallow" in reference to God.

Thy Kingdom Come

1. St. Thomas joins the seven *gifts of the Holy Spirit* with the seven petitions of the Our Father. How does he bring in the gifts of fear and piety?
2. Why do we pray that the "kingdom of God may come," since it has always existed?
3. The word "kingdom" here means the rule of God in the hearts of men by His grace, and the reign of God in all society and in every nation by His law. Discuss this.
4. How do we assist the foreign missions when we pray "Thy kingdom come"?
5. In another sense, "kingdom" means the glory of heaven. Explain.
6. We also pray that we may one day live in the kingdom of God because of its perfect justice, its perfect liberty, and its great riches. Explain and discuss this.
7. In what ways can we cooperate in the advancement of the kingdom of God on earth?

Thy Will Be Done

1. Explain how the gifts of knowledge and wisdom teach us to pray that God's will be done on earth as it is in heaven.
2. God wills of us that we gain eternal life, and that we keep the Commandments. Discuss this.
3. "God has made man without the help of man, yet He cannot save man without his coöperation." What does this mean?
4. "Thy will be done" is our prayer that we obey the will of the spirit and not the will of the flesh or of the world. Discuss this.
5. The final object of this petition is that we pray for the bliss and happiness of "those who mourn." Explain this and notice the references from the Scriptures.

Our Daily Bread

1. What is the relation between the gift of fortitude and this petition of the Lord's Prayer?
2. Notice how we ask only for spiritual things in the first three petitions of this prayer, and we ask for our temporal necessities in the fourth petition.
3. "Give us this day our daily bread" includes our prayer to avoid five sins associated with the temporal needs of man. What are these sins, and what are the means of avoiding them?
4. What does St. Thomas say about excessive solicitude for the things of this world? What well-known sermon of Our Lord does he recall? (See Matt., vi. 24-34.)
5. "Bread" here means all our temporal wants and our spiritual needs as well. Explain how this refers particularly to the Holy Eucharist.
6. Does the "Word of God" also have a share in this petition? How?

Forgive Us Our Trespasses

1. Through the gift of counsel we pray that God may "forgive us our trespasses." Explain this.
2. Discuss how "trespasses" are our debts or sins.
3. Explain how the virtues of fear and hope arise out of this petition.
4. The answer of this prayer for forgiveness is had first of all in the Sacrament of Penance. Discuss this.
5. Discuss the means of remitting the temporal punishment due to sin.
6. Explain the last part of this petition, viz., we pray to forgive others the offenses they commit against us. Is this not included in a good confession?

What Is Temptation?

1. How is this petition connected with the previous petition?
2. What is temptation? Discuss how it refers to performance of good and to avoidance of sin.
3. Discuss the ways in which man is tempted by the world, by the flesh, and by the devil.
4. What is the chief safeguard against temptation?
5. Do we ask to be delivered entirely from temptations? Or do we pray that God may give us grace to overcome temptations?
6. Does God actually lead us into temptation? Explain this.

Deliver Us from Evil

1. In this final petition do we not pray for deliverance from all sins and from all conceivable evils?
2. How does St. Thomas explain our deliverance from adversity and afflictions in this world?
3. What is the virtue of patience, and how do we practice this virtue?
4. How does this prayer secure peace for us?
5. Explain the meaning of "Amen."
6. Discuss how the Lord's Prayer contains all that we ought to desire and all that we ought to avoid.
7. Discuss how the Our Father has all those excellent qualities of prayer which St. Thomas says belongs to all prayer. The qualities are: confident, ordered, suitable, devout, and humble.

The Hail Mary

1. What parts of the Hail Mary were contributed by the Angel Gabriel, by St. Elizabeth, and by the Church?
2. Recall the words of the "Angelus" prayer, and discuss how it recalls the Annunciation.
3. Discuss how the Blessed Virgin was truly "full of grace" (see footnote 11).
4. Explain the difference between the Immaculate Conception and the Virgin Birth.
5. How is Mary the "Mother of Christians"?
6. Explain and discuss the title: "Mediatrix of all graces" (see footnote 20).
7. "The Lord is with thee" are words of greatest possible praise and honor to Mary. Explain this.
8. Discuss the Angel's words: "Blessed art thou among women."
9. What are the penalties of sin, and how was the Blessed Virgin entirely free from them?
10. Explain Mary's beautiful title: "Star of the Sea."
11. Make a comparison between Mary and Eve.
12. Describe the visitation of Mary to Elizabeth, and explain the words: "Blessed is the fruit of thy womb."
13. The last part of the Hail Mary was added by the Church. Explain this prayer.
14. How is the Mother of God also our Mother? Recall the words of Our Lord to Mary spoken while He was dying on the cross (John, xix. 25-27).

INDEX